Liberalism without Democracy

POLITICS, HISTORY, AND CULTURE
A series from the International Institute
at the University of Michigan

SERIES EDITORS: George Steinmetz and Julia Adams

SERIES EDITORIAL ADVISORY BOARD:

Fernando Coronil	Nancy Rose Hunt	Julie Skurski
Mamadou Diouf	Andreas Kalyvas	Margaret Somers
Michael Dutton	Webb Keane	Ann Laura Stoler
Geoff Eley	David Laitin	Katherine Verdery
Fatma Müge Göcek	Lydia Liu	Elizabeth Wingrove

Sponsored by the International Institute at the University of Michigan and published by Duke University Press, this series is centered around cultural and historical studies of power, politics, and the state—a field that cuts across the disciplines of history, sociology, anthropology, political science, and cultural studies. The focus on the relationship between state and culture refers both to a methodological approach— the study of politics and the state using culturalist methods—and to a substantive one that treats signifying practices as an essential dimension of politics. The dialectic of politics, culture, and history figures prominently in all the books selected for the series.

Liberalism without Democracy

Nationhood and Citizenship in Egypt, 1922–1936

Abdeslam M. Maghraoui

Duke University Press
Durham & London 2006

Printed in the United States of America
on acid-free paper
Designed by Jennifer Hill
Typeset in Quadraat by Keystone Typesetting, Inc.

Library of Congress Cataloging-in-Publication Data appear
on the last printed page of this book.

Duke University Press gratefully acknowledges the support of Hicham Ben
Abdellah, founder of the Transregional Institute for the Study of North Africa,
the Middle East, and Central Asia at Princeton University, who provided funds
toward the production of this book.

To my twin daughters Sarah and Lena

Who taught me the meaning of signs in
establishing authority, ownership, and difference

A bdelfattah Kilito, a Moroccan fiction writer and classical Arabic literature specialist, tells the story of a Bedouin who strayed at night and got
lost in the desert.[1] To find his way, the Bedouin began to imitate a dog
barking, hoping to induce scavenger dogs around nearby camps to bark
back so that he could follow their echoes to human habitation. The night-
time itinerant is caught in a dire situation: he must mimic a dog to become
human again, but mimicry can have a steep price. Imagine if you will,
ponders Kilito, that our *mustanbih*—"he who provokes the barking of dogs
by imitating them"—returns to civilization and begins to bark in earnest
because he has lost his human language. How would his tribe react if he
barked in response to their questions? What should his tribe do if he actually
adopted canine habits and started chasing cats and gnawing bones? What if
his kinfolk accept him, as strange as he might be, but then he begins
yapping and groaning during community meetings where serious matters
are discussed, or during sacred ceremonies where dogs' barking is most
improper?

Kilito presented this parable at a conference on bilingualism in Morocco
in 1981 as an allegory for the alleged alienation of North African intellectuals
who write in French. The central question at hand, then, was whether writing in the language of the colonial other disfigures one's identity and the
perception of one's own culture and society. Contrary to what one might
expect from a writer who draws insight for his tale from al-Jahidh, an
almighty literary figure in ninth-century Baghdad, Kilito does not advocate
cultural or linguistic uniformity in the name of an authentic language or
literary tradition. He is thoroughly bilingual and bicultural and embraces his
dual position completely. Yet Kilito takes us into a playful and engrossing

maze of risks and possibilities, through the Bedouin's uncertain journey, to expose the strategic limits and literary mediocrity of mimicry.

The lot of the lost Bedouin in the wilderness may be comparable to the challenges that Muslim societies have been facing for the last century and a half: What happens when modernity is appropriated through the language of the other and through colonial conquest? Were the early efforts by Arab and Muslim reformers who attempted to mimic the language of the "civilizing mission" just a "bark in the dark"? What role did language and identity play in the failure of Western-inspired liberal experiments in the Middle East after independence? What is the connection between language and politics? This book addresses these general questions in the context of the liberal experiment in Egypt after independence in 1922. I emphasize the overlooked interplay between politics, culture, and language by focusing on the ideas and writings of a group of liberal reformers in Egypt who hoped to change their society by adopting the language of the colonial other.

The bulk of this book was written fifteen years ago as a doctoral dissertation in Princeton University's Department of Politics. It was an attempt to draw on history, literature, linguistics, and critical theory to explain resistance to, and accommodation of, modern politics in the contemporary Middle East. For years, the argument attracted little professional attention. Two developments revived interest in the book's subject matter and analytical approach. The invasion and occupation of Iraq in 2003 reinvigorated the debate about "liberal imperialism" and the salutary interventionism of empire, and the perestroika movement within the American Political Science Association opened up new theoretical frontiers within the field of comparative politics.

I was a visiting scholar at Princeton University between the invasion of Iraq in March 2003 and the end of June 2004, when plans about engineering democracy through occupation were in full swing. In lectures and campus meetings about the war, I found it difficult not to draw parallels between the Bush administration's policy of "regime change" in Iraq and Napoleon's invasion of Egypt in 1798, or the British navy's bombardment of Alexandria in 1882, or the British misadventure in Iraq in the 1920s. In all these spurts of colonial expansion in the region, the rationale for invading and occupying a country to liberate its people from local despots turned into new forms of violence and domination that hindered rather than encouraged the emergence of modern, democratic politics.

The United States' current venture in Iraq is conspicuously reminiscent of the centuries-old imperial ventures. The Bush administration advanced several reasons to rationalize the invasion and occupation of Iraq in March 2003. But the most enduring and consistent justification for the war has been the self-appointed mission to "liberate" the Iraqi people from Saddam Hussein's tyranny, "democratize" their government, and make their nation a "beacon of freedom" for all other nations in the Middle East. In a speech on the eve of the invasion, President Bush rationalized the war on Iraq as a neo-Wilsonian mission to democratize the entire Middle East. "A liberated Iraq can show the power of freedom to transform that vital region, by bringing hope and progress into the lives of millions," said the president. "A new regime in Iraq would serve as a dramatic and inspiring example of freedom for other nations in the region."[2] In what many considered a historic speech at the National Endowment for Democracy a few months after the invasion, the president reiterated and elaborated on his grand mission for democratic transformation in the Middle East: "Sixty years of Western nations excusing and accommodating the lack of freedom in the Middle East did nothing to make us safe—because in the long run, stability cannot be purchased at the expense of liberty," he said. "Therefore, the United States has adopted a new policy, a forward strategy of freedom in the Middle East. . . . From the Fourteen Points to the Four Freedoms, to the Speech at Westminster, America has put our power at the service of principle."[3]

As it turns out, postwar Iraq is hardly a model for how to promote democratic values and institutions anywhere. But this is not surprising, given the Bush administration's astonishing strategic mistakes following the invasion. The current debacle in Iraq seems simply to confirm what the old colonial strategists knew all along: misguided or badly executed imperial policies can break empire. Yet it is misleading to blame the current crisis in Iraq only on miscalculations, mistaken policies, or poor execution, as the U.S. liberal press and think tanks that rallied behind the "democratization mission" have tried to do.

What is indeed also striking about past and present conquests is the rallying of liberal thinkers, politicians, and commentators behind imperial interventionism. Liberalism's historical complicity with colonialism in India, Algeria, Egypt, sub-Saharan Africa, and elsewhere is well established. Still, it is puzzling that prominent American liberal figures remained silent about the military invasion of Iraq and didn't rise to oppose the targeting of innocent Arab and Muslim Americans at home following the terrorist attacks on September 11, 2001. A declaration by sixty leading American intellectuals, including many prominent liberal thinkers and politicians, that qualified military action after September 11 as a "just war" was an unambiguous "liberal endorsement" for the invasion and occupation of Iraq, even though there was no connection whatsoever between Saddam Hussein and September 11, and even though the United States had supported Hussein's regime for more than a decade to counter Iran's ideological influence in the region. Furthermore, during the debates on whether the reactions to September 11 met the criteria of a "just war," there was hardly a mention of the United States' direct and indirect contribution to the emergence of the Taliban regime to counter Soviet influence in Afghanistan in the 1980s. At home, despite several reports by the International Red Cross about the illegal detention of hundreds of Muslims in U.S. custody, the broadening of interrogations of Arab and Muslim Americans and immigrants, and the outsourcing of interrogations to countries known for human rights violations, the liberal establishment remained by and large unconcerned and ineffective. The Patriot Act, which Congress passed in 2001 and renewed in 2005, compromises key constitutional articles and amendments, establishes legal procedures that leave individuals no recourse to proper defense or fair trial, and allows secret searches, detention without limit or criminal charges, and wide discretionary executive powers. The immobility of liberals in the face of these deteriorations is not circumstantial; it reveals a deeper problem within liberalism: despite its claim to rationality, emphasis on cultural neutrality, and valorization of individual choice, liberalism can become parochial and prone to "collective groupthink" when it encounters unfamiliar cultures. The fallout of September 11 exposed liberalism's cultural biases and enduring tendency to justify imperial conquest despite the negative historical legacy of the old "civilizing missions."

Why is it that liberal thinkers from John Stuart Mill to Michael Walzer are tempted by the "liberating" scheme of empire? I argue that liberalism's inattentiveness and incapacity to grasp the contradiction between "occupation" and "liberation" are rooted in biased cultural assumptions about self and other. This argument is important because it calls into question liberalism's claim to cultural neutrality. I argue, moreover, that language provides an extraordinary, yet neglected, field to explore and understand liberalism's biased and contradictory cultural assumptions. This argument is important because it situates strategies of political domination and resistance within language rather than within a presumed objective reality that can be controlled and manipulated through sound imperial policies. Liberalism's problem with cultural difference is still relevant and particularly important today because liberalism remains the dominant political framework within which cultural pluralism in democratic society is theorized.

A second development that gave impetus to this book is the perestroika movement within the American Political Science Association. The growing appreciation of political studies that borrow from social and cultural history, political anthropology, literary criticism, religious studies, and philosophy— disciplines that were previously considered irrelevant to political analysis— has loosened the hold of "value free" social scientific approaches in political science and opened up new methodological and theoretical possibilities. Not that the discipline has never before confronted questions about theory, method, and truth—the works of Hans-Georg Gadamer, Jürgen Habermas, Paul Ricoeur, Charles Taylor, and Sheldon Wolin are familiar to students of politics. But these questions were largely confined to the field of political theory, and students of comparative politics in particular have been "shielded" from challenging questions raised by theorists. The gradual recognition of these theoretical and methodological debates by the discipline at large provides a great opportunity for a work that "belongs" to the field of comparative politics but draws insights from critical theoretical questions.

In this book, politics are not limited to the formal institutional process, culture is not a variable that can be measured and quantified to establish some causal relation, and language is not just a technique of communication. Instead I attempt to explain how culture and language are themselves pregnant with rich and important political matter that escapes the analytical grid of standard political science. To carry on with these theoretical issues within a specific political and historical context, the work of Anne Norton, a major contributor to the movement of methodological innovation within North American political science, was a great source of inspiration.[4] In addition to broadening the boundaries of the political beyond the officially structured, and clarifying the relevance of culture and language to politics, Norton's work was immensely helpful for explaining the suitability of the empirical evidence that is the foundation of my interpretation of the liberal experiment in Egypt. My grounding of liberal politics in Egypt during the 1920s and 1930s in culture and language called for sources and textual materials that go beyond the standard fare of analysts of political science. When Egyptian liberal reformers argued, for example, that Egyptian literary critics should not concern themselves with Arabic poetry because it was alien to Egyptian culture, or when they claimed that the traditional fez was unhealthy, and discouraged people from wearing a symbol of "Oriental backwardness," they were making meaningful political statements about what aspects of Egyptian national identity should be repressed and what aspects should be represented. Debates about Egyptian literature, the proper national attire, and the subversive nature of popular ceremonies such as mourning or Sufi rituals are much more interesting and relevant to my argument than negotiations and bargaining among competing political parties. Newspaper articles on controversial social and cultural issues, memoirs, biographies, cartoons, poems, literary works, and artifacts can provide great insight into what exactly happens when liberal ideas and principles travel across cultural and geographic boundaries. The sphere of investigation covered in this book thus lies outside the arena of social structures and political institutions such as classes, interest groups, parties, governments, and the state.

Because the approaches of political science claim to provide objective explanations that focus on verifiable social, economic, and institutional facts, they are epistemologically blind to a whole area of investigation that is essential to understanding the failure of the liberal experiment in Egypt. Missing from their analyses is a consideration of the meaning that the Egyptian liberal reformers attached to liberalism. I am not concerned here with the objective, material, or ideological conditions that presumably caused the failure of the liberal experiment in Egypt. I am concerned, rather, with collective subjective meaning: what the Egyptian liberals thought was important to their being in the appropriation of colonial political institutions regardless of the epistemological coherence, strategic value, or even historical veracity of their statements or actions. For this reason, analytical categories such as the state, classes, political parties, civil society, and their corresponding conceptual frameworks and methodologies are not directly relevant to the interpretive approach I propose here. A *fait divers* that in a newspaper recounts a traffic accident and triggers exchanges among alarmed specialists on the problem of public order in the new Egypt is more revealing in this context than the most accurate descriptions of formal power relations between the British, the king, and the Parliament. A prominent poem that exalts Pharaonic arts, or a celebrated "scientific" finding that claims that Egyptians are not a Semitic people, provides better evidence for my purpose than empirical data on the social base of the postcolonial state.

A parochial fait divers, a reflective poem, a fictitious scientific claim—all may be dismissed as too eccentric and subjective to provide adequate material for an objective, social scientific approach. But the purpose of this book is not to dispute the findings of political scientific inquiries on Egypt; rather, it aims to shed light on the unthought, or the epistemologically censured (to use Althusser's and Balibar's formulation), which eludes their approaches.[5] Often the unthought and unproblematized are not merely individual, arbitrary events and enunciations. What determines the value of the sources chosen here is precisely their function as fragments of discourses that integrate in their structure interlocutors who are saying and perceiving something meaningful about their being. Hence I treat these events and enunciations as parts of a signifying system in which the signifier—a poem, a constitutional passage, or a statue—is linked to a signified that has characteristics and content to be identified and analyzed. Such an approach is necessarily interpretive, for my purpose is to go beyond the Egyptian nationalists' overt claims of defending Egypt's glorious Pharaonic past or promoting social progress to expose the barely dissimulated, contradictory categories of cultural, racial, and social exclusions that these claims carry with them.

We can observe the working of this dissimulation most clearly in the discursive efforts that Egyptian reformers made to construct images of modern Egyptian nationhood and citizenship that strove to approximate the image of a European nation and people. To exonerate Egypt from the negative European portrayals of the Orient, the Egyptian liberal nationalists did not contest those essentialized images per se; instead, they accepted European depictions as adequate representations of Oriental cultures and people. They objected instead to including Egypt geographically in the Orient by emphasizing its Mediterranean location and challenging the historical rationale of treating it as a non-Western cultural entity by recalling the grandeur of Egypt's Pharaonic past. Ironically, Egypt, which was the birthplace of the Pharaonic civilization that European historians and Egyptologists glorified and claimed as part of the Western heritage, had now to ascertain its spatial and temporal links to it. The reiteration of Egypt's Mediterranean orientation and the attempt to revive the Pharaonic past during the 1920s and 1930s allowed the Egyptian nationalists to make the case for their country's integration in Europe's geographic and cultural space.

So the nationalists sought to reinstate the "true" image of Egypt by reconstructing the historical and ideological boundaries of a nation that excluded all remnants of Arabic and Islamic cultural traits. The heated discussions on the abolition of the Islamic caliphate, for example, were not about theological matters. The seemingly irrelevant debates on the influence of Arabic poetry in Egyptian literature were not just about literature. Likewise, the virulent attacks in Egyptian newspapers on popular Sufi rituals were not triggered by social concerns alone. These debates were constituents of the political battle to redefine Egyptian national identity in opposition to, and as a negation of, the essentialized image that European descriptions attached to Egypt. Literary critics were urged to revive Pharaonic literature and ignore Arabic poetry because proponents of liberalism thought that the resurrection of ancient Egyptian arts and sciences brought Egypt closer to its Western origins. Hence, while defending Egypt's cultural anchorage in Europe and denying the Egyptianness of certain "backward" social and cultural practices, the liberal nationalists reproduced the same cultural biases and racist stereotypes that colonial liberalism smuggled in its language as it claimed to liberate the natives and inculcate them with European democratic principles. The duplication of these biases was especially prevalent in the debates on the meaning of modern citizenship.

How the Egyptian liberals delineated the boundaries of the nation naturally influenced their definition of citizenship. The meaning of citizenship was structured by the myth that the Egyptian nation and people were an extension of Europe, rendering membership in the new political community and citizenship rights conditional on conformity with a European origin. Because such a conception assumed a kind of individual who literally approximated the modern European man or woman, initiation into citizenship was essentially reduced to mimicking Europeans in every aspect of life. Here again, the most important and interesting debates about citizenship in interwar Egypt were centered not on political participation and representation or individual rights; these concerns were rather marginal and only scantily addressed. More revealing are the heated discussions on the need to alter the social practices, cultural values, and moral priorities of the Egyptian masses to mold them after the Europeans. For example, Egyptians were taught that wearing the modern European hat instead of the traditional fez was a symbol of freedom and modernity. Popular cultural and social manifestations, whether of mourning or of celebration, in public or in private, became suspicious because they were considered backward, sometimes decreed "unhealthy" by the medical authorities, and generally unsuitable for the newly defined Egyptian nation. Any sign that recalled the Oriental image of Egypt, from the most innocuous cultural artifact to open religious expressions, was viewed as incompatible with Egypt's Western orientation.

This conception of citizenship, which legitimates the West's claim to cultural and moral superiority and reduces Egypt to an undifferentiated entity, is reminiscent of the prevailing European constructions of the Orient. In colonial literary crusades, Egyptians are stigmatized as "idle," "morally weak," "culturally backward," "irrational," "stubborn," and "ignorant" owing to their fanatic attachment to Islam. The Egyptian liberals believed

that to overcome the negative images associated with "the Egyptian character," Egypt had to mark its distance from the Orient and reattach itself to the
West. The constitution that Egypt adopted in 1923 formally inscribed that
commitment to reunion when its preamble declared that to join the ranks of
the civilized world, Egypt had to embrace a form of government modeled
after those of Western nations.

—— *acknowledgments*

R esearch for this book began in Dar al-Kutub, the Egyptian National Library, in Cairo. The staff in the reading room and the microfilm service were most friendly, knowledgeable, and accommodating. I am indebted to them. While in Cairo, I had access to the library facilities at the American University in Cairo thanks to the good offices of Walid Kzihah and William Sullivan. I am obliged to Jean-Claude Vatin, Alain Roussillon, and 'Ali Adham for letting me share whatever small space was available at the CEDEJ offices in Cairo. I would like also to thank the editorial board of the *Journal of Mediterranean Studies* for allowing me to reprint a section on Frantz Fanon in chapter 2. The paper was published in 2004 under the title "Negotiating Identity in the Post-colonial Arab World: Clues from Psychoanalytic Theory."

Funding for research in Cairo was provided by grants from the Near East Studies Program, the Council on Regional Studies, and the Center for International Studies at Princeton University. I am indebted to Professors Carl L. Brown, Ezra Suleiman, and Henry Bienen for their interest and encouragement. The Ford Foundation's Middle East Research Competition program provided a one-year grant for further research and writing. I am most thankful to the Ford Foundation's Cairo scientific staff for their support. A one-year fellowship at Princeton's Institute for the Transregional Study of the Contemporary Middle East, North Africa, and Central Asia allowed me to devote precious time to rewriting and refining the manuscript. I want to take this opportunity to thank Greg Bell, program assistant at the Transregional Institute, for his friendship and diligent service.

I was very fortunate to have inspiring and rigorous scholars read different versions of the manuscript. I am particularly grateful to John Waterbury, Anne Norton, and Diane Singerman for their detailed comments and pointed critiques. Their insights and encouragement were invaluable. Any misinterpretation or mistakes in fact or judgment are mine alone. Thank you.

Last but not least, my profound appreciation goes to Rachel Kranton for her unrelenting support throughout the years. Her perceptive comments and helpful suggestions at all stages of writing were instrumental to my refining and completing the book. May she find in these pages the expression of my deep gratitude.

This book is about liberalism in the context of imperial domination in the modern Middle East. It describes Egypt's liberal experiment during the 1920s and 1930s, a vibrant period whose political leaders and literary figures drew inspiration from European liberal political and philosophical thought. The book focuses on why and how the Egyptian liberal reformers felt compelled to degrade local cultures and identities to accommodate liberal principles. The liberal experiment ultimately failed, and the book underlines the problems of cultural incompatibilities. But rather than confirming the familiar tensions between local cultures and customs and liberal universal values, this book reveals liberalism's own cultural prejudices and parochialism in an imperial context. This finding is significant because current debates and policies about exporting democracy to the Muslim world continue to misread and misrepresent the role of culture and therefore fail to comprehend why a poor people might be willing to die for asserting who they are, but not for an alien political system that promises good schools and hospitals. There is a long history in the region of "noble" Western interventionism that stretches from the French "civilizing mission" in Egypt in 1798 to Operation "Iraqi Freedom" in 2003. Yet despite different international power relations, different personalities and war technologies, and dissimilar local social and economic conditions, the justifications, language, and foolish ambitions of these imperial interventions have one thing in common.[1] Whether in Iraq under American control (March 2003–present) or under British rule (1917–24), whether in French Algeria (1930–62) or in Cromer's Egypt (1882–1922), advocates of Western civilization and liberal democratic values see no contradiction between liberating the natives and subverting their cultures and traditions.

The period following Egypt's formal independence from Britain in 1922 is particularly interesting because it demarcates a period of nation building and national identity formation, a moment of political conflict and cultural negotiation that reveals the cultural foundations of politics. Any emerging nation-state strives to invent an absolute sense of national identity and persuade its members to adhere to it. To be successful, emerging nation-states suppress other competing communal identities that might threaten their claim to collective representation. What cultural elements nations exclude and accommodate during the "laboring" trauma of national identity formation provide great insights into the cultural underpinnings of politics. In the context of colonial or imperial domination, the process of constructing a national self-image after independence highlights cultural tensions and contradictions within both the dominant nation and the colonized society and culture.[2] The two decades following Egypt's independence witnessed an unprecedented upsurge of political, historical, and literary works mostly by Muslim Egyptian authors influenced by Western secular ideas and principles. Questions about political rights, civil liberty, individual autonomy, the role of religion in society, and the extent of state interference to mold a collective identity led the Egyptian liberal reformers to reject not only local cultural and social practices that might or might not be incompatible with liberalism, but also Islam and local traditions as a whole. During the two decades I studied, I identified more than one thousand articles, letters, editorials, and opinion pieces from a dozen leading Egyptian newspapers on Islam's compatibility or incompatibility with modern politics. A large number of these articles, written by influential liberal thinkers, denigrated Islam and the Arabs and celebrated Europe's superior social habits, ethical values, and even Aryan race.

The Egyptian liberals' emphatic downplaying of Egypt's Islamic and Arab cultural roots during this period could be explained simply as an effort to reassert Egyptian national sovereignty after centuries of oppression under non-Egyptian Arab and Muslim rulers.[3] From the Arab conquest of Egypt (639–1250) through the rule of the Mamluks (1250–1516) to integration into the Ottoman Empire (1516–1882), Egyptians were governed by rulers whose ethnicity and language were alien.[4] The Arab-Islamic domination marginalized Egypt's Christian Copts, who were already suffering from religious discrimination under Byzantine Christians. The Mamluks, slaves, and mercenaries in the military service of the princes were of Turco-Circassian and Greek origin, and the Ottoman viceroys who continued to rely on the Mamluks to govern were Turkish. Hence native Egyptians were effectively excluded from positions of power and authority for centuries. But this does not adequately explain why the Egyptian liberal reformers wanted to construct an Egyptian national identity that is ardently non-Islamic and non-Arab. For one, by the time Muhammad 'Ali became governor of Egypt in 1805, the influence of the Ottoman sultan had already begun to weaken and was gradually reduced to ceremonial formalities. Muhammad 'Ali was in fact proclaimed governor of Egypt by Egyptian religious scholars, or 'ulama, who mobilized the population to depose the governor that the Ottoman sultan had appointed by decree. Thus with Muhammad 'Ali (1805–46) it is already questionable to speak of Muslim rulers in Egypt as alien, even though the legitimacy of the Ottoman sultan remained strong. More importantly, however, the process of Islamization has been so long, deep, and widely accepted that it has become difficult to distinguish "Egyptian" from "Arab" from "Islamic" cultural traits, let alone dismiss the latter as alien. Simply put, the idea that Egyptians considered themselves non-Muslim or identified with a pre-Arab, pre-Islamic Egyptian culture does not square with everyday anthropological reality. While Egyptians speak mostly a colloquial dialect, an informal variety of spoken Arabic, the five daily prayers at home or in mosques are conducted in formal Arabic. Hence switching from one language or identity to the other is a daily occurrence that blurs the demarcation between what is "Egyptian" and what is "Arab" or "Muslim." Last, if the Egyptian liberals' devaluing of Egypt's Islamic traditions and Arab cultural influence was simply a backlash against alien domination, it is odd that they did not articulate the same discourse toward French or British invaders. After all, British imperial domination was more recent and had more immediate relevance to Egypt's national sovereignty than the Islamic expansion in 639 AD. Yet Egyptian advocates of liberalism went to great lengths to prove—through archaeological findings, biological arguments, and literary traditions—that Egypt was a European nation and that Egyptians were not a Semitic, Oriental people. For these reasons, the Egyptian liberals' attempt to invent a European self-image for Egypt is all the more puzzling.

This book traces the Egyptian liberals' biased cultural conceptions of modern nationhood and citizenship to European rationalist thinkers and liberal theorists. I argue that the Egyptian liberals' perceptions of Egypt and local cultures and traditions are grounded in the contradictory tendencies of imperial liberalism—associated in this book with the political and philosophical tradition that emerged in full swing in the eighteenth century to legitimate colonial conquest in the name of civilizing and emancipating backward natives. I argue further that colonial liberalism's contradictions are not the result of the immediate colonial situation where the colonizer suddenly feels alienated from the "strange" habits and practices of the colonized. Rather, these contradictions reflect deep, conflicting cultural perceptions of "self" and "other" before the objective reality of the colonial event. I illustrate how the Egyptian liberal reformers—by embracing the language of liberalism as their own—adopted new social prejudices and cultural biases that informed their notions of nationhood and citizenship during the 1920s.

This argument builds on Frantz Fanon's enormous theoretical contribution to identifying language as a semiotic and cultural field that offers possibilities for both resistance and self-deceiving emancipation. I view Fanon's theoretical legacy as part of an earlier critical tradition that began with Aimé Césaire and Albert Memmi and continued with postcolonial theorists such as Edward Said, Gayatri Spivak, and Homi Bhabha. This is important because the analysis of colonial historical conditions, considered to be the domain of the earlier tradition, and the study of colonial texts, the domain of the latter, are more intertwined than we think.

In this book, I employ the idea of "culture" in the manner of Jacques Lacan, referring to a preconceived "order of language" in which human beings are caught up at birth, and from which they incompletely emerge as conscious, autonomous selves through complex patterns and contradictory emotions.[5] I use Lacan's insight on the importance of language during a person's laborious journey for self-emancipation as a metaphor to explain the occupied nation's use of, and fixation on, culture and language as the means to reclaim its own identity and independence. The word *metaphor* is to be taken seriously, for it refers to a figurative technique of reading that draws insight from a dynamic or a process that has no objective relation to the historical situation I analyze. This book, then, does not provide a psychoanalytic explanation of colonial relations whereby colonial domination damages or produces the colonized "cultural unconscious." Psychoanalytic theories of colonialism have their merits and problems, but this book is not concerned with those analyses per se. The concept of culture as language and in language, or, as Lacan would have it, culture as a "symbolic order," provides an account of the logic and mechanics of the colonized's intricate and ambiguous responses to colonial liberalism. I contextualize Lacan's theoretical insight on the importance of language within Fanon's empirical analysis of French colonialism in Algeria, where colonial culture was violently rejected, and more elaborately within the context of interwar Egypt, where Egyptian advocates of liberalism embraced colonial culture in a manner that Fanon would call a "performance of self-deluding emancipation."[6]

I will discuss these methodological and theoretical issues throughout the chapters to come; now, however, it is important to provide examples from different historical colonial settings to illustrate my general argument that colonial liberalism's contradictory tendencies are rooted in conflicting cultural constructions. The example I have chosen—the colonial liberal experiment in Egypt during the 1920s and 1930s—presents many historical tricks, methodological challenges, and theoretical twists on this basic idea. In terms of history, Egypt was formally independent in 1922, and British rule was relatively short and its cultural impact quite insignificant. Therefore my referring to colonial liberalism after independence may be questionable. My methodological challenges concern the general use of culture, rather than, say, politics, as an explanatory variable. Numerous works on Egypt during the period have shown that structural and institutional factors provide straightforward and convincing accounts of the failure of liberalism in Egypt, so adding cultural explanations to the mix might seem unnecessary. Moreover, using culture to explain liberalism's failure in a Middle Eastern country situates my work within the Orientalist tradition that Said associates with imperial domination. Also, the substance of my theoretical argument— that politics are grounded in culture, which is in turn shaped by language— could be seen as untenable, since the Egyptian liberal reformers, predominantly Arabs and Muslims, quite enthusiastically embraced the liberal ideas and principles that I claim denigrate native culture.

Each of the following chapters works its way through these historical, methodological, and theoretical challenges. Each highlights the interplay of politics and language that largely evades social scientific and Orientalist accounts.

Chapter 1 provides the theoretical framework and methodological assumptions that govern my reading of the liberal experiment in Egypt. Here I situate my reading of Egypt's colonial history within critical studies of colonialism. I argue that colonial and postcolonial scholarship, whether empirically grounded or theoretically oriented, implicitly or explicitly converges on the prism of culture and language in colonial relations. I borrow Jacques Lacan's linguistic rendering of a child's entanglement in the Oedipal drama as a structural metaphor to explain the political implication of the fragmented, incomplete differentiation of self from the other.[7] I contextualize this framework within Frantz Fanon's empirical analysis of French Algeria to show the importance of reclaiming a cultural "self" in his writings and the prominent role of language in that process. The purpose of discussing Fanon in contrast to the Egyptian liberals' devaluation of local cultural and social practices is to emphasize the importance of language in redefining identity in colonial situations, regardless of ideological outlook and political strategies.

The complicity of liberalism with colonial conquest clashes with the principles of cultural tolerance and self-determination that we often associate with liberalism. British liberal thinkers, including Jeremy Bentham, James Mill, John Stuart Mill, and John Robert Seeley, enthusiastically embraced the British Empire's territorial expropriations in the name of civilizing the world's "primitives" and "barbarians."[8] The liberals' justification of colonial servitude would be uninteresting if their advocacy of universal emancipation, at least since the eighteenth century, was a literary ruse to hide their prejudice. But that was not the case. As Uday Mehta argues in his study of British liberal ideas, although liberal thinkers depict colonial subjects as "strange," "childish," and "irrational," they also allow for human "understanding" and "sympathy." In fact, the belief in transhistorical, transcultural, and transracial progress through legislation and education is a central category in the liberal rationalization of colonial conquest.[9] The confluence between liberalism and colonial oppression of native cultures and peoples, whether in French Algeria or British India, cannot be seen simply as practical colonial constraints alien to liberal theorizing. In the case of British India, Mehta convincingly argues that the connection between liberalism and empire, though intuitively puzzling, is not at all surprising. Within liberal theory, he identifies an "internal" epistemological "urge" to dominate and impose a particular version of history, reason, and rationality on the "strange" and the "unfamiliar."[10] Mehta's analysis is insightful because it speaks to the artificial separation between historical colonialism and literary ideas about colonization—in this case, abstract political theorizing. But while Mehta grounds British liberal writings on India in a cultural construct —the widely used metaphor of human evolution from childhood to adulthood to refer to civilization's hierarchies—his overall analysis seems to privilege theoretical abstractions disconnected from the cultural contexts that produce them. Mehta faults British liberal thinkers for lacking a normative understanding of the colonial situation as a human experience. But he does not fully explain why and how cultural traditions, religious sentiments, or ambivalent identities can produce this result. This apparent decoupling of the historical and the literary speaks to normative and epistemological squabbles that beset colonial and postcolonial studies.

Chapter 2 provides a historical background to the liberal experiment in Egypt. I discuss various episodes of colonial encounter in Egypt to illustrate how the colonial missions of "liberation" and "liberalization" were rooted in cultural prejudices that predated the material conditions of colonization. The dissimulation of these prejudices in Egypt's first constitution after independence indicates the continuing dominance of colonial culture and language and anticipates future political conflicts. Textual analysis of Egypt's 1923 Constitution reveals irreconcilable contradictions between the document's allegiance to universal liberty and equality and the political community it purports to speak to, constitute, and represent. I explain why and how the appropriation of Western liberal institutions and concepts in postcolonial Egypt can be read as an effort to erase the negative, essentialized image that the "other," colonial Europe, attached to the Orient. In their attempt to define an Egyptian national identity that is culturally, racially, and geographically removed from the Orient and attached to Europe, the Egyptian liberal nationalists reproduced the same hierarchies of exclusion that liberal colonialism smuggled in through its language of emancipation and progress.

I am not suggesting that the power imbalance between occupying authorities and natives simply crumbles once "authentic" figures such as al-Jabarti, Ayatollah Ali al-Sistani, or Gandhi wave around local texts and traditions. Nor am I disregarding the possibility of interpreting the same local texts and traditions to justify tyrannical rule, as the Ottoman government did when it denounced Napoleon's distortion of religious doctrine. Rather, I suggest that colonial conflicts go beyond formal institutions of power and occupation. They are inscribed in textual contests over cultural traditions. In the face of overwhelming power and methods, all that al-Jabarti has, like Systani in Najaf, is his pen and traditional knowledge of the Qur'an. The cultural claims of the colonized cannot, then, be dismissed as futile attempts to retrieve a legendary past and escape the reality of imperial power. As Fanon would put it, cultural claims in the colonial context, though disorderly and incoherent, though partly conscious and partly unconscious, disrupt colonial narratives because they reestablish the human experience of the colonized—an experience the colonial discourse attempts to render strange or deny altogether.

Said, who eloquently argued the confluence between textual and historical colonialism, remarked that the "Napoleonic invasion of Egypt . . . was in many ways the very truly scientific appropriation of one culture by another, apparently stronger one."[11] The establishment of the Institute of Egypt with its laboratories and the publication of the *Description de l'Égypte* with its twenty-three volumes on Egyptian history, culture, and customs were not just scientific and literary productions. They were discursive strategies to displace local cultural narratives and project new power relations. Although Said marvels at al-Jabarti's literary efforts in the face of such colonial scientific and military power, Said considers al-Jabarti's resistance to cultural displacement, like that of Algeria's Emir Abdel Kader or Afghani's rebuke of Ernest Renan's racial theories, to be a futile attempt to revive a pure native origin.[12] Along with Bhabha, Said sees the potential for resistance in the workings of "mimicry" and "hybridity" that emerge from cross-cultural fertilization, not in a return to "authentic" texts. Yet, considering Egypt's impressive historical record in laboring to embrace the principles of European civilization—at least since the reforms of Muhammad 'Ali (1805–48)—the workings of "mimicry" and "hybridity" as counterhegemonic strategies should permeate Egyptian history. Egypt does not lack epic figures and heroic episodes of resistance to European influence or colonial domination. But these episodes do not seem to conform to the anticolonial and postcolonial dynamics that Said and Bhabha describe. I argue that the Egyptian reformers who most contributed to the myth of a pure Egyptian cultural origin and reproduced the stereotypes of the colonial narrative during the 1920s and 1930s were sophisticated, Westernized liberal thinkers. They emerged from a long tradition of cross-cultural fertilization. Because they were caught up in the language of the other, to use Lacan metaphorically, I argue that these Egyptian reformers were hardly more successful in articulating counterhegemonic discourses than those who understood their colonial experience through local cultural traditions.

Chapters 3 and 4 provide evidence for how the adoption of liberal principles and institutions in interwar Egypt was grounded in relentless literary efforts to redefine national identity and renegotiate the boundaries of the political community. Hand in hand with writing a modern constitution, founding a parliament, and advocating the principles of liberalism, the Egyptian liberal reformers declared the birth of a new nation—a nation that they claimed had roots in Europe.

Chapter 3 documents and analyzes how the liberal reformers attempted to validate claims to a European origin on the basis of "scientific" theories about race, culture, and history. To construct a nation modeled after its

European counterparts, Egyptian liberals went to great lengths to minimize Egypt's Arabic and Islamic heritage and emphasize links with Western society and civilization. The adoption of Western liberal institutions was linked to the redefinition of national identity and the demarcation of new political boundaries. Loyalty to the Islamic community and identification with a larger cultural entity such as Arab heritage were to be abolished. The Egyptian people were now to owe allegiance to a nation whose roots lay in Europe. Much of Egyptian liberal discourse was directed at disguising difference with the West and denying resemblance to the "uncivilized" Orient. Political liberalism in Egypt, I will show, began with the effacement of "self" as the constructed "other" of the European.

This effort to suppress the influence of Islam and the Arabs in Egypt's history and culture was at once inevitable and counterproductive. It was inevitable because the attempt to establish modern political institutions in Egypt was structured by the same discourse that legitimated modern political authority in Europe and therefore reproduced a worldview after the European self-image. Thanks to critical research in anthropology and psychoanalysis, we now have a better idea of how colonial depictions and treatments of the colonized, whether as "noble savage" or as "intimate enemy," but always as outcast, were essential to constructing and redefining European self-images.[13] Thus as the Egyptian liberal reformers embraced the basic principles of colonial liberalism, they also embraced its implicit and explicit racial, social, and cultural hierarchies of proximity.

But the Egyptian liberals' effort to repudiate cultural references, historical memories, and religious myths, even if they were in disharmony with the modern notion of "nation," was politically counterproductive. Max Weber, who remains the clearest and most systematic theorist of modern political legitimacy, regarded the "community of memories" as the ultimate constitutive element of "national consciousness."[14] In other words, the legitimacy of modern political authority also depends on the citizens' understanding of themselves as constituting a collective, the basis of which cannot be "legal norms" alone.[15]

To define a political community disconnected from European images of the Orient, Egyptian liberals imposed boundaries that were alien to the people who were supposed to constitute that community. Moreover, the majority of Egyptians could not be incorporated as equal citizens in the new political community because citizenship rights were also predicated on certain social and cultural attributes that privileged the European lifestyle. The Egyptian population, therefore, could not be attached to the newly defined nation by any feeling of "responsibility," "emotion," or "common political destiny," to use Weber's words.[16]

This negation of constitutive community helps explain why the concern with establishing liberal democracy in Egypt was accompanied by another seemingly unrelated discourse on Egyptian history, culture, geography, and race. The purpose of such a discourse was twofold: (1) to remove any doubt of the wisdom of adopting the cultural, moral, and ethical values of the European as a sovereign subject; and (2) to present the political qualities of liberalism as operative only insofar as the Egyptian people were reformed and could identify with the newly defined Egyptian nation. In other words, justice, equality, and freedom could be guaranteed only if the Egyptians, individually and collectively, rejected what Weber considers the sole potential basis of a political community: their own "common memories."

Chapter 4 demonstrates that citizenship rights in Egypt's liberal colonial context were predicated on exclusive European cultural requirements. If the purpose of redefining Egyptian national identity was to bring Egypt closer to Europe, then nothing was more troubling to liberal reformers than reminders that the vast majority of Egyptians did not fit the image of the new nation. Any manifestation or sign of native culture, in private or in public, in celebration or in mourning, by a group or an individual, was considered a serious threat to the newly defined political community. This equation of citizenship with European culture was based in the belief that European culture, moral values, social institutions, and way of life were superior.

Chapter 5 considers the liberal experiment in Egypt in comparative perspective to highlight the cultural assumptions of social scientific research. I conclude that the conceptual tools of the democratization literature, both the structurally determined and agency-oriented models, miss an important dimension of politics because they take for granted the normative appeal of Western liberalism and focus on the structural and institutional factors that impede its actualization.

The colonial context and conflicts of identity that informed the Egyptian liberals' notions of nationhood and citizenship, which I consider essential to understanding the failure of the liberal experiment in postindependence Egypt, continue to escape social scientific accounts of contemporary politics in the Middle East. Despite the reformulation of their conceptual tools on the basis of new empirical research and comparative theories, social scientific approaches to Middle Eastern politics still assume a universal process of political change that is largely the result of structural factors and strategic actors whose rational action can impede or advance the development of modern institutions of pacts and negotiation. The culture and language that give meaning to citizenship and political community are left out of the social scientific paradigm.

For the past fifty years, scholars of Middle Eastern politics have disagreed on how best to capture and explain politics in the region (Binder 1957; Zartman 1976; Bill 1995; Tessler 1999; Anderson 1999).[17] The methodological and theoretical divide became particularly acute (Salame 1994; Tessler 1999) as the region lagged behind the "Third Wave" of democratization.[18] Two general research orientations compete for dominance. On one side of the methodological divide, cultural approaches attempt to link authoritarian institutions to a set of popularly held values and attitudes that inform political life. On the other, proponents of structural and institutional explanations emphasize social and economic constraints to democratic institution building.

Scholars who focus on culture to explain political change in the Middle East draw theoretical insight from Max Weber's seminal 1905 analysis of Protestantism and capitalism.[19] They maintain that dominant cultural norms, social customs, and religious values shape political behavior and institutions. According to this approach, prospects for democratization in the region depend ultimately on the disappearance of primordial values and norms thought to be fundamentally incompatible with modern democratic principles. Because of the theoretical and methodological difficulties that surround the concept of culture, cultural approaches to Middle Eastern politics have often been simplistic and essentialist. Hence scholars such as Raphael Patai (1973), Fatima Mernissi (1975), Fouad Ajami (1981), David Pryce-Jones (1989), Elie Keddouri (1992), and Bernard Lewis (2002) have suggested that the "Arab mind," the "Muslim psyche," "Islam," or the overall "fatalist character" of Middle Eastern peoples are fundamentally incompatible with modern democracy.[20] Although a number of political studies that use culture as an explanatory variable are not so reductive and are based on sound research, a basic causal relationship between culture and political outcome is assumed. The political scientists William Quandt (1969), John Waterbury (1970), Marvin Zonis (1971), Michael Hudson (1977), Robert Bianchi (1984), and the historians Philip Khoury and Joseph Kostiner (1990) focus on sociocultural factors such as family networks and primordial loyalties to explain how patronage politics infiltrate modern institutions and undermine democratization.[21] Still, these works have questioned the old established dichotomy between modernity and tradition taken for granted in political science. A more recent variant of the cultural approach to explaining political change is the focus on civil society. The connection between culture and the emergence of a public sphere leading to democratization (John Hall, 1985) became the focus of intense debates among Middle East specialists in the 1990s.[22] Orientalist scholars such as Ernest Gellner (1991) and Bernard Lewis (1993) have argued that Islamic societies, unlike the West, have no tradition of legal, corporate bodies independent from the state.[23] Others, including Ellis Goldberg (1993) and Richard Norton (1994, 1995) have demonstrated that autonomous associations are not at all alien to Muslim cultures and social traditions.[24] They maintain that exogenous factors, not cultural hostility, prevented civil society from carving out an autonomous public sphere in Muslim societies.

While attentive to culture, I question the idea that there is a single, enduring culture that can be identified and correlated empirically with the endurance of authoritarianism in the region. As Diane Singerman's painstaking 1995 study of local politics in a popular Cairo neighborhood has shown, there are at least four sources of political cultural reproduction: formal religion (Islamic orthodoxy, established religious traditions and institutions, etc.), local milieu (neighborhood networks, street activists, the influence of popular religious figures, etc.), modern national integration (social mobility, education, political adherence, etc.), and global influences (international migration, diverse media outlets, new consumption patterns, etc.).[25] Each one of these components may contain potentially democratic as well as antidemocratic attributes and may interfere with other components. Because so many different interactions between several variables can be taking place simultaneously or at different times, it is a huge methodological task to sort out what aspects of "culture" influence the political process, and to what extent.[26]

A second body of literature has focused on economic and social structures as determinant of political change. Scholars here argue that prospects for democratization in the Middle East will depend on long-term economic growth, the size of the middle classes, the state's dependence on taxation or on "rent," and the strength of independent entrepreneurs. In this perspective, economic imperatives, both domestic and international, will force political regimes to undertake economic and political reforms that favor the development of civil society and lead to democracy. Scholars such as Hazem Beblawi (1987), Giacomo Luciani (1988), Nazih Ayubi (1992), Rex Brynen (1992), Robert Springborg (1993), Daniel Brumberg (1995), and Alan Richards and John Waterbury (1996) have explored this connection.[27] More recently, scholars dissatisfied with traditional case studies of democratization in the Arab world have emphasized the need for a more cohesive, comparative approach. From a conceptual perspective, Bahgat Korany, Rex Brynen, and Paul Noble (1995, 1998) seek to establish a rigorous methodology to study and evaluate the connection between political liberalization and democratization.[28] They find that the region is too diverse and at the same time too similar to other developing regions to single out cultural specificity or economics as the determinant variables. From a historical institutional perspective, Abdo Baaklini, Guilain Denoeux, and Robert Sprinborg (1999) focus on the increasing, but widely ignored, role of legislatures in Arab politics.[29] The recent resurgence of legislative politics, they found, is in fact part of an older tradition of representative institutions.

My book departs from the existing literature. I contend that social, economic, and formal political institutions are misleading indicators of democratization when they are decoupled from the substantive issues of citizenship and political community. To be sure, there are growing signs of political and economic change that seem to favor democratization throughout the region. According to the Civil Society Center in Cairo, some seventeen countries were "liberalizing" or "democratizing" in 1993. However, the examples of Morocco, Egypt, Jordan, Tunisia, Algeria, Yemen, and Iran show that it is possible to initiate and implement political and economic reforms without actually democratizing. This is not a new observation. However, this study suggests a new place to look to understand what is going on. Social and economic interests certainly explain why specific groups oppose or support reforms, but they do not determine the outcome. In Morocco, for example, it is easier to pass a labor law contested by business representatives or proceed with a socially costly privatization program than to settle whether sovereignty resides with an abstract notion of the monarchy or directly with the people. Progress toward democracy is not simply a matter of political constraints, timing, or sequence of political and economic reform. It is above all a complex cultural process of negotiation to reconcile multiple, conflicting identities with the identity of the nation-state that claims to represent them all while suppressing their hegemonic temptations.

one

Colonialism as a Literary and Historical Phenomenon

L iberalism's historical connivance with colonialism to promote free markets and individual liberty overseas contradicts the principles of cultural
diversity and self-determination we generally associate with liberal theory.
The British Empire's territorial expansions to "civilize" natives in faraway
lands found political rationale and moral justification in liberal theorists
from Jeremy Bentham to John Robert Seeley. Yet, as Uday Mehta argues, the
complicity of British liberal thinkers with colonial conquest was grounded in
a genuine philosophical passion and confidence in the possibility of universal human flourishing.[1] Inattentiveness to the contradiction between liberalism and empire in classical liberal thinking lies somewhere else. Mehta
identifies what he calls an "internal" epistemological "urge" within liberal
theory to convert the "alien" into a familiar image. His analysis of British
imperialism is pertinent because it speaks to a crucial debate within colonial
and postcolonial studies on the nature of the colonial encounter and its relevance to understanding relations of domination and resistance in general.

Critics and Theorists of Colonial Relations

With the publication of Edward Said's *Orientalism*, postcolonial theorists
such as Homi Bhabha and Gayatri Spivak have privileged the "semiotic

field" of language and enunciation as the means by which to conceptualize relations of domination and resistance.[2] But because of their common suspicions of hegemonic, nationalist cultural claims, these authors are ambivalent about the semiotic field of the colonized as a uniform, coherent arena for native resistance and "self" assertion.[3] This oversight, though more applicable to Said than to Bhabha or Spivak, lends credence to the criticisms launched by the more empirically oriented postcolonial writers, such as Abdul JanMohamed, Aijaz Ahmad, Arif Dirlik, and Benita Parry. These critics charge postcolonial theorists with a new form of complicity with colonial discourse for confining the discourse critiquing Western hegemony to "semiotic squabbles" about colonial texts. Postcolonial critics privilege the historical domain, focusing on the daily struggles of the oppressed and breaking away from what they consider a new political agenda of the dominant West, reincarnated in postmodernism and poststructuralism. Such criticism, I hold, is not valid because postcolonial theorists are equally convinced of the importance of local cultures in the process of self-emancipation. The problem with postcolonial theory lies elsewhere. I suggest here that analyses of colonial and postcolonial relations, whether empirically grounded or theoretically oriented, by engaged nationalists or more distant scholars, are acutely aware of the confluence between the cultural and historical production of colonial relations. This awareness is clearly articulated in the writings of theoretically oriented scholars such as Said, Bhabha, and Spivak, and by the early critics of colonialism such as Aimé Césaire and Frantz Fanon. I bring out this convergence in the prolific writings of Fanon, a psychiatrist and militant activist during the Algerian war of liberation, to argue, in opposition to Said and Bhabha, that the use of culture in Fanon's writings cannot be reduced to crude nationalism.[4] Fanon is fully aware of "the pitfalls of nationalist consciousness," to which he devotes an entire chapter in The Wretched of the Earth. In opposition to postcolonial critics who pledge allegiance to Fanon, however, I maintain that while Fanon's critique of colonial relations, especially in Black Skin, White Masks, is based on extensive empirical observation, it is grounded in an abstract understanding of culture as language. The unmistakable theoretical influence of Jacques Lacan's psychoanalytic linguistics on Fanon's thinking allows him to consider culture as constitutive of consciousness and emancipation without falling into essentialism.[5]

Fanon is certainly the most distinguished of the first colonial writers, but he was not alone in inferring colonial practices from colonial texts and culture. Writing in the 1950s about French colonialism, Aimé Césaire explains that colonial regimes survive by resorting to two strategies: brute force and dehumanization.[6] He sees the relationship between the colonizer and the colonized as one of violence, brutality, and punishment (20–21). But advocacy of naked repression in the colonies, Césaire argues, is not the exclusive domain of colonial soldiers; it is legitimated in the writings of politicians, humanists, and idealist philosophers as well. His extensive references to Carl Siger and Ernest Renan, among others, as well as to less prestigious texts and practices drawn from his native Martinique, highlight Césaire's attentiveness to colonial writings and colonial policies. More importantly, many of the writings illuminate a general predisposition to violence and prejudice that has nothing to do with practical political problems such as establishing institutions of representation and emancipation in "illiberal cultures." He quotes, for example, Carl Siger, a colonial autocrat and author of *Essai sur la colonization* (1907), whose justification of violence in the colonies reflects a wider cultural complicity that recalls impulses behind the torturing of Iraqi "hajis" in Abu Ghraib:

> The new countries [colonies] offer a vast field for individual, violent activities which in the metropolitan countries would [be forbidden] but in the colonies . . . affirm their worth. Thus to a certain extent the colonies can serve as a safety valve for modern society. Even if this were their only value, it would be immense. (21)

Now consider the sentiments expressed by Ernest Renan, whose justification of colonial conquest is rooted in a quest to validate the superiority of certain European races and languages. Césaire quotes from Renan's *La reforme intellectuelle et morale de la France* (1871):

> The regeneration of the inferior or degenerate races by the superior races is part of the providential order of things for humanity. With us, the common man is nearly always a déclassé nobleman, his heavy hand is better suited to handling the sword than the menial tool. . . . Pour forth this all-consuming activity onto countries which, like China, are crying aloud for foreign conquest. Nature has made a race of workers, the Chinese race . . . a race of tillers of the soil, the Negro . . . a race of masters and soldiers, the European race.[7]

Siger and Renan may well represent extreme rationalizations of colonization. But Césaire situates these extremist views in the general trend of humanist philosophy whose advocates claimed to defend universal human values. These advocates defended the colonial project in the name of eliminating absolutism but did not mention the colonial authorities' cooperation with local tyrants. They applauded colonialism for introducing progress and rationality to the indigenous populations but never considered the immorality or consequences of destroying local cultures. They listed the number of roads, schools, hospitals, and factories that the mother countries built, but never noticed that the colonized peoples were largely deprived of services provided for the European communities.[8] Anticipating future works by Said, Bhabha, and other critical theorists, Césaire also argues that the philosophical links between Western liberal democracy and totalitarian ideologies—he refers specifically to fascism—are less shocking when we examine Renan's racial categories and consider the ruthless exercise of power in the colony. Thus Césaire's *Discourse on Colonialism*, though largely ignored by theorists of colonialism, inaugurated a field of research devoted to exposing not-so-subtle complicities in the cultural domain, a domain that operates simultaneously as the symbol of oppression in the colony and the repository of enlightened reason and individual emancipation in liberal thinking.

Césaire's critical reading of the prominent role of culture in the colonial context cannot be dismissed as an ideological, nationalist diatribe that viewed colonial relations in simplistic, clear-cut binary oppositions. Situated within the same critical tradition as Césaire, Fanon, C. A. Diop, and G. G. M. James,[9] the analyses of W. E. B. Du Bois and Albert Memmi, who both agonized greatly over their national identities, are no less attentive to culture as a privileged domain of resistance and domination.[10]

Du Bois, who was acutely aware of the material estrangement of Diaspora African Americans from the daily experiences and political struggles in Africa, recognized the difficulty, if not the impossibility, of escaping the African cultural heritage. More than a color-based nationalism, Du Bois's description of two conflicting souls—one African and oriented toward communal identity, the other American and reflecting national identity—represents the continuing, and perhaps never ending, cultural investing of political identity. Beyond formal political status and civil rights concessions, Du Bois saw in African American culture an affective political force that does not erode with the passage of time or estrangement from Africa's material life. Thus Du Bois associated African American emancipation not only with formal political emancipation in the "host" country but more importantly with the freeing of African cultural heritage as a whole from European colonialism in Africa.[11]

Memmi, a Tunisian Jew whose identity in French North Africa is neither colonial nor nationalist, displays a sense of ambivalent allegiance similar to Du Bois's "two souls." As a Jew in a colonized Muslim society, he belongs to a relatively privileged group. Yet Memmi's privilege depends on a colonizer who gives the "hope" of integration into European society while denying the actual possibility of that provisional concession. Memmi captures this colonial economy of inclusion and exclusion in the realm of culture. As a young student of philosophy at the Sorbonne, he heard rumors that he would not be allowed, as a Tunisian, to sit for the examinations. When he asked the president of the jury to let him take the exam, he was told, "It is not a right. It is a hope. Let us say it is a colonial hope."[12] Tunisian Jews, like all other Tunisians, were treated as second-class citizens, excluded from basic civil services and deprived of political rights. But unlike Moslems, Tunisian Jews aspired to identify with the French. What made that "hope" possible was not material privilege, which was derisory, according to Memmi, but cultural initiation and resolve: learning to speak and write in French, wearing Italian clothes, adopting European social habits, and carrying on even when these attempts were often laughable within the Jewish community, duplicitous in the eyes of fellow Tunisians, and ridiculed by the colonizer. One might add, with Memmi, that these cultural efforts are consequential political acts that redefined political boundaries and challenged both native and colonial authorities.

The culture-focused anticolonial views of Césaire, Du Bois, and Memmi are neither exhaustive nor necessarily analogous. But their diverse grounding of colonial relations in cultural efforts reflects a concern with a common human condition that is deeper than the familiar nationalist impulse: it concerns the tortuous, painful, and often complex process of self-emancipation. The elements, workings, hesitations, and bitter conflicts that characterize this process of self-emancipation are, I believe, at the center of recent colonial and postcolonial theorists from Bhabha to Said.[13] In this critical theoretical tradition, analyses that focus on language, whether in psychoanalytic or literary studies, are particularly insightful because they are less inclined to dismiss demands for cultural recognition as a rudimentary nationalist impulse.

Building on the psychoanalytic tradition of Fanon, Memmi, and Octave Mannoni, Ashis Nandy, a psychiatrist and social critic, studies the cultural and psychological distortions of colonialism on the colonizer and the colonized beyond the formal retreat of empire. For Nandy, the conflicting logic of colonial relations is most palpable not in the political system or the economy but in minds and cultures. He identifies the complex and surprising workings of colonial logic in two contrasting sets of biographies and literary and historical commentaries. On one side, the biography of Rudyard Kipling, who repressed memories of his Indian childhood to pass for an "authentic" Englishman, untainted by native culture, represents the maturity and masculinity of British rule.[14] The British in India, argues Nandy, rationalized their imperial hegemony on the basis of two exaggerated polarities: masculinity versus femininity and adulthood versus childhood (4–16). Through a fascinating juxtaposition of Kipling and Indian texts, Nandy shows that the colonized were also trapped in the colonial construction of natives as feminine and childish (51–62). He focuses on the works of Indian writers such as Madhusudan Dutt, Bakimchandra Chatterjee, and Rammohun Roy to show how they reinterpreted Hindu traditions to counter colonial discourse, emphasizing themes of masculinity, martial valor, and monotheistic divinity in the Indian texts. Nandy shows that the reformulation of India's traditions under pressure to be the manly obverse of the colonizer is a cultural trap that reproduces, though in a different way, the colonial narrative. He notes that colonialism "colonizes the minds in addition to bodies and it releases forces within the colonized societies to alter their cultural priorities once and for all. In the process, it helps generalize the concept of the modern West from a geographical and temporal entity to a psychological category. The West is everywhere, within the West and outside, in structures and in minds" (xi).

Yet Nandy does not surrender to the power or ubiquity of colonialism. A more promising counternarrative to colonial cultural construction, he argues, is represented by the biography of Aurobindo Ackroyd Ghose. A native of Bengal whose parents gave him an English middle name and sent him to be schooled in England, secluded from indigenous culture and language, Ghose rejected his English "self" to become a mystic revolutionary in the Hindu tradition. Nandy suggests that Indians who worked within local values and strove for cultural authenticity (e.g., Ghose, Mahatma Gandhi, Ishwarshandra Vidyasagar) provided a more creative and defiant response to colonial and postcolonial cultural domination. Yet their locally based cultural response was neither culturally exclusive nor incompatible with the West (48–51). Gandhi, the most eloquent representative of Indian authenticity, advocated simple human values and was not the antithesis of the English. Rather, he brought forth "the soft-side of human nature, the so-called non-masculine self of man," repressed in Christianity and censured in "Western self-concept" (49).

Nandy's intricate thesis is insightful because he explores the emancipating role of local cultural traditions within the critical philosophy of Foucault, Derrida, Kristeva, and Lyotard, whose works radically subvert Western cultural self-representation. In this sense, Nandy's two essays reflect a paradigmatic transition from the early historical treatments of colonialism to postcolonial theorizing heavily influenced by French radical thought.

But it is Edward Said's *Orientalism* that most symbolizes this paradigmatic shift. Drawing insights from the writings of Michel Foucault, Said was a pioneer in attempting to systematically locate historical imperialism in literary practices. He employs Foucault's notion of discourse to study Orientalist texts as a set of "discursive formations" that display two main characteristics: a dubious relationship to empirical reality and a built-in will to dominate. Said defines Orientalism as a "style of thought based on an ontological and epistemological distinction made between the 'Orient' and . . . the 'Occident.'"[15] This imaginary binary opposition between East and West has informed a large mass of European works, not only in academic disciplines and administrative documents but also in the arts, literature, and the media. Said makes it clear, however, that the connection between Oriental scholarship and imperial power is direct and concrete. He methodically deconstructs Orientalists' texts to show how Orientalism has been at the service of Western governmental policies and institutions since the early twentieth century. He focuses on the strategic dissemination of a "discursively produced Orient" via universities, professional societies, geographical services, and various circles of cultural influence. In parallel, he documents the appointment of prominent Orientalist scholars, travelers, and "experts" on the Orient as advisors and administrators in various positions of power. By the late nineteenth century, the Orientalist whom Said portrays is a "special agent of Western power" who had managed to get "beneath the films of obscurity" surrounding the mysterious East. For Said, then, Orientalism as an academic and literary tradition cannot be separated from the political strategies of the colonizer or imperialist. There is an unmistakable Orientalist imprint in the production of a "broadly imperialist view of the world" (15).

Said does not claim that all Oriental studies—a composite field of scholarly research dating back to the Middle Ages that includes history, philology, ethnography, and the study of Oriental texts—are unequivocally driven by conquest. But he argues that since the late eighteenth century, Oriental studies, specifically in France, England, and the United States, have become overtly complicit with colonial and imperial schemes in North Africa and the Middle East. Behind the claim to scientific knowledge and intellectual objectivity, Orientalist scholarship has systematically used pseudoscientific theories about race and human biology to validate the cultural notions of Oriental inferiority:

Thus the racial classifications found in Cuvier's *Le Regne animal*, Gobineau's *Essai sur l'inegalite des races humaines*, and Robert Knox's *The Races of Man* found a willing partner in latent Orientalism. To these ideas was added second order Darwinism, which seemed to accentuate the "scientific" validity of the division of races into advanced and backward, or European-Aryan and Oriental-African. Thus the whole question of imperialism . . . carried forward the binary typology of advanced and backward (or subject) races, cultures, and societies. . . . Since the Oriental was a member of a subject race, he had to be subjected. (206–7)

The problems with Said's arguments in *Orientalism* are well known. There is a tension between his grounding of discourse in agency, governed by a will to dominate, and Foucault's notions of discourse grounded in invisible, authorless networks of power. This tension is at the core of a series of untenable claims that Said seems to make: the incorrectly expected causal relation between Orientalism and imperialism cannot be established; the dualism between the "real" Orient and the "discursive" Orient is counterproductive; the "totalizing" homogeneity that Said imposes on the colonizer and the colonized contradicts his own arguments; and the absence of any voices of resistance is puzzling given Said's faith in human agency and the capacity to resist structures of power. But these are analytical tensions, not irreconcilable epistemological contradictions. Said's two most important theoretical propositions—that the reality of historical colonialism and imperialism can be inferred from Oriental texts that precede the actual colonial encounter, and that seemingly objective historiography is in fact complicit with colonialism—are still valid and particularly relevant to understanding the analogous literary and political revival of liberal imperialism after 9/11. Said's argument that colonialism and imperialism were justified and legitimated by Orientalist scholars before colonial conquest does not exclude material considerations, whether economic, political, or military, as rationales for the territorial annexations in the eighteenth and nineteenth centuries. Contrary to the claims of Said's empiricist detractors, *Orientalism* is not a book about establishing monocausal relations between a literary and a historical phenomenon. His general point is that Western knowledge about "other" peoples in Asia, Africa, and other parts of the world is not value free; rather, it distorts, and is associated with power. Conventional historical studies of colonialism have neglected this confluence. It is a moot point to fault Said, for example, for excluding German Orientalists from his study because Germany was not an imperial power in the Middle East and therefore invalidates his entire theory. As for the distortions, partiality, and complicity with colonial power that Said diligently associates with Orientalism, they do not imply an ontological prejudice toward the "native." Like Uday Mehta's British liberals, Said's Orientalists are caught up in an epistemological trap.

Clearly, however, Said is not satisfied with epistemological explanations alone. His search aims for deeper cultural details and possibilities of resistance that he discovers not with Foucault's "discursive formations" but with Fanon's phenomenological approach to culture, and not in Orientalist discourse but in Third World writings. In *Culture and Imperialism*, Said states at the outset that his purpose is to pursue what he left out of *Orientalism*: literary forms of resistance to Western domination in the Third World.[16] He acknowledges resistance to imperial domination within the West and softens some his harsh comments on Western literary figures in *Orientalism* but wants to pay special attention to decolonization narratives in nationalist struggles. Said's new emphasis on the importance of writings from the "historical experience" or the "*voyage in*," to describe the intellectual efforts of writers in the peripheral world, clearly recalls Fanon's phenomenological notion of the "lived experience of the black" as a strategy to disrupt the colonial narrative.[17] Yet Said hesitates. Suspicious of reductive categories such as race, religion, ethnicity, and national identity, he privileges the "hybrid" writings of exiled Third World intellectuals who live in the former metropolis to the writings of nationalist critics, whom he considers still trapped in the unproductive colonizer-colonized dichotomy. Ultimately, Said is more comfortable with metropolitan voices such as the Irish poet William Butler Yeats and the Indian migrant novelist Salman Rushdie than with the "voices of resistance" from within.

The contradiction between efforts to recover local counterknowledge and the postmodern suspicion of claims to cultural origins and authenticity is even more pronounced in the works of Homi Bhabha and Gayatri Spivak, who, more so than Said, aim to identify and recover marginalized subaltern voices along less essentialist lines. Modern colonialism, according to Bhabha, did not owe its survival to what Césaire calls the "dehumanization" of the colonized, or what Fanon considered "psychotic dependence." Rather, it survived through its ability to establish intermediary structures between the colonial authority and the natives, to legitimate and perpetuate the colonial project. For Bhabha, "Mimicry emerges as one of the most elusive and effective strategies of colonial power and knowledge."[18] In post-Enlightenment English colonialism, for example, the colonial project relied on the partial reformation of a class of natives to serve as intermediaries between the colonial authority and the colonial subjects. Colonial authorities pursued partial reformation because complete reformation would imply equality between the colonizer and the colonized. Analyzing the text of Charles Grant's "Observations on the State of Society among the Asiatic Subjects of Great Britain," published in 1792 by the East India Company, Bhabha writes:

> Caught between the desire for religious reform and the fear that the Indians might become turbulent for liberty, Grant implies that it is in fact the "partial" diffusion of Christianity, and the "partial" influence of moral improvements which will construct a particularly appropriate form of colonial subjectivity. What is suggested is a process of reform through which Christian doctrines might collude with divisive caste practices to prevent dangerous political alliances. . . . In suggesting, finally, that "partial reform" will produce an empty form of "the imitation of English manners which will induce them [the colonial subjects] to remain under our protection," Grant mocks his moral project and violates the Evidences of Christianity. (127)

Thus to support the colonial order, the native "interpreter" class was "to be Anglicized, but emphatically not to be English." As such, the natives were not to become exactly like the colonizer but to mimic him—become "almost the same, but not quite" (128). Yet in mimicry lay the hidden but potentially revolutionary threat to the colonial order. The desire for only partial reform disclosed the ambivalence of colonial discourse and disrupted its authority.[19] Mimicry was a form of resemblance that did not hide the identity of the person assimilating European civilization. Mimicry was a powerful colonial strategy and at the same time a threat to the colonial project because it continued to be an incomplete representation of the colonizer. The native interpreters created by the colonizer became themselves the agents and object of colonial surveillance. Hence for Bhabha, the colonial encounter was ambivalent from the start, and the differences between colonizer and colonized were not radically oppositional.

Perhaps more important, Bhabha argues that this ambivalence continues to inform postcolonial relations decades after independence to suggest complex patterns of cultural survival and real possibilities of intellectual renewal in the Third World.[20] In this sense, Bhabha's work is a relentless effort to break away both from Said's conception of and "fixation" on the ubiquity of Western power in Orientalism and from what Bhabha considers Fanon's reductive portrayal of the colonized.[21] While Bhabha's critique of Said is convincing, his reading of Fanon's works is less so. Bhabha credits

Fanon for using Lacanian theory in Black Skin, White Masks to understand colonial relations at the intersubjective level but faults him for focusing on economic exploitation or repressive laws in The Wretched of the Earth, a focus that Bhabha claims detracts from the larger issue of human emancipation. As I will explain later, this reading of Fanon is arbitrary, because Fanon remains consistently committed, though in a different way, to exploring issues of language, cultural authority, and emancipation in his later works as much as in his earlier writings. What Bhabha really objects to is Fanon's interest in "nationalist" cultures and identities that do not engage or necessarily speak to the colonizer. Like Said, Bhabha is suspicious of nationalism and weary of cultural self-containment.

Though admittedly eclectic in the range of authors, selective in the choice of texts, and schematic in connecting the covered topics, this overview is nonetheless sufficient to underline the importance of culture as language in the writings of both early critics of colonialism and more recent postcolonial theorists. Of course, there are significant differences not only between the two traditions but also within them that should not be overlooked. My point, however, is simply that the importance of culture in colonial relations and the confluence between literary and historical colonialism is assumed in both sets of writings. I argue next that Fanon represents the most coherent and convincing case of that confluence.

The Importance of Language in Fanon's Views on Emancipation

Writing during the 1950s, when the colonial conflict in French Algeria reached a dramatic point, Frantz Fanon wanted to expose the psychic structure of colonial relations. Fanon was responding to a newly published book by Octave Mannoni, Prospero and Caliban: The Psychology of Colonization.[22] The central thesis of Mannoni's book, according to Fanon, is that "the confrontation of 'civilized' and 'primitive' man creates a special situation—the colonial situation—and brings about the emergence of a mass of illusions and misunderstandings that only psychological analysis can place and define."[23] Mannoni asserts, however, that "when an adult Malagasy is isolated in a different environment, he can become susceptible of the classical type of inferiority complex; [this] proves almost beyond doubt that the germ of the inferiority complex was latent in him from childhood [rather than caused by his encounter with the colonialist]" (Fanon, Black Skin, White Masks, 84).

Fanon welcomes Mannoni's undertaking a psychological inquiry into col-

onization but rejects his postulate that the inferiority complex of the colonized exists before colonization. Fanon argues that the sense of deficiency
internalized by the colonized is created by the Europeans' feeling of supremacy: "It is the racist who creates his inferior" (93). The moment the
colonies are conquered and subjugated, the natives cease to exist as equal
people, for their identity becomes defined primarily as nonwhite, with all the
degrading notions that appellation entails. The reaction of the indigenous,
as Fanon describes it, is "hallucinatory whitening," whereby men of color
literally dream of becoming white men (99–103). By exposing the psychological dimension of colonialism, which constructs black as the opposite and
inferior pole of white, Fanon seeks to cultivate the revolutionary potential of
the binary implied in the colonial relationship. Hence in later works, Fanon
provides directions for the constitution of native self-identity, which would
motivate and enable colonized subjects to resist and reject the submissive
position assigned to them in the colonial order. Just as colonization was
based on the spatial, cultural, and racial differentiation between two peoples,
so decolonization would be the product of violent conflict between two
forces that the colonial experience had condemned to eternal opposition.[24]

Fanon speaks distinctively to the thesis that the colonized people need to
carve out their own language of resistance and liberation. In Black Skin, White
Masks, he writes:

> I ascribe a basic importance to the phenomenon of language. That is why I find it
> necessary to begin [the book] with this subject, which would provide us with one
> of the elements in the colored man's comprehension of the dimension of the other.
> For it is implicit that to speak is to exist absolutely for the other. . . . To speak
> means to be in a position to use a certain syntax, to grasp the morphology of this
> or that language, but it means above all to assume a culture, to support the weight
> of a civilization. . . . A man who has a language consequently possesses the world
> expressed and implied by that language. What we are getting at becomes plain:
> Mastery of a language affords remarkable power. (17–18)

When he wrote this, Fanon was addressing the dilemma of natives from
Martinique, and no doubt also his own dilemma, of whether or not to use
the language of the colonizer to subvert colonialism on its own terms. Fanon
is well aware of the potential power of speaking French, for he equates
mastering that language in the colonial context with material control. But in
the end, he argues, natives who adopt the language of the colonizer will not
necessarily escape racial discrimination. Natives, including the eloquent and
well-respected Aimé Césaire, who was "French enough" to run for a deputy

seat in the French parliament, are conspicuously reminded of their black-ness. As Fanon put it, "ready-made phrases [such as] 'a Negro with a univer-sity degree,' or 'a black man who handles the French language as no white man today can,' have a hidden subtlety, a permanent rub" (39). Fanon criti-cized the people of Martinique, who, unlike the Algerians, were all too eager to drop their Creole and adopt the French language to entertain "white" illusions and dream of "white" ambitions. This illusion—natives thinking of themselves as white Europeans because they spoke French—explains, ac-cording to Fanon, why colonial conflict in the West Indies never reached the moment of re-creation and emergence of self that results from violent re-sistance to oppression.

Yet Fanon is also aware of the potential trap of claiming to restore an identity based on an "authentic" language and culture. He stood apart from the negritude movement of the 1940s and 1950s that claimed the glories of "authentic" African tradition and identity to confront the denigration of black culture and people in colonial discourse. The controversy concerning the political need, or even epistemological possibility, of recovering a black "self" or "consciousness" in early anticolonial writers cannot be dismissed as postmodernist or poststructuralist squabbles, since they predated these theories and were linked, rather, to immediate historical and theoretical concerns. Historically, early anticolonial writers were tied to the ongoing struggles for emancipation in Africa and Asia; theoretically they were influ-enced by the growing moral and philosophical disillusionment with the Enlightenment within European intellectual circles in the aftermaths of Naz-ism and fascism. Hence to ask which language, identity, or conception of the human can articulate postcolonial subjectivity is tied to the same questions that the negritude movement and later the works of Césaire, Fanon, and Memmi addressed in their own way.[25] At the heart of these queries is the dilemma of either emphasizing cultural identities and risking falling into essentialism or adhering to the notion of universal political emancipation and risking legitimizing a hegemonic political paradigm that in any case cannot escape the cultural imprint of the dominant group.

Fanon's deep ambivalence on this question—apparent in his vacillation between the strategic claim of black identity in Black Skin, White Masks and the call for a new revolutionary humanism in The Wretched of the Earth—anticipates current divergences on the pitfalls and liberating potential of what is today labeled "identity politics."[26] In Black Skin, White Masks, Fanon's primary concern is to explore what it means for a black man—who is "sealed in narcissistic blackness" as a result of white racism—to claim an identity.

He summarizes this personal dilemma as follows: "As I begin to recognize that the Negro is the symbol of sin, I catch myself hating the Negro. But then I recognize that I am a Negro. There are two ways out of this conflict. Either I ask others to pay no attention to my skin, or else I want them to be aware of it" (197). Fanon's thinking about how to escape this dilemma seems incoherent at first, as he appears to endorse the claim of black identity at the beginning of the book only to undermine it later by embracing a transcendental conception of being. In the first three chapters, Fanon juxtaposes two conflicting attitudes of the black man toward the "white world": to hide behind a white mask by appropriating the language, culture, and consciousness of the Other, or to assume one's true color and search for a black identity. At this stage he believes that a black man "who is driven to discover the meaning of black identity" can overcome the alienation that racial discrimination produces, whereas a black man who seeks to become white remains trapped in a psychologically unstable position. Against the colonizer's denigration of African culture and rejection of the black man, Fanon insists on the importance of emphasizing difference: "I resolved, since it was impossible for me to get away from an inborn complex, to affirm myself as BLACK. Since the other hesitated to recognize me, there remained only one solution: to make myself known" (115). In this respect at least, Fanon seems to share the identity claims of negritude poets and essayists whose glorification of the "natural qualities" of the black man he quotes at length.

At the same time, however, one senses a brutal irony in Fanon's tune when he joins the chorus on "black humanness" or "closeness to nature," as when he cites Césaire in these verses:

Those who invented neither gunpowder nor the compass
Those who never learned to conquer steam or electricity
Those who never explored the seas or the skies
But they know the farthest corners of the land of anguish . . .
. . . But those without whom the earth would not be the earth
My blackness is neither a tower nor a cathedral
It thrusts into the red flesh of the sun
It thrusts into the burning flesh of the sky . . .[27]

Fanon rejoins sarcastically: "The tom-tom chatters out the cosmic message. Only the Negro has the capacity to convey it, to decipher its meaning, its import" (124). Fanon does not find solace in the dichotomous image of the black man's closeness to nature and the white man's growing alienation in industrialized society. He does not want the black man to be appropriated as an evanescent distraction for the alienated Other, even if that appropriation brings some kind of recognition of black humanness. "When the whites feel that they have become too mechanized," he complains, "they turn to the men of color and ask them for a little human sustenance. At last I had been recognized, I was no longer a zero" (Black Skin, White Masks, 129). The recognition that Fanon is looking for is different indeed from the native essentialism that he later attributes to Césaire and Léopold Senghor.

Yet, as much as Fanon feels uncomfortable with the sentimental, reactive images that negritude's defenders project on African peoples and cultures, he is painfully aware of the strategic value of negritude in the long struggle for self-emancipation. In Black Skin, White Masks, Fanon condemns Sartre for dismissing negritude as a secondary moment in the world revolutionary movement, although he himself later relinquishes negritude for an abstract conception of freedom. When introducing Senghor's L'anthologie de la poésie nègre et malgache, Sartre writes: "In fact, Negritude appears as the minor term of a dialectical progression: The theoretical and practical assertion of the supremacy of the white man is its thesis; the position of negritude as an antithetical value is the moment of negativity. But this negative moment is insufficient by itself. . . . It is intended to prepare the synthesis or realization of the human in a society without races. Thus negritude is the root of its own destruction" (133). Fanon felt that he had "been robbed of [his] last chance." The claim to a white identity proved to be an unhealthy illusion, and now Sartre, a "friend of the colored peoples," "snatched away" from him the purpose of reclaiming a black identity. "Not yet white, no longer wholly black, I was damned. . . . I needed to lose myself completely in negritude. One day, perhaps, in the depths of that unhappy romanticism. . . . In any case I needed not to know. . . . Sartre, who remains The Other, gave me a name and thus shattered my last illusion" (133–37).

Fanon does not believe for a moment that Sartre is wrong in reducing negritude to a fleeting romantic moment. Still heavily influenced by Sartre's transcendental conception of freedom in Being and Nothingness, Fanon wants to believe in the possibility of an abstract consciousness: "I am not a potentiality of something, I am wholly what I am. . . . My Negro consciousness does not hold itself out as a lack. It is. It is its own follower. The Negro is not. No more than the white man is" (135, 231). However, he reproaches Sartre for being inattentive to l'expérience vécue du Noir, "the lived-experience of the black," by which Fanon means something different from what Charles Markmann translates as "the fact of blackness" in Black Skin, White Masks.[28] The lived-experience is a subjective, psychological "processing" of a fact or an objective condition that is not immediately accessible to Sartre, the Other. This idea could be interpreted to mean that only a black man ultimately understands the black condition and therefore only a black man can represent or speak in the name of the black condition. However, this interpretation is not what Fanon has in mind, since he insists that it is possible and necessary to "go beyond the historical" to comprehend the human condition.

One is then tempted to ask, "What kind of recognition does Fanon really want?" to rephrase his famous question about the black man at the book's beginning. At this stage of his writings, Fanon is concerned with reestablishing what I would call, following Lacan, the phenomenological "I." According to Fanon, the black is not considered an ordinary or natural phenomenon in an environment dominated by white man because of the darkness of his skin and the impossibility of hiding it behind a white mask.[29] He rejects fixing the black man into either a white mask or a black skin, both of which ultimately lead to "a zone of non-being." "No, I do not have the duty to be this or that. . . . I have no wish to be the victim of the fraud of a black world. . . . I am not a prisoner of history. I should not seek there for a meaning of my destiny," he forewarns by way of conclusion in Black Skin, White Masks (229). Consistent with his analysis of black-white relations ultimately immersed in personal "lived-experience," Fanon first situates the struggle for black self-emancipation in the realm of subjective recognition and affirmation independently of a "racialized" black body.[30] In his treatment of what he calls "black psychopathology," Fanon concludes that the alienation of the Antillean, who after thinking of himself as a white man suddenly "discovers" that he is black when he encounters white fear and rejection, is linked to the symbolization of the body. To explain the black child's alienation from his own body, that is, when he identifies himself as a "body-for-others," Fanon turns to Lacan's concept of the mirror stage, which would allow him to distinguish between the symbolization of the black body and the imago.[31]

In a long footnote on Lacan, Fanon discusses the importance of the mirror stage for the constitution of the (white) subject. "The subject's recognition of his image in the mirror," he quotes Lacan, "is a phenomenon that is doubly significant for the analysis of this stage: The phenomenon appears after six months, and the study of it at that time shows in convincing fashion the tendencies that currently constitute reality for the subject; the mirror image, precisely because of these affinities, affords a good symbol of that reality: of its affective value, illusory like the image, and of its structure, as it reflects the human form" (Black Skin, White Masks, 161). But access to the symbolic is barred to colonized black people, Fanon argues, because white Negrophobia is grounded in the biological, the imago. The black person "symbolizes the biological danger. To suffer from a phobia of Negroes is to be afraid of the biological. For the Negro is only a biological" (165). Hence the futility of attempting to explain the alienation of the Antillean in psychoanalytic terms, for his alienation is not neurotic. "Since the racial drama is played out in the open, the black man has no time to 'make it unconscious.' . . . The Negro's inferiority or superiority complex or his feeling of equality is conscious. . . . In him there is none of the affective amnesia characteristic of the typical neurotic" (150). To unlock the black man's entry into the symbolic, that is, to free him from what Fanon calls "the epidermalization of his inferiority," he underlined early in the book the priority of changing the "social and economic realities" of black people (10–11).

In subsequent works, notably in The Wretched of the Earth, Studies in a Dying Colonialism, and Toward the African Revolution, Fanon appears to have abandoned the search for self-recognition and affirmation in language; but in fact he never did. To be sure, his involvement in the war of liberation in Algeria influenced his view on the necessity of achieving emancipation through violent transformation of the material conditions that sustain colonial domination, yet Fanon's objective never ceased to be "subjective" self-emancipation. His "therapeutic" notion of violence is meant to reestablish the colonized's shattered symbolic order, that is, the order of culture and language in the Lacanian sense, without which self-emancipation remains unattainable.

Although Fanon does not explicitly state this, the elements and even strategies to reestablish that symbolic order are scattered throughout his writings.[32] Fanon's distinction between national culture and national consciousness, his analysis of the colonizer's efforts to unveil Algerian women, the revolutionary potential he unfashionably concedes to Algerian peasants, and the transforming power he accords to The Voice of Algeria can all be read as strategies to reestablish the colonized's symbolic order. Fanon valorizes national culture, achieved through liberation, over national consciousness, which he associates with formal independence, because national culture implies the destruction of the colonizer's culture and language and the rehabilitation of the colonized's system of reference, whereas national consciousness implies merely establishing national sovereignty over inherited colonial institutions.[33] The objective of restoring the colonized's symbolic order is not to recover some sacred heritage or authentic identity, as advocates of negritude would have it. Rather, Fanon's aim is to achieve a new subjectivity on the basis of a conception of man that departs from the moral and philosophical foundations of Western humanism, now shaken up by the advent of colonialism and the Holocaust.[34]

As an example of the colonizer's determination to destroy native social and cultural systems of reference, Fanon points to the immense efforts and resources that the French colonial administration invested to unveil Algerian women.[35] Fanon interprets the French colonial formula in Algeria—"Let's win over the women and the rest will follow"[36]—not just as another shrewd and flawed policy but as a strategic battle between Muslim and colonial European symbolic orders that colonialism was bound to lose. Long before the colonial authorities realized it, unveiled Algerian women became unsuspected bearers of arms and bombs into French quarters hitherto inaccessible to Algerian revolutionaries. The revolutionary potential that Fanon attributes to Algerian peasants—a heretical view among French avant-garde revolutionaries at the time—is accordingly linked to their relative insulation from colonial culture. Unlike the Westernized town dwellers, including the working classes, and the nationalist elites whom Fanon ridicules for imitating the colonizer's lifestyle, rural folks remain attached to their social customs and are therefore more motivated to transform a war of national independence into a total war of colonial liberation.[37] Here again, Fanon's objective is not to advocate a moral or aesthetic attachment to peasant culture, since he recognizes that it could be retrogressive; rather, his point is that the colonized should not be trapped in that "zone of non-being."

Finally, for Fanon, the radio broadcast called The Voice of Algeria was not just an innovative appropriation of alien technological tools to resist alien rule but a material process to retrieve native speech.[38] Colonial settlers had their Radio-Alger to sustain "the occupant's culture, [mark] him off from the non-culture, from the nature of the occupied. . . . The radio [was] a symbol of French presence . . . a material representation of the colonial configuration" (71–73). In the same way, The Voice of Algeria "that speaks from the djebels" provided "the possibility of hearing an official voice . . . to tell the story of the liberation march, and incorporate it into the nation's new life. . . . This voice, often absent, physically inaudible, which each one felt welling up within himself, founded on an immense perception of the fatherland, became materialized in an irrefutable way" (82–85). Fanon's interpretation of The Voice of Algeria recalls the prohibitive voice of the absent father, the author of the Law and master of the symbolic order.

But it is Fanon's concept of violence that most clearly displays his intuitive concern with the symbolic order. His insistence that the colonized carve out their own language is most dramatically expressed in his revolutionary theory and fascination with violence for which he was criticized by liberal humanists.[39] Though morally compelling, such criticisms seem to miss the point. Fanon's liberation strategy is not based on a theory of violence for the sake of physically harming or exterminating the enemy but on a specific conception of violence.[40] He talks about creative rather than destructive violence, which inspired the Mujahidins in Algeria, and which Fanon regards as the ultimate sign of both demarcation and re-creation: demarcation from the culture, concepts, logic, and civilization that gave credence to colonial domination, and re-creation of destroyed native institutions, language, and system of reference. He saw in jihad the articulation of an ethical language of resistance, not "holiness," as Marie Perinbam appears to suggest. So when Fanon prescribes the use of violence as a necessary strategy of emancipation, he does so with a keen, even if implicit, awareness of the language that structures it.

There is another reason why the meaning of violence in Fanon's writings defies conventional moral judgments. Despite his quite open endorsement of violence, physical coercion as such was morally repulsive to him as a psychiatrist. Fanon was clearly tormented by the contradiction between his profession and his political endorsement of armed insurrection. And he was painfully aware of the psychological disorders engendered by violence and wrote extensively about them. But this did not alter in his eyes the value of violence for resisting and transforming the colonial situation, for violence in this context had to be "primitive" and "natural," and therefore an "ethical" language: the only language that could effectively liberate the colonized and subvert the logic of colonialism. It is total rupture with the institutions of colonization and re-creation based on a new language that Fanon has in mind, it seems, when he tells former colonized people that "humanity is waiting for something other from us than . . . imitation, which would be almost an obscene caricature. [We therefore] must turn a new leaf, we must work out new concepts, and try to set afoot a new man."[41]

The Relevance of the Familial Metaphor

I have argued that Césaire's, Memmi's, and particularly Fanon's privileging of culture and language as the source of power and resistance is not necessarily incompatible with the anti-essentialist views of postcolonial theorists such as Said and Bhabha. I would moreover suggest that Jacques Lacan's familial paradigm of the emerging subject—the male child who utters "I, you, he, she" to distinguish himself from his parents—is a useful metaphor to capture the most primary act of self-emancipation. The appropriation of the grammatical "I," which empowers the child to take a grip on himself as not-other and negotiate a "full" place in existing discourses and social practices, allows us to conceive of identity not as a metaphysical essence that can be "objectively" retrieved and actualized. Rather, here, identity is an interactive, discursive process with multiple interlocutors (oneself, mother, and father in the familial triad) and from multiple positions (from the child's initial identification with his body's image, to being the mother's object of desire, to having a phallus of his own).

This explanation of identity invites reflection on the paradoxical humanizing and alienating effects that Jacques Lacan attributes to the acquisition of language and resolution of the Oedipus complex. In his writings, Lacan distinguishes two important "phases" or moments of transition in the constitution of the human subject: the Imaginary Order and the Symbolic Order.[42] The Imaginary corresponds to Freud's primary identification, which Lacan calls the *stade du miroir*, where a child searching for self invests with narcissistic libido the image of another human being—his own in the mirror, his mother's, or another child's—with which he merges in a pre-Oedipal, dyadic relationship. This encounter is salutary, says Lacan, because it is the child's first step toward the appropriation of the corporeal "I," that is, toward physical self-recognition, by discovering complete representation of a hitherto fragmented biological entity (93–96). But this is also the beginning of alienation in the Imaginary.[43] Cognizance of the totality of one's own body is deceptive because the body, still dominated by narcissistic identification with images of the other, is external to the self. At the mirror stage, a child is his own double rather than himself: he would cry when he sees another child fall, misconstruing the image of the other child for himself; and in his mother, he sees nothing but a peer with whom he merges. Because the infant's body infringes on the mother's from the beginning and the initial "lack" of being emerges from this undifferentiated union, the phallus stands as the signifier of completeness. In this "intransitive" relationship, a child cannot take a grip on himself as a singular subject because "he is prisoner of the signifier, a prisoner of his ego's image or the image of the ideal. A child effectively lives by the other's gaze upon him and he is unaware of this."[44] If a child remains prisoner of the Imaginary, he risks becoming like an animal, not able to distinguish himself from the world that surrounds him. This would constitute an instance of the Lacanian psychosis: the inability to distinguish image from self, the signifier from the signified.[45] The child is forced to interrupt the quest of self in the other when the Symbolic father, the author and guarantor of the Law, disrupts the mother-child union and imposes the Name-of-the-Father that institutes the prohibition of incest. The result of this encounter with the *nom du père* results in the child's precipitation into the Symbolic Order.

In the Symbolic Order, a term Lacan borrows from Claude Lévi-Strauss's symbolic function to connote the rules that sustain a human collectivity, the child integrates the triangular structure of the familial order, where child, mother, and father are assigned names and places and assume their roles in society as singular subjects. Hence the superiority of the Symbolic over the Imaginary in Lacan's thinking. The Symbolic constructs what the image has denied the child in the mirror stage, that is, awareness of self as a human entity distinct from other human beings. Equally important, entry into the Symbolic involves a confrontation with paternal interdiction, which the child either negotiates by internalizing preestablished cultural norms and social rules and hence surviving the Oedipal drama, or refuses to submit and laps back into the Imaginary and falls ill.[46] Thus we are introduced to another characteristic paradox of Lacanian psychoanalysis in the long battle for subjectivity: humanization is attained at the cost of the circumscription of individuality. In both processes, language plays a central role.

The importance accorded to language in psychoanalytic studies does not originate with Lacan. Although not familiar with Ferdinand de Saussure's modern linguistics, Freud had already identified in speech what he called "nodal points" of discourse, the equivalent of a secondary "signifying system," to explore conscious and unconscious processes.[47] This signifying system is secondary in the sense that the language that interests psychoanalysts has a subjective logic and basis of organization and is therefore distinguishable from *la langue*, the "neutral" or primary form of social communication, on which speech nonetheless relies. The originality of Lacan lies in his confounding the Symbolic Order, that is, the order of social norms, codes of behavior, et cetera, with the order of language, the signifier-signified structure, which allowed him to articulate his famous thesis that "the unconscious is the discourse of the Other."

For the purpose of my argument, which is to draw a parallel between Egypt's struggle to situate itself (politically but also historically and culturally) between Europe and the Orient and Lacan's linguistic rendering of the Oedipal problem, the thesis is crucial. If we roughly translate the "Other," with a capital O, as the world of rules into which every child is born and must submit to, the thesis carries three meanings. First, it implies that what is repressed in the unconscious does not originate in the unconscious but finds its way there after being symbolized through language. Hence Lacan's formula "Language is the condition of the unconscious."[48] Second, the thesis means that human subjects are constituted by the impersonal reality of language, an idea that Lacan substantiates in another important formula, "The child is caught up in language from the time of his birth." Finally, in conflating the unconscious with the Other, Lacan extricates the unconscious process from the sphere of brute biological instinct or "Need" and anchors it fully in "Desire," which, he says, has to be symbolized before it makes its way into the unconscious. Hence Lacan's third, most important formula, "Desire is the desire of the Other."

If we extend Lacan's linguistic rendering of man's never quite complete transition from the Imaginary to the Symbolic Order to Egypt's flustered fascination with Europe and rejection of the Orient, then we can grasp the relevance of Lacanian notions to reinterpreting Egypt's liberal experiment during the interwar period. To reduce the appropriation of Western political institutions to some objective reality, whether social, economic, or cultural, would be equivalent to confusing "desire," which is mental, with "need," which is physical, thereby privileging biological instinct over meaning in the march toward achieving emancipation. If appropriating a modern political system is conceived as a message to the Other, in this case as a desire to be recognized and identified with Europe, then it is at the level of discourse and its lacunae that such a motivation, conscious or unconscious, is to be located. As in the patient's speech for Lacan, what is said is as important as how and when it is said, for the purpose is not to retrieve an objective "truth" but to uncover the logic that structures Egyptian liberal discourse. Lacan does not view tribulations during the Oedipal drama, under whose spell all humans remain vulnerable for the rest of their lives, as a mental illness to be treated clinically or as a crime that society can tolerate or punish. He sees the "Oedipal moment" as an odyssey into the unconscious to be "unrealized" by reestablishing its Imaginary and Symbolic dimensions.[49] Similarly, the Egyptian liberals' claim to cultural closeness to Europe in opposition to the Orient could be seen as an epic wandering that can be neither rejected nor accepted on the basis of some "objective" criteria but rather must be understood or recognized by restoring its Imaginary and Symbolic dimensions. However, on what basis can we assume a parallel between an incomplete or derailed Oedipal experience and the Egyptian liberals' drive to identify Egypt as a European entity? I suggest that the liberals' rejection of any symbolic representation of the Orient—the fez, Arabic poetry, or blood connection with the Semites (symbols that had already been denigrated by Europe)—amounts to a rejection of the Name-of-the-Father's two commandments: to the child, thou shall not sleep with thy mother; and, to the mother, thou shall not reappropriate thy product.[50] If the mother does not accept the father as the author of the Law, as the colonized cultures denied the authority of colonial Europe, the child does not recognize the paternal interdiction and remains fixated with the mother's image. That bars the child's access to the Symbolic Order and to language, which allows him to differentiate himself from the world that surrounds him and to pronounce the "I" that sets him apart from other human beings. If the mother accepts the father as the author of the Law, the child submits and gains access to the father's speech, which establishes the prohibition of incest.

I suggest that Lacan's linguistic rendering of emancipation is relevant to understanding liberal colonialism, particularly John Stuart Mill's view of colonialism as a force of emancipation guided by the "European family of Nations"[51]—that is, a liberalism based on a political and moral philosophy that legitimates colonial conquest in the name of liberating backward communities from local despotisms and "training [them] in what is specifically *wanting* to render them capable of a higher civilization."[52] In this sense, colonial liberalism is less a theory of political emancipation than an ideology of assimilation that promises to educate and civilize only to impose on the natives a national identity of proximity that confirms Europe as the (familial) dispenser of culture, authority, and sovereignty. The Egyptian liberals' interpretation of liberalism, even if largely intuitive, corresponds to Mill's general view. If the Egyptian people were to become free and civilized, they had to rectify a primary lack by partaking in the manners of Europeans and surrendering to the culture and will of "Mother Europe." The appropriation of modern European political concepts, nationalism, secularism, and constitutionalism, like the discarding of the traditional fez and the adoption of the English hat, symbolized for the Egyptian liberals the recovery of an imaginary European identity that was lost following the Islamic conquest of Egypt.

two

The Colonial Encounter in Egypt

A lthough the French occupation of Egypt was not formal colonization and lasted only three years (1798–1801), its impact was profound because, more than anything else, it was an effort to rewrite a cultural order. "The conquest of Egypt was not an ordinary matter of cupidity," commented the French romanticist Jules Michelet on the Napoleonic invasion of Egypt in 1798; "rather, it was the sublime hope of human resurrection."[1] In a letter to General Kleber shortly after the French invaded Egypt, Bonaparte reflected the same faith and eagerness: "What is happening here is of the utmost interest, and will have immense effects on trade and civilization. Great revolutions will date from this epoch."[2] Notwithstanding Napoleon's universalizing message and the use of local discursive conventions to rationalize the occupation, the French army's repressive measures exposed the inherent contradictions of the first modern colonialist excursion in the Middle East. To be sure, the French found a country torn by feuding Ottoman Mamluks and devastated by overtaxation, plague outbreaks, and natural disasters. The Egyptian chronicler al-Jabarti leaves no doubt about the dismal social and economic exploitation of Egyptians at the hands of Ottoman viceroys before the French military expedition. Al-Jabarti puts the blame for the French invasion squarely on the tyrannical rule of the Ottoman beys, especially Murad and Ibrahim (1775–98). Still, the French authorities added extra economic burdens, and the political benefits for the Egyptians were rather thin. Cut off from supplies by the British-Ottoman forces, the French imposed additional taxes on merchants, artisans, and peasants; their soldiers looted markets for food and implemented harsh repressive measures against resisting populations, local authority figures, and religious institutions. The suppression of the Cairo uprising in October 1798, the hanging of Muhammad Kurayyim, the governor of Alexandria, the harsh repression of rebellious rural communities along the Nile Valley, and ultimately the bombardment of al-Azhar, a traditional institution of religious learning and a symbol of resistance, all epitomized in the eyes of the Egyptians the stark reality of Napoleon's "liberating" mission.[3]

Napoleon's Expedition:
Asymmetries of Power and Language

Napoleon's institutional attempts to "emancipate" native Egyptians were also limited. His direct appeal to indigenous Egyptian notables, merchants, and local leaders to "participate" in a colonial administration that excluded the Mamluks may be considered a first step in self-government. After securing his military positions, Napoleon established a Diwan, or administrative council, to which he appointed by decree Egyptian religious figures, prominent merchants and artisans, and members of influential urban families. But the Diwan was just a formal institution, and its members were powerless when the French decided to limit its activities or even suspend it, as they did for two months after the Cairo revolt. The Diwan's powers were limited to decisions on civil government in Cairo only; the rest of the country was run by Napoleon's appointed Provincial Councils. Even in Cairo, every decision required the approval of the French authorities, and important matters—such as appointments of officials, the creation of legislation, the reform of inheritance laws, civil and judiciary matters, and the revision of the land distribution system—clearly lay in the hands of French officials. Yet these limitations are "ordinary" in the colonial context, and it is not illuminating to evaluate Napoleon's political design for Egypt by focusing on the Diwan's lack of formal prerogatives. What is compelling in the story of Egypt's encounter with Napoleon Bonaparte, and later with the British, is not just financial expropriation or the semblance of political emancipation but also the meta-inscription of colonial conflicts in texts, both literary and material.

"In the name of Allah, the Merciful, the Compassionate; there is no god but Allah, He has no offspring and no partner in His kingdom." Thus began the Arabic proclamation circulated by Napoleon in Alexandria the day after his troops invaded Egypt, on an early July morning in 1798. To Egyptian people in the streets, Napoleon presented himself as the savior come to free Egypt from the despotic Ottoman sultans who had been ruling Egypt since the early sixteenth century. The pamphlet continues:

> O ye Egyptians, they may say to you that I have not made an expedition hither for any other object than that of abolishing your religion; but this is a pure false-hood. . . . Tell the slanderers that I have not come to you except for the purpose of restoring your rights from the hands of the (Mamluk) oppressors and that I more than the Mamluks serve God—may He be praised and exalted—and revere His prophet Muhammad and the glorious Qur'an.[4]

Ironically, while the proclamation proceeds to confirm that the French nation, on whose behalf Napoleon speaks, is "based upon the foundation of freedom and equality," the first two articles immediately set the tone and conditions of the French "liberating" mission. Article 1 asserts: "All inhabitants situated within three hours distance from the . . . French army . . . are required to . . . announce that they submit and that they have hoisted the French flag which is white, blue, and red." Article 2 declares: "Every village that shall rise against the French army shall be burnt down."[5]

Commenting on the arrival of the French expedition in Egypt, the Egyptian chronicler al-Jabarti wrote that "the year 1213 [1798] marked the beginning of epic battles, tremendous events, disastrous deeds, frightful calamities, total confusion, the overthrow of the natural order of things, revolutions, continual terror, social disorders, political discord, and general devastation."[6] Napoleon's "trick," his use of Islamic discursive conventions to introduce a new discourse of political order and domination, apparently did not fool this witness of the French expedition. In a witty and revealing passage, al-Jabarti scrupulously commented on the style of the Arabic declaration, suggesting that Napoleon's Arabic text, with all the errors it embodied, could only be the work of a corrupt author. What is most striking in al-Jabarti's critique is his distinction between the Egyptian's world from the conqueror's world—the natural versus unnatural "order of things"—on the basis of the written word. From the aberrations of the Arabic text, he deduces the aberrant character of the French authorities. Commenting on the grammatical and stylistic errors of Napoleon's declaration, al-Jabarti writes, for example:

[In Napoleon's] statement *Fahadara* (therefore has come) there is no reason for this *fa* here. Good style would require *wa-qad-hadara* [it has come]. His statement *bta'al-Mamalik* [belonging to the *Mamluks*] is despicable and a banal and trite word. The word *mutma'in* should be *mutma'inan* because it is a *hal* [circumstantial expression] and converting it to the *raf'* [normative] incorrectly is an indication of the [sorry French] state, and their insignificance.[7]

The ironic composition of Napoleon's declaration, in that it uses local discursive conventions to impose political domination, merits special attention because it reflects the tensions characteristic of colonial liberalism. Written in a mixture of scriptural and colloquial Arabic, the proclamation begins with the Qur'anic invocation of God and continues with an explicit guarantee of protection for local religious beliefs. Yet despite its simulation of Islamic style and references, the proclamation was clearly meant to displace the authority of the local religious traditions it allegedly set out to protect, and to establish a new authority in their place. The document proclaimed liberty but was the product of the propaganda organs of a threatening invader; it promised liberation from foreign, Ottoman despotism but imposed a new, alien form of control and surveillance; it declared equality but demanded submission and established a hierarchy of literal, spatial proximity to the French army posts.

Sensing the deterioration of relations between the French authorities and Egyptian populations, Napoleon decided to reconvene the Diwan two months after it had been prorogued. In a public statement to the people of Egypt, Napoleon explains his reason for reestablishing the council in terms that invoke two contradictory textual traditions: the French republican value of deferring to the people (a value that in practice was largely ceremonial and manipulative), and references to fictive Qur'anic verses that allegedly demanded the subordination of Egyptians.[8] In his statement, Napoleon says that Allah had ordered him to show compassion to the Egyptian people even though some of them had gone astray and had caused much harm and chaos in the country. He further claims that in the sacred Qur'an, many verses prophesied his conquest of Egypt and therefore any opposition to his rule would be tantamount to a renunciation of God's will. Thus Napoleon presented collective, unwavering subordination as a divine order and as a condition for a vague notion of "representation" by the few in the Diwan.

This odd rationalization of political authority from an invader who represents a modern order bent on abolishing the sacred authority of kingship lends itself to two different but complementary readings. A member of the

French expedition provides a political reading of the statement: he recollects that the move to revive the Diwan had nothing to do with political representation or initiation in self-government; rather, it was a failed device to bring back native Egyptian leaders who had lost faith in Napoleon and formed their own revolutionary committees around mosques.[9] Despite this potential political reading, al-Jabarti challenged Napoleon's statement on literary, not explicitly political, grounds. In a commentary that recalls his reading of Napoleon's first Arabic proclamation, which raised doubts about his real intent for invading Egypt, al-Jabarti rejects Napoleon's references to Egypt in the Qur'an as "gross falsifications and depraved delusions that can be readily dismissed without much examination."[10] As with his earlier critique, al-Jabarti astutely infers political trickery from a literary distortion.

This is not to suggest that local texts and traditions can't be oppressive or that the imbalance of power between colonizer and colonized simply disintegrates once "authentic" figures such as al-Jabarti, the Ayatollah Ali al-Sistani, or Gandhi resort to local discursive traditions. Rather, the story brings to mind the inscription of power relations and domination in textual contests that strive to establish ownership of cultural traditions. It is difficult indeed to imagine how al-Jabarti in sixteenth-century Cairo, like Systani in today's Najaf, could face the overwhelming force and technological power of a vastly superior army. In both cases, their traditional knowledge of the Qur'an proved more effective in subverting the legitimacy and authority of foreign invaders. Hence, using local discursive traditions to resist colonial claims to cultural superiority and domination cannot be written off as a pointless, desperate attempt to ignore the reality of imperial power by falling back on some mythical past. As Fanon discovered in French Algeria, even though cultural expressions look rowdy and disjointed, they reestablish the colonized human experience that colonial discourse attempts to render inhuman and unattainable.

Yet Edward Said, who is attentive to the connection between textual and historical colonialism, did not think highly of local traditions and responses to colonial conquest. He considers al-Jabarti's resistance to cultural domination through language contestation, like that of Algeria's Emir Abdel Kader or Afghani's response to Ernest Renan, as naive efforts to retrieve a native "origin."[11] Like Homi Bhabha, Said is skeptical about the liberating possibilities of authentic texts and finds salvation in "mimicry," or hybrid culture, that emerges from colonial cross-cultural fertilization. But Egyptian liberal reformers from the eighteenth century through the first part of the twentieth century were hardly local, traditional figures. In fact, the Egyptian reformers who revived the myth of a "pure" Egyptian race and culture and accepted disparaging colonial claims at face value were sophisticated, Westernized liberal thinkers. They were the product of a long tradition of cross-cultural fertilization between Egypt and Europe. Caught up in the language of the "other," to use Lacan metaphorically, Egyptian reformers who privileged Western concepts were hardly more successful in articulating counterhegemonic discourses than those who thought about their colonial experience within the confines of local cultural traditions.

After the French departed in 1801, Egypt remained "sovereign" until the British occupation in 1882. Although Egypt was nominally reintegrated as a province of the Ottoman Empire in 1841, its leaders retained wide political and administrative autonomy. Muhammad 'Ali, who defeated other Mamluk contenders to emerge as Egypt's leader in 1805, extracted political privileges from the Ottoman sultan and virtually ruled as a sovereign *wali*, or viceroy. He continued the far-reaching administrative, legal, and agrarian reforms Napoleon had started, and introduced the massive use of European technology to run industry, public works, and state functions.[12] 'Ali's reforms, known as *nizam jadid*, or "new order" (a name also used by Ottoman writers to refer to the Napoleonic regime), were modeled after military discipline and methods and were actually carried out under the supervision of French army officers and engineers.[13] As in any formal colony or protectorate, the rebuilding of Egyptian towns and villages, the organization of the modern Egyptian army, and the introduction of standardized, state-controlled public schooling involved a reshuffling of cultural priorities and the displacement of large populations and communities. Peasants and farmers were uprooted from their fields and cultivations to be conscripted in distant army posts and public construction sites. Qur'anic schools and traditional seminaries that dispensed religious teachings and basic social and technical skills, though still preponderant, lost power to discipline-oriented instruction. Small artisanal workshops that could have developed progressively into more efficient production units were devalued in favor of monopolistic, state-oriented industries. Religious figures and institutions who could have fostered the notion of consultation and accountability between rulers and ruled became subservient legitimators of the now centralized, despotic rule of *walis* (viceroys) and *khedives* (sovereign rulers). Vast resources were diverted to finance grandiose projects with questionable value and to service loans with exorbitant interest and fees contracted by European banks. All of this recalls the classic, formal colonial process we see elsewhere.

The point of this discussion is not to lament the passing of a traditional order, which was culturally and intellectually stagnant under Ottoman rule, or deny the dynamism of the modernization process. Rather, the point is that the modernization reforms were linked to a colonial discourse that exaggerated the need for cultural transformation to the point where self-denial became a prerequisite for reform. The colonial impact of the Napoleonic expedition was deep and lasted for at least a century, though the occupation itself was brief and not considered formal colonization.[14]

What follows from the reforms undertaken by Egyptian rulers after Napoleon is that opposition to, and accommodation of, reforms are best understood as contests over cultural identities, not principled ideological positions on modern political change. Hence religious figures and traditional leaders who resisted reforms were not necessarily archaic or antimodernist, and the Western-oriented rulers and elites who advocated social and cultural change to emulate Europe were not necessarily political liberals. Curiously, al-Azhar—the institution that most symbolized Egypt's Islamic identity, most needed reform, and could have contributed greatly to political renewal and cultural renaissance—was marginalized and left to decay. From the reign of Muhammad 'Ali in 1805 to the rule of Khedive Ismail in 1879, the rulers of Egypt became increasingly Western oriented and decreasingly accountable to Istanbul, though they continued to pay a symbolic tribute to the Ottoman imperial treasury. The substitution of Arabic for Turkish as Egypt's official language in 1856, the decreeing of the line of succession to the Egyptian throne in 1866, and the access of native Egyptians to most positions of state power all formalized the separation between Egypt and the Ottoman Empire. The Egyptian ruler was no longer a wali, or representative of the sultan, but a sovereign bearing the formal title of khedive. There was still a powerful pro-Ottoman group among the so-called Ottoman-Egyptians, but its members were even more enthusiastic about opening Egypt to European economic and political influence. Ironically, as Juan Cole notes in his study of the social and cultural origins of Egyptian nationalism during this period, the pro-European "Ottoman-Egyptians" advocated autocratic rule, whereas the pro-Ottoman group advocated consultative government.[15]

Finally, while Ottoman influence was, ironically, revived after the British occupation in 1882, the caliphate was just a symbol that lost all political relevance with the collapse of the Ottoman Empire in World War I. At that time, oppression was clearly associated with the European powers that supported and manipulated Egypt's despotic rulers, not with the Ottomans. In sum, by 1922, when Egypt gained formal independence after more than a century of modernization reforms, the so-called Ottoman-Egyptian elites were by and large "Egyptianized," and the Ottoman threat was nonexistent. It seems odd, therefore, that the Egyptian liberal elites after independence associated the viability of liberal political institutions with the censure of Islamic and Arab influence in Egyptian history and culture. The efforts of the Egyptian liberal reformers in the 1920s and 1930s to create the myth of the European cultural origin of Egypt cannot be explained in terms of political anti-Ottoman sentiments.[16] Something that resembles Kilito's imaginary *mustanbih*, the Bedouin who howled like a dog to rejoin human society but lost his speech and appropriated canine behavior and identity, is at work.[17]

The writings and ideas of the European Enlightenment that made their way to Egypt through educational missions greatly contributed to the formulation of the myth of a pure Egyptian origin. The impact of reforms initiated by Napoleon and continued by Muhammad 'Ali (1805–48) and Ismail (1863–79) went beyond the material reordering of Egyptian society and its economy. Though the initial purpose of missions abroad was technical (military, engineering, and commerce), scores of European-educated Egyptians, including teachers, doctors, engineers, and public officials, were trained to teach natives the social manners and cultural customs of modern European life. Beginning in the 1820s, Egyptian student missions were sent to France, Italy, and England; they trained in the modern educational system; became familiar with the ideas of the Enlightenment; read Rousseau, Montesquieu, Auguste Comte, Saint-Simon, and the French Constitution; then went back home, translated and wrote books, and launched an active campaign to reform their society. Some of the Egyptians who went to Europe on educational missions, such as Rifa'a al-Tahtawi, 'Ali Mubarak, and 'Abdu'llah Fikri, were appointed to prominent administrative positions in the Egyptian government in the 1860s and 1870s. "In the introduction of [European] ideas and processes," writes Nubar Pasha, a prime minister of Egypt under the British, "authority alone has no power. Power resides in persuasion. One cannot take one-by-one four or five million individuals to convince them that such thing is better than another."[18] Organized public education, which was emphatically introduced as a separate realm from the religious and social spheres, became a model of how to transform loosely linked traditional communities into a homogeneous, modern nation.

Though modern public education was the main vehicle or model for reordering Egyptian culture and society, it was not the only one. Constitutional politics were also seen as an important instrument for inculcating European manners. The convening of the Consultative Assembly of Deputies in 1866 by Khedive Ismail was viewed as just another step in that direction. "Our parliament is a school by means of which the government, more advanced than the population, instructs and civilizes that population."[19] Hence the main purpose of the early experiments with political parties, legislative bodies, and representative government was not public participation in decision making or political manipulation by rulers to galvanize the support of the social, religious, and financial elites for their policies. Neither Muhammad 'Ali's Advisory Council of 1829 nor Ismail's Consultative Assembly of 1866 had any real legislative power. Both 'Ali and Ismail wanted to appear as modern monarchs because absolutism was associated with Oriental backwardness, and Egypt, in the words of Ismail, was now a part of civilized Europe. This monarchic model does not mean that there were no conflicts of interest, demands for power sharing, or debates about policies within these assemblies or that constitutional politics did not matter. I am simply suggesting that the development of liberal constitutionalism in Egypt during the 1860s and 1870s, and its maturation in the 1920s and 1940s, cannot be fully appreciated outside the problematic construction of modern Egyptian identity. Opposition to Ismail's semiconstitutional rule was spearheaded by Jamal al-Din al-Afghani, who founded an influential reformist movement that included religious figures, political leaders, intellectuals, and other notables.

Afghani's seemingly contradictory positions reflect the complex process of negotiating native identity under European encroachments: He rebuked Renan's prejudiced views about Islam but advocated the spread of modern knowledge, including the education of girls. Afghani mobilized a generation of Egyptian religious figures, intellectuals, and political leaders against European power and influence in Egypt, but he also advocated constitutionalism. He defended Islamic cultures and traditions, yet he severely criticized Ottoman despotism, which he blamed for cultural and intellectual decline among Muslims. He called for social, political, and cultural reforms in Egypt but alerted Egyptians to the threat of European-induced reforms on religion and culture.[20]

In a brilliant illustration of the exercise of colonial power in both representation and the material world, Timothy Mitchell uses Michel Foucault's description of the panoptical model of discipline, surveillance, and containment to analyze the emergence of modern politics in Egypt during the mid-nineteenth century.[21] Mitchell shows how, beginning in the 1830s, the Egyptian people were confined to their villages and were subjugated to a new

form of control through the establishment of regional and provincial Bu-
reaus of Inspection. Mitchell traces this practice to the rule and "reforms" of
Muhammad 'Ali.

The main characteristic of the "new order" was the organization of Egyptian society, villages, cities, households, its system of education, and the
private life of the individual according to the rigid and disciplined model of
modern military control.[22] A number of military schools, established and
administered with the help of French military engineers of l'École Poly-
technique de Paris, provided the models and methods of how to organize
Egyptian society. "The new methods of power," writes Mitchell, "sought to
police, supervise and instruct the population individually. It was a power that
wanted to work with 'known individuals' and 'noted characters,' who were
to be registered, counted, inspected, and reported upon" (98). These new
technologies of power, which made the corporeal body the object of their
practices, aimed to establish permanent colonial control over the material
space within which the population moved and operated. The displacement
of political control from the "personal command of a master," and its diffusion through military-like institutions, made the exercise of political power
and obedience less and less visible (175).

Mitchell's real insight is that the functioning power of colonialism in
Egypt extended beyond the material control of the population to encompass
the colonization of the mind. "[This colonizing power] seemed to construct its object as something divided into two separate concerns, body and
mind. . . . This very division was something new. . . . It was produced by the
new methods of power and . . . the essence of these methods was in fact to
effect such separation" (95). Just as the organization of material space—
exemplified by the construction of modern cities in colonial Morocco and
Egypt—was conceived by the paradoxical safeguard and exclusion of the
medinas, the production of the colonized mind and character reflected a
similar paradox. The colonized could be conceived only by positing a series
of differences between the European self and the Oriental opposite. Thus the
indolence and fatalism of the native was the negative shadow of the industriousness and motivation of the European character. "Identity now appears
no longer self-divided, no longer contingent, no longer something arranged
out of differences; it appears instead as something self-formed, and original. What is overlooked, in producing this modern effect of order, is the
dependence of such identity on what it excludes" (167). Hence, in addition to
the confluence between the disciplinary mechanisms of colonial power and
writing and representation, Mitchell suggests a paradoxical articulation of

difference according to which European identity is at once the absolute opposite and an integral part of the native. But Mitchell does not pursue this analysis further to explore its relevance for self-emancipation. Like Said, Mitchell seems to overlook the trap inherent in locating the potential of resistance in the native's appropriation of the colonizer's methods of instruction and discipline (171). This strategy of appropriation merely duplicated European images of an Orient that lacked its own methods of organization, all within a society that remained, despite Mitchell's portrayal of overwhelming modern power, nonliterate or literate only in basic Islamic norms and traditions.

The new identity that the Egyptian modernizers strove to construct, like Ashis Nandy's Hindu revivalists who invested Brahminist heritage with manly values and monotheistic principles, was primarily defined in opposition to, and in negation of, European images of the Orient. Curiously, the great majority of the first nontechnical books translated into Arabic and widely read among the Egyptian reformers were the works of European Orientalists and ethnographers. These works posited the essential superiority of the European race and the equally innate indolence of the Oriental, Asiatic, and African peoples.[23] Among these books were Edward Lane's *Manners and Customs of the Modern Egyptians*, Georg Bernhard Depping's *Aperçu historique sur les moeurs et coutumes des nations*, Samuel Smiles's *Self-Help, with Illustrations of Conduct and Perseverance*, Edmond Demolins's *A quoi tient la supériorité des Anglo-Saxons*, and François de la Mothe-Fénelon's *Aventures de Télémaque*. The rediscovery of Egyptology by Egyptians and the renaissance of Islamic studies and classical Arabic literature during this period, while creative and prolific, were influenced by European Orientalist views. Thus an influential segment of the Westernized Egyptian elites began to view their own people through the lens used by European chroniclers, historians, and ethnographers.

The British in Egypt: The "Terrible Turk"

Egyptian rulers, modern intellectuals, and European-trained administrators were active for nearly a century attempting to turn their country into a non-Oriental nation. By the turn of the century, Khedive Ismail felt confident enough to tell a European financial control commission: "[Egypt] is no longer in Africa, it is part of Europe." Despite Egyptian efforts, or perhaps because of them, other noble missionaries, the English this time, felt that Egyptians were still incapable of self-government. Like Napoleon's, the Englishman's civilizing mission began with the bombardment of Alexandria, in the early morning of July 11, 1882. By five-thirty in the evening, the city was silent and buried under rubble. The bombardment was justified "not merely on the narrow ground taken up by the British Ministry, namely, that it was necessary as a means of self-defense but because it was clear that in the absence of effectual Turkish or international action, the duty of crushing 'Arabi [in reference to the nationalist revolt led by 'Urabi] devolved on England."[24] As in 1798, the principal claim for the British occupation, despite assertions of both its political motive and its impermanence, was to acquaint the natives with Western democratic ideals and liberal values. "The Englishman . . . came to Egypt with the fixed idea that he had a mission to perform," wrote Lord Cromer, the most distinguished figure of the colonial enterprise in Egypt. "With his views about individual justice, equal rights before the law, the greatest happiness of the greater number, and similar notions, [the Englishman] will not unnaturally interpret his mission in this sense, that he is to benefit the mass of population."[25]

But the English "civilizing mission" in Egypt was fraudulent and lacked the imagination and playfulness to conceal it. Not only were the "justice" and "equality before the law" it promised predicated on the use of naked violence and insistence on unconditional surrender, but its language, saturated with religious hatred and racial prejudice, invalidated the principles it announced. British colonial accounts of Egypt tend to be parched and lacking in compassion—in many ways reflecting uninspiring colonial policies— but they lend themselves to a humorous reading, especially when they are addressed to the French. The views and thoughts of Lord Cromer, the architect of the colonial project in Egypt, are particularly indicative of the British apathy and bitterness. Commenting on the Europeanized Egyptians whose ambition it was to establish Western parliamentary institutions by themselves, Cromer makes the point that the Europeanized Egyptians are really not fully Europeanized; they are " demoslemized Moslems and invertebrate Europeans."[26] Cromer explains what it would take for the Europeanized Egyptian to become fully civilized. He explains that in Europe, Christian morality provides the deep-rooted basis of truthfulness and tolerance. According to Cromer, Christian morality constituted the foundation of Western civilization, and in its absence the Europeanized Egyptian would remain incompletely civilized:

> There is an essential difference between the de-moslemised Moslem and the free-thinker in Europe. The latter is surrounded with an atmosphere of Christianity. . . .

The fact that he is a free-thinker does not cut him off from association and co-operation with his friends, who may not share his disbelief or his doubts, his reason, his associations, and his hereditary qualities alike impel him to assert, no less strongly than the orthodox Christian, that the code of Christian morality must form the basis to regulate the relations between man and man in modern society. That morality has, indeed, taken such deep root in Europe that if, as would appear probable, the hold which revealed religion and theological dogma has on mankind is destined to be gradually relaxed, no moral cataclysm is to be anticipated. . . . Far different is the case of the Egyptian freethinker. . . . Neither his past history nor his present associations impose any effective moral restraint upon him. . . . The society in which he moves does not seriously condemn untruthfulness and deceit. . . . He rushes blindfold into the arms of European civilization, unmindful of the fact that what is visible to the eye constitutes merely the outward signs of that civilization, whilst the deep seated ballast of Christian morality . . . is difficult of acquisition to the pseudo-European imitator of the European system. (231–32)

Having ungraciously denied Europeanized Egyptians the bliss of full membership in the community of civilized men, Cromer nonetheless admits that they are essential for reforming their society by erasing their religion and instilling a higher moral code:

It is conceivable, as time goes on, the Moslems will develop a religion, possibly a Deism, which will not be altogether the Islamism of the past and of the present, and which will cast aside much of the teaching of Mohammed, but which will establish a moral code sufficient to band society together by bonds other than those of unalloyed self-interest. (234)

In a twist of invectiveness that reflects inter-European rivalries, Cromer excoriates the French, who exerted their influence in Egypt for fifty years but with no success. The reason, he says, is that the French lack the inductive philosophy of Bacon. The Englishman "instinctively rejects a priori reasoning," while the Frenchman "will advance some sweeping generalization with an assurance intemperate by any shadow of doubt as to its correctness" (237). In every respect, Cromer contends, the Englishman is superior to the Frenchman. It is the Oriental predisposition to take only the worst and miss the most valuable from European civilization and morality. It is the "light intellectual ballast" of the Egyptian that causes the pseudo-Europeanization of the Egyptian. "Such . . . is the Europeanised Egyptian. His intellectual qualities have, of late years, certainly been developed. His moral characteristics have generally been little, if at all, improved by contact with Europe"

(242–43). In Cromer's vision, the French training had failed to rectify the defects of the Egyptian character, and now it was the Englishman who had taken over that mission. The task of the Englishman, Cromer tells us, is a difficult one because "the mind of the true Eastern is at once lethargic and suspicious; he does not want to be reformed" (161). Moreover, the Eastern languages are written backward: the "Turk, the Arab, and the Persian begin to write on the right side of the page; the short vowels are almost always omitted. European alphabets, on the other hand, are simple. The European begins to write on the left hand side of the page" (163). If Orientals write "backward," their civilization is necessarily backward.

Despite these seemingly insurmountable problems, Cromer's Englishman is a hardworking, ambitious, and confident person who has the proven moral and intellectual qualifications for the task:

> There lie those nine or ten million native Egyptians at the bottom of the social ladder, a poor, ignorant, credulous, but not . . . an unkindly race. . . . It is for the civilized Englishman to extend to them the hand of fellowship and encouragement, and to raise them, morally and materially, from the abject state in which he finds them. And the Englishman looks towards the scene of other administrative triumphs of world-wide fame, which his progenitors have accomplished. He looks towards India, and says with all the confidence of an imperial race—I can perform this task; I have done it before now . . . (130)

What kind of colonial relations may one infer from Cromer's colonial diatribe? Manifestly, Cromer believes that the Egyptians, including the most Europeanized, cannot govern themselves, and the French, who lack the moral and intellectual qualifications to civilize, gave the natives faulty political ideas. But this mode of thinking is not Cromer's alone. Events leading to the occupation and British colonial policies suggest consistent and unequivocal opposition to liberal reforms and constitutional politics when these might compromise their interests. As early as 1879, religious figures, notables, and members of the Assembly drafted a manifesto that spoke about the sovereignty of the Egyptian nation and the rights of the Egyptian people to run their government independently from European influence. While not calling for representative democracy—the signatories saw themselves as "representatives of the Egyptian umma [nation]"—the manifesto alarmed Lord Cromer, who decried it as a dangerous coup d'état.[27] A related suggestive decision was the forced abdication of Khedive Ismail, the ruler who truly "Europeanized" Egypt and laid the foundations of constitutional politics, in favor of his young son Tawfiq. With the support of other European powers,

England and the Ottoman sultan forced Khedive Ismail to abdicate in 1879 when he acquiesced to financial policies recommended by the Assembly. With this move, England not only violated a basic democratic belief; it also reestablished the principle of vassal relations with the Ottoman Empire and opened the door for potential Ottoman claims on Egypt, which lasted until the fall of the Ottoman Empire in World War I.

After Ismail's abdication, the British government pressured young Khedive Tawfiq to suppress a modernizing nationalist movement in 1881 and to shut down newspapers that supported its causes and leaders. The 'Urabi revolution of 1881 to 1882—named after its leader Ahmad 'Urabi Pasha, minister of war in two cabinets before the British occupation—was not just an agitation by violent army officers hungry for power, as British historiography and official accounts portray it.[28] Jacques Berque's and Juan Cole's studies of the period, using Egyptian sources and American consular dispatches, describe a much broader social and national movement with specific reformist and constitutionalist demands.[29] 'Urabi, who called himself "al-Misri," the Egyptian, wanted constitutional reforms to check the powers of the khedive and the cabinet, cautioned against the neglect and subordination of local cultures under the onslaught of European influence, and demanded the withdrawal of British gunboats from Alexandria's harbor, whose presence was used to pressure the khedive's compliance on financial matters. 'Urabi had the support of political leaders within the government and the Assembly, intellectuals, army officers, merchants and artisans, and the rural and urban middle classes.[30] When demands for a constitution were gaining momentum in early 1882, and Tawfiq appeared to waver on demands by the Assembly's deputies in the spring of that year and reinstated the cabinet that the European powers had pressured him to dismiss, the British decided to intervene forcefully.[31]

Ironically, it was under orders from the liberal government of William Gladstone and Lord Granville, known for their anti-imperialist sentiments and support for universal justice and liberty, that England bombed Alexandria and occupied Egypt. Apparently, 'Urabi's "violent" and "despicable" character, as portrayed in the English press and consular accounts, reminded the English so much of the "Terrible Turk" who was repressing Christian populations in the Balkans that even a liberal could not remain unmoved.[32] Gladstone had indeed led a campaign in the 1870s on the "Balkan massacres" and made wild predictions about an "impending war in Europe between a Muslim and a Christian power" that would lead to "communal tensions in the Ottoman Empire, including Egypt."[33] Thus the mythical image of the Terrible Turk and the partial recollection of events in the Balkan massacres, inscribed in the memory of Englishmen from the "sublime" liberal Gladstone to the "mediocre" Major Baring (later Lord Cromer), informed the British occupation of Egypt. Conventional historical accounts that focus predominantly on imperial ventures, Anglo-French rivalries, Ottoman intrigues, or the waning of the khedives' power tend to overlook the cultural assumptions that inform colonial relations.

One need not look too hard to see the moral and cultural workings of liberal colonialism in Egypt. The political project of Lord Dufferin, who initiated and established the Legislative Council and General Assembly in Egypt in 1883, is revealing. "Under British superintendence," wrote Dufferin, "the legislative bodies might be fostered, and educated into fairly useful institutions, proving a convenient channel through which the European element in the government might obtain an insight into the inner mind and the less obvious wants of the native populations."[34] From the start, the so-called parliamentary institutions were conceived as instruments of manipulation in the hands of the colonial administration that Lord Cromer described extensively and suggestively as a "machinery" of political control.[35] Native parliamentary institutions, Cromer believed, were "of necessity a mere *decor de theatre*."[36] Lord Cromer and his three successors Eldon Gorst, Lord Kitchener, and Lord Allenby governed Egypt with an iron fist to establish a "good government" based on an efficient administration and Christian virtues.

Jacques Berque, who is equally critical of French colonialism in North Africa, summarized British rule in Egypt as follows: "The British were Machiavellian *faute de mieux*. In this land of paradox, so disconcerting to the Westerner, they simply strove to counter the unintelligibility of the East with the common-sense and accuracy of the accountant, the engineer's efficiency and—why conceal it, since they made no secret of it?—the virtues of the Christians."[37] In the words of Lord Cromer himself, the priority of the departing conqueror should be to leave behind "a fairly good, strong, and—above all things—stable government, which will . . . prevent the Egyptian question from again becoming a serious cause of trouble to Europe. . . . It is essential that, subsequent to the evacuation, the government should . . . act on principles which will be in conformity with the commonplace requirements of Western civilization."[38]

The 1923 Constitution, Egypt's first foundational political text after independence, seems to have been written with Lord Cromer's wish in mind. The failure of the liberal experiment in Egypt during the 1920s and 1930s cannot fully be understood in separation from the cultural impulses and identity conflicts that emerge from the colonial encounter. The writing of a modern constitution, like the reinterpretation of Egyptian history and national culture, or the adoption of European dress and manners that I examine in chapters 3 and 4, were meant to reintegrate Egypt into a mythical European origin that is emphatically non-Oriental.

Text and Polity:
A Reading of the 1923 Constitution

In April 1923 the Egyptians drafted a constitution to establish a political community that corresponded to the image the Egyptian liberals had created for their nation. The new constitution, however, resembled yet another covenant between the colonizer and the colonized. This covenant inscribed in words the permanence of Western presence and domination over an Oriental nation. With its reliance on modern European constitutional law and its emphatic depreciation of Egypt's Arabo-Islamic heritage, the first Egyptian Constitution legitimated Britain's claim of civilizing the Egyptian native and normalized the native's accountability to the European master.[39] The Constitution became the symbol of a reformed "self" who adopted the principles of "modernity," "order," "progress," and "liberalism" but also adopted an identity that alienated the basic cultural and historical qualities of the Arabo-Islamic "self."

The specific question that concerns us here is what kind of justice, equality, and freedom the Egyptian citizens could expect from the political community the Egyptian liberals offered. I suggest that by accepting and normalizing the European colonial claims on the natives, the discourse of Egyptian liberalism authorized the alienation of the basic political principles of liberalism: respect for individual freedom and the exercise of authority in the interest of all citizens. Political liberalism could not possibly succeed in Egypt because of the Egyptian liberals' failure to grasp the centrality of individual and collective identity in its relation to freedom, equality, and authority. The end result was a political experiment that was ironically liberal in its forms, institutions, and ideals, but illiberal in its practice: it denied basic individual rights in order to grant nominal rights. In other words, to become eligible for the "privileges" of modern citizenship in a liberal society, the Egyptian individual had to be appropriated, transformed, controlled, and alienated from his or her identity.

My analysis will focus on the kind of political community the first Egyptian Constitution purported to establish and the relationship it assumed with the people it claimed to represent. My argument is that the political and civil rights the Constitution professed were operative only in the context of the specific political community the Egyptian liberals sought to establish.

On February 28, 1922, Britain granted formal independence to Egypt. The British imposed four restrictive provisions on Egyptian sovereignty and independence: (1) the protection of imperial communications in Egypt; (2) the protection of Egypt from any external aggression; (3) the protection of foreign interests and minorities in Egypt; and (4) the custody of the Sudan, which was an Anglo-Egyptian condominium, to remain under the imperial administration. The decision to grant Egypt independence was a compromise between the British government, not willing to give more than a limited internal autonomy to the Egyptians, and the Egyptian sultan and his men, who were ready to comply with Britain's demands. This arrangement was unacceptable to the nationalist leaders of the Wafd Party, who enjoyed immense popular support but failed to deliver independence to their people after a series of aborted negotiations with the British government. To protect their interests from eventual nationalistic turmoil, the British insisted that an Egyptian government draft and promulgate a constitution that would establish in writing the Egyptians' acceptance of the four terms of independence. An atmosphere of political tension and uncertainty prevailed in Egypt, and the British required, or at least expected, the formation of a "friendly" government that would keep Saad Zaghlul and the Wafd Party, known for their strong opposition to the four provisions on independence, out of power.[40]

The British government believed that if they introduced the constitutional regime, Saad Zaghlul and his nationalist colleagues of the Wafd would be isolated. Accordingly, the declaration of independence specified exactly what kind of government Egypt should have.[41] And while there was no mention of what kind of a constitutional regime Egypt should adopt, the British high commissioner in Egypt, Lord Allenby, made recommendations to Sultan Fu'ad concerning the draft of an Egyptian constitution.[42] The Egyptians formed a Constituent Committee to draft a constitution, but Saad Zaghlul's immediate reaction was to denounce it as the *lajnat al-ashkiya*, "committee of wretches," because it was a nonrepresentative body and incapable of standing up to Britain's intransigence. When the first draft of the Constitution was submitted, designating King Fu'ad as "King of Egypt and the Sudan," the British opposed it because Fu'ad's claim to the Sudan conflicted with the provisions of the February 28 declaration. The controversial article was finally removed from the constitutional text under British pressure.[43] The satisfactory settlement of this first incident validated Lord Allenby's assurances to his government that granting Egypt formal independence would not jeopardize British interests.

Behind the obvious mechanism of continuous British domination over the Egyptian nation, however, hid one that was elusive and expansive and hence more powerful: the imposition of political conventions that on the surface advocated the notions of individual freedom, equality, and justice but in fact took advantage of these very conventions to protect imperial interests. The logic and purpose of duplicating these political conventions in non-Western societies have not been addressed by students of non-Western politics. Scholars take for granted the impartiality of introducing European political values and establishing modern European political institutions in the non-Western world. Thus, if the effigy of Western democracy did not work in non-Western societies, native cultural traditions and unfavorable political and economic circumstances were to blame. Both political scientists and the ruling elites in Third World nations who are opposed to democratic changes advance this explanation.

Previous analysts of the 1923 Egyptian Constitution have centered their criticism on the misdistribution of powers between the Parliament and the Egyptian monarchy.[44] In their view, the extensive legislative and executive powers entrusted to the king perpetuated the traditional consultative character of Egyptian assemblies. The common assumption of these studies is that the 1923 Constitution was the political product of an arrangement between two trends inside the commission that was charged with drafting the constitutional text. One "autocratic" faction led by supporters of King Fu'ad argued that the Egyptian people had not yet reached the required level of education and maturity necessary for European-style government, and therefore the Constitution must confer on the king extensive powers to govern the country. The other, "democratic" faction, led by supporters of Tharwat Pasha, president of the Council of Ministers, insisted on limiting the powers of the king and establishing a constitution that duplicated the modern European constitutions in every aspect.

Well-founded as they may be, these analyses reduce the crisis of constitutional life in Egypt to a technical political problem that could have been solved through a coherent redistribution of legislative and executive powers between the king and the Parliament. These solutions overlook the significance of the link between politics and language in the constitutional enterprise and assume the neutrality of language in constituting a political community. Consequently, previous readings fail to see that the primary purpose of the 1923 Constitution was not to describe a covenant between a sovereign and a people on how to organize a political community—despite the fact that the text of the Constitution clearly orders Egyptians to constitute themselves according to specific political principles and values.[45] My concern, however, is not whether these principles were effectively applied. We know that they were not. My objective is to clarify the conditions under which the principles advocated by the Constitution would be realized.

These principles and values are important not because of their abstract theoretical meaning but because of the meaning they generate within the structure of the constitutional text.[46] The most important objective of the first Egyptian Constitution was its attempt to "write" Egyptians as a people who could identify with the civilized Europeans by adopting their political conventions. The Constitution was thus a covenant between Egypt and colonial Europe that inscribed in words the permanent presence of Western authority hidden under the guise of constitutional language and the promise of "independence." That is to say, if direct colonial rule was displaced, the political authority of the British was nonetheless guaranteed through a "mimic representation" of European constitutions.

As a written text, a constitution implies the construction of a political community through a written arrangement of words. Constitutions do not describe an already existing political order; rather, they narrate a political order into words, and it is the text itself that binds people together into a community. The first purpose of a constitutional text is to create a community of readers who will come to speak the language of the constitution. My use of the term "language" follows James Boyd White's idea of a "language [which is the product of a specific] culture [and] structured way of thinking and talking and being by which value and character are defined and community is constituted."[47] This idea of language means that a constitution succeeds in creating a "political community" only if it succeeds in creating a "textual community"; that is, if it can engage readers to speak its specific language and to adopt its discourse.[48]

The power of any written text, such as a constitution, therefore depends on the capacity of its language to persuade its readers of the validity and legitimacy of the world it claims to describe and represent.[49] Political language, then, refers to the system and procedures of thought by which certain political values are defined, expressed, and given priority over others. The dilemma of the Egyptian liberals was that they had to address two audiences: Britain, to show that the perpetuation of Western presence could be guaranteed through the appropriation of European political conventions; and their own people, to convince them that their interests would best be served by espousing the modern European ideals, and to teach them the political language of the civilized European. The simultaneous publication of the Constitution in Arabic, English, and French is indicative of this dual audience. Priority, however, was given to the European audience. The comments of one Western observer who had every reason to celebrate the triumph of Western political values and institutions in an Oriental kingdom reflect the ambiguous status of the Egyptian Constitution:

> For an Eastern country, a constitution involves a break with the past and the replacement of an ideal. There were still pious objectors who denounced this secular initiative as useless and indeed impious, on the grounds that the religious law provided for everything. As it happened, they had good reason to be anxious. The constitution was too closely modeled on a Western pattern. But that was part of its attraction: its symbolic value was more important than its functional value. . . . Perhaps, nevertheless, the Egyptian constitution banked too much on the people's docility and neglected, or even dreaded, their fundamental strength, their collective potential.[50]

Predicated on the assumption that politics derive meaning and authority from language, I read the 1923 Constitution as a literary text that founds a polity. Semiology has taught us that a text, any text, is a system of signs that implies a relationship of signifier and signified. This relationship is of fundamental importance to understanding the meaning of the text.[51] In living speech, what the speaking subject says (the sentence), how he or she says it (tone of voice), and what he or she does by saying it (the effect the speaker wants to produce) make it possible for the interlocutor to understand the meaning of the discourse. These three levels of the speech act can be codified and inscribed in written discourse.[52] The spoken sentence can be transformed unaltered into a written text. How the sentence is said can be reflected partially in a grammatical form through verbal modes, punctuation, or other relevant signs of expression. Finally, what the speaker does by saying, though less easy to inscribe, can be interpreted just as the interlocutor in the speech act understands the effect the speaker wants to make.

The 1923 Constitution supplies us with signs that presuppose a conjuncture between signifier (the visible document of words and articles) and signified (the transcendent structure of the political order signaled by the document). According to this paradigm, the 1923 Constitution seems to establish a political order of a different kind—an ordering of relations between Egypt as a backward Eastern nation and Egypt as a civilized European nation. Here arise elementary discursive questions that have not received any attention in previous readings of the Constitution.[53] Who is speaking? Whom does the Constitution address? And what claims does the Constitution make by "saying"?

Answers to these questions can yield great insights into the meaning of establishing a constitution in Egypt and what kind of community the Egyptian Constitution strove to create. Let us begin with the preamble, where the text immediately indicates the speaker, the reader, and the political claims that the author makes on his audience:

We, Fouad, the first King of Egypt,

Whereas, since our succession to the throne and our undertaking to guard the trust given us by the Almighty, all our efforts have constantly been directed toward assuring the well being of our people and its guidance toward the way which we know would lead to happiness and progress and thus to assure for it the benefits enjoyed by all free and civilized people;

Whereas, this result cannot truly be attained except through the possession of a constitutional regime similar to all modern and perfected constitutional regimes, which would result to the people in a happy life, prosperity and freedom, and would guarantee them effective participation in the administration of public affairs together with the elaboration and confidence in the present and the future while at the same time safe-guarding the national spirit—qualities and distinctive traits which have been the historically glorious heritage of our people;

Whereas, it was there that rested our highest ideal and the principal object of the efforts which we exert with a view to raising our people to a level commensurate with its glorious past history, a level to which its intelligence and aptitudes accord it the right to aspire and with a view to enabling it to maintain with dignity its rightful place amongst the peoples of the civilized worlds.

We order [the following].[54]

The first sentence of the preamble designates the speaker by the first-person plural pronoun used by a monarch, "We . . . King of Egypt." This reference must be qualified for a number of reasons. We know that the text of the Constitution was drafted collectively by a "Committee of Thirty," which included Egyptian intellectuals, notables, government officials, businessmen, and religious scholars.[55] We also know that during the six months of discussions that preceded the declaration of the Constitution, members of the commission examined the constitutions of various European countries before they finally decided to adopt the Belgian model.[56] Last, according to

Berque, members of the commission relied extensively on the works of Leon Duguit, a professor of law at the University of Bordeaux, to write the Constitution.[57] The point is that the multitude of writers behind the indicated speaker complicates the relationship between the speaking subject and the discourse. In this case it is not the subjective intention of the indicated speaker that matters, but rather what language the designated author is speaking.

As a written text, a constitution is intended to go beyond the life of the original speaker to impose its own meaning and will independently from the author. The text itself leaves no doubt as to who is speaking: not the individual reader (in the U.S. Constitution, the reader becomes speaker subsumed in the plural, "We the people"), and not the people at large (most constitutions are supposed to represent the will of the people). The speaker is a single authoritative figure who orders the readers to constitute a political community on the basis of a specific language.

The first aim of the speaker, then, is to create a "textual community" where the reader is taught and initiated into the language and discourse of the Constitution. The object of this discourse is to make the reader believe that "well-being," "happiness," "progress," "prosperity," "freedom," "peace," "confidence," "intelligence," "aptitudes," and "dignity" are traits and rights of "civilized [read European] nations." (We will see in chapter 4 what the new social and cultural notions of "order," "security," "prosperity," "intelligence," "happiness," "good health," "love," and "death" meant in the Egyptian liberal discourse.) Once the reader begins to speak the language of the Constitution, the boundaries of discourse are set: the choice is either to accept the path to civilization or to reject it. The Constitution assumes a readership that considers, or will come to consider, European civilization a sublime goal and offers a "way" to "raise" the readers, the Egyptian people, toward it. "This result cannot truly be attained," says the Constitution, "except through the possession of a constitutional regime similar to all modern and perfected constitutional regimes."

This goal is not difficult to achieve, the Constitution tells the reader, because the Egyptian people have "qualities" and "distinct traits" that are shared by the civilized people of Europe, thanks to the glorious heritage of the Egyptians. The reference here is to an ideal ancient Egyptian civilization that had been used to reinforce the historical and cultural linkages between Egypt and Europe. Of course, there is nothing liberal, democratic, or constitutional about that past. The Pharaonic revivalist movement was used as a bridge to link Egypt and Europe via the Greek heritage. The Egyptian liberals believed that the historical, cultural, and racial reconstitution of Egypt was necessary to constitute a political community according to the principles of European liberal democracy. Just as liberal Egyptian historians, linguists, artists, and men of letters and science claimed membership in the European club of civilized nations on the basis of the Pharaonic past, so the 1923 Constitution made the same claim for Egypt as a whole. The author of the Constitution reminds the Egyptian people of their nation's ancient grandeurs and glories and presents the historical accomplishments of the ancient Egyptians as proof that entitles contemporary Egyptians to live like the civilized peoples of Europe.

The conspicuous absence of the traditional Islamic invocation "Bismi allah al-Rahman al-Rahim" (In the Name of God, the Merciful, the Compassionate), which accompanies official state declarations in Muslim countries, clearly indicates who the relevant audience is: those who can speak, or can be persuaded to speak, a new language, assume a new function in society, and begin a new life.[58] Like the literary, historical, and social writings of Taha Husayn, Husayn Haykal, and Salama Musa, the Constitution was yet another attempt to amend Egyptian culture and identity and reconstruct the community in which they lived through the implementation of a new constitutional language.

The relationship that the speaker, the sovereign king, maintains with the readers, the Egyptian citizens, throughout the text of the Constitution is itself informed by the concern to teach the readers a new language of political authority: an odd combination of legal rational conventions and God-given privileges. The speaker begins his discourse by claiming divine rights and duties, apparently inherited from ancestors, to manage the life of the people. The speaker thus uses the imperative mode, "Amarna bima huwa atin" (We order [the following]), to set the political tone of the Constitution. The speaker addresses the audience from the point of view of authority where the readers are expected to accept unconditionally the message and to follow orders with no opportunity for independent thinking or questioning. The text assumes readers who do not know themselves, and therefore offers to teach them how to read and interpret their own history. The readers are not expected to add or contribute anything to the propositions of the Constitution; rather, citizens are only expected to actively participate through reading and consenting—the minimum required for the Constitution to be effective.

On the basis of this reading of the preamble, the discourse of the 1923 Constitution might appear fundamentally antiliberal. Most students of Egyptian politics of the so-called liberal period have noted the shortcomings of this experiment. No one has claimed that the Constitution instituted a successful parliamentary democracy. But the explanations of the failure of constitutional democracy in Egypt miss two fundamental problems addressed in this chapter: (1) the unequal, removed, and authoritative political relationship that the Constitution as a linguistic artifact assumes between the author of the Constitution and its reader; and (2) the attempt to create a community on the basis of conventions that do not recognize or consider the culture or sentiments of the people of that community.

The preceding analysis should provide an idea about the character of the political community that the Egyptian Constitution aimed to establish: one not based on shared moral values and understanding but defined in accordance with British interests. The elaboration of this political community can been seen in an examination of key articles of the Constitution. Article 1 states: "Egypt is a sovereign state, free and independent. Its rights of sovereignty are indivisible and inviolable. Its government is that of a hereditary monarchy; it has a representative form." The actual meaning of the words "sovereign," "free," "independent," and "representative" lies in the structural circumstances of the constitutional text. They immediately follow the preamble, whose aim is to tell Egyptians that Egypt deserves a place in the civilized world where it once belonged and where it would be today if it were to adopt a constitutional regime. The first article of the Constitution establishes Egyptian independence and sovereignty, yet the preamble remains curiously silent about the very recent historic event of Egypt's independence from Britain. The "sovereignty," "freedom," and "independence" of the Egyptian nation could mean a proclamation of detachment from the Islamic Umma, since the modern concept of nation-state rules out any political dependence on a larger religious entity.[59] The "indivisible and inalienable" sovereignty of Egypt could be violated by no other state, except Britain, in accordance with the provisions of the 1922 declaration of "independence." Article 1 renders any other claim on Egypt, on religious or cultural grounds, illegal.

Accordingly, after Article 1 declares Egypt a sovereign, free, and independent state, Article 2 affirms that "Egyptian nationality is determined by Law." This juxtaposition is not coincidental. Article 2 means that to become a member of the community the Constitution wants to establish, Egyptians can no longer identify with the Islamic Umma or Arab culture but rather must identify with what the Constitution defines to be an Egyptian.

It is peculiar indeed that the Egyptian Constitution defines its political community with minimal attention to the two most important elements of that community: Islam and Arab culture. The only reference to Islam and the Arabic language appears in Article 149, in the last section of the Constitution, called "General Arrangements." The article states, "Islam is the religion of the state; Arabic is the official language." This does not mean, however, that the Constitution wants to establish a secular democracy where religious matters are separated from state affairs. Rather, the Constitution entrusts the state with the sole power to regulate and instruct on religious concerns and to control those who decide among Muslims what is morally right and wrong. Article 153, for example, states:

> The Law regulates the manner in which the King exercises his power, in accordance with the principles of the present Constitution, in so far as concerns religious foundations, the appointment of heads of religious bodies, the wakfs property entrusted to the management of the Ministry of Wakfs and, in general all matters concerning the fates admitted in the country. In the absence of any legislative revision, these powers will continue to be exercised in accordance with the rules and usages at present in force.[60]

Where the relationship between religion and the state is most explicitly articulated, the Constitution stipulates the submission of religious matters and institutions to the state. Therefore, contrary to what one might expect from a constitution based on liberal political principles, the text of the Egyptian Constitution recommends state intervention in religious affairs.

The Constitution thus uses religion in two convenient manners: obscuring it as the primary trait of Egyptian national identity, and making it subservient to lawmakers who can manipulate it to justify their policies and actions. For example, Article 13 stipulates: "The state protects, in accordance with the practices established in Egypt, the free exercise of the rites of all religions and creeds, on condition that they are not prejudicial to public order or morality." The last clause is a very important one. A great deal of popular cultural and many religious practices were deemed corrupt, dangerous, and contrary to public order and morality because they betrayed the new self-image of Egypt as a European nation. Therefore, when the Constitution guarantees individual liberty (Article 4), inviolability of the home (Article 8), liberty of opinion (Article 14), and liberty of association (Article 20), these rights are not guaranteed in isolation from the kind of political community the preamble professes to establish. The Constitution makes explicit in each article the exceptions regulated by law. When the Constitution thus provides the protection of certain rights, it implies the rights of those who have specifically accepted becoming part of the political community the Constitution is seeking to create: those who can identify with its language, moral codes, interpretation of history, and view of the world. This conception of rights would leave out all those who do not necessarily accept the superiority, or even understand, the Western conceptions of morality, ethics, love, friendship, happiness, well-being, intelligence, dignity, and civilization.

Again, while the Constitution guarantees in Article 3 that "all Egyptians are equal before the law [and] enjoy civil and political rights, and are equally subject to public duties and responsibilities, without any distinction of race, language, or religion," the equality it claims to protect is paradoxical. The Constitution establishes an elaborate hierarchical structure backed by other conditions stipulated by the electoral law. To be elected or appointed senator, for example, according to Article 78 one has to belong to one of the following categories:

1   Ministers; diplomatic representatives; presidents of the Chamber of Deputies; under secretaries of state, presidents and judges of the court of appeal or of jurisdictions or superior legal standing; procureurs general; batonniers of the order of advocates; government officials of the rank of director general or above, still in service or retired.

2   High representatives of the ulema and the clergy; retired army officers of the rank of lewa or of higher rank; deputies who have been members of the chamber during two of its legislative periods; property owners paying taxes of no less than LE 150 yearly; persons having an annual revenue of at least LE 1500 and engaged in financial, commercial, or industrial enterprises, or following professional career—all the foregoing, under reserve of the incompatibility of functions stipulated by the Constitution or by electoral law.[61]

The first Egyptian Constitution professes to guarantee formal civil and political rights that were compatible with the most liberal constitutions in Europe at the time. Yet the Constitution assumes a political community whose members are individuals who relinquish their personal identities and where citizens enjoy rights because they adhere to a specific view of the world. In the following two chapters, I discuss the cultural assumptions that informed the Egyptian liberal reformers' notions of political community and citizenship.

three

Defining the Boundaries of the Political Community

I n a memorandum presented by the Egyptian delegation to the European powers at the Paris Peace Conference in 1919, a small paragraph criticized the West for having divided the world into civilized and uncivilized nations along cultural and racial lines. The excerpt denounced the subjugation and colonial domination of the peoples of the Orient who were deemed "uncivilized" by the European powers.[1] But the Paris Conference may not have thought that Egypt was quite "civilized," for the long-term purpose of the British invasion was to "liberate" the country from the "principles of the Mohammadan faith which [the European powers considered] antiquated, obsolete, and opposed to commonplace ideas of modern civilization."[2] Yet an Egyptian journalist covering the peace conference for *Wadi al-Nil* reported in his memoirs that before the Paris meeting, the Egyptian delegation, despite its critique of Europe, had declined to join the Society of Eastern Nations. Various delegations from the East had attempted to form a common front with the goal of presenting a unified position to the colonial powers.[3] Members of the Egyptian delegation gave a legalistic explanation for their refusal to participate in the Society of Eastern Nations: "The mandate of the Wafd," they said, "related only to the independence of Egypt and nothing else."[4] It appears, however, that when the Egyptian delegation pleaded for national independence, the Egyptians wanted to minimize any affiliation with the East. Instead they emphasized the unique character of Egyptians as distinct from all other peoples of the Orient. The assumption was that the West would consider this distinction as a valid basis on which Egypt could be granted political self-rule. The declared purpose of the memorandum was "to introduce the true image of Egypt; a country of advanced culture having the right, in all respects, to benefits which have been granted to nations, however, less important and less civilized." The reference was to Britain's support of the independence of Hijaz (Saudi Arabia) after the sharif of Mecca revolted against Ottoman rule in 1918.[5] "Among all peoples of the Orient," the memorandum continues, "Egyptians have been and are the most eager to seek European cooperation and to leave the doors of their country widely open to Europe."

Ironically, even though the intent of the declaration was to assert Egypt's right to independence, its spirit echoed the feelings of an earlier generation of reformers who began to view Egyptians as Europeans but portrayed them as "weak in character," "deceitful," "fearful of authority," and lacking the moral virtues to live a good life. The works of religious leaders and public educators such as Shaykh al-Sharqawi (Tuhfat al-nazirin fiman waliya Misr mina al-wulat wa al-salatin [A Survey of the History of Governors and Sultans], 1865), and Shaykh Rifaʿa Rafiʿi al-Tahtawi (Al-Murshid al-Amin li-1 -banat wa-1 -banin [A Guidebook for Boys and Girls], 1872), who greatly contributed to reformist thought and practice in Egypt, already bore the seeds of this denigrating trend. This is not to deny the contribution of these reformers to Egypt's cultural and intellectual renewal, but rather to point out that modernist reformism was already pregnant with prejudiced cultural and moral assumptions. But this understanding of self, seen through European eyes, became a systematic and coherent discourse with the second generation of liberal reformers such as Taha Husayn (1889–1973), Muhammad Husayn Haykal (1889–1956), and Tawfiq al-Hakim (1899–1987). They all spent extensive time studying in Paris and marveled at the achievements of French culture and civilization. Being part of Europe turned out to be the main justification of their demand for political independence, cultural renaissance, and social emancipation and became the raison d'être of interwar Egyptian liberalism.[6] As Egypt became more European than Oriental in the eyes of the Egyptian liberals, the adoption of the modern "European principles of order, progress, and liberalism" took on an existential significance: the principles became the sacred symbols of the new national identity, which the Egyptian liberals laboriously attempted to fabricate and validate on the basis "scientific" studies and theories.[7] Although efforts to anchor Egypt in

Europe had gained political significance as early as Khedive Ismail's rule, they became politically dominant only after formal independence.

During the 1920s and 1930s, after Egypt gained nominal independence, native Westernized elite who had been influenced by contemporary European ideas took on the ambitious and sensational task of directing and completing their own version of the "civilizing mission." To be sure, the colonial powers imposed their particular view of man, society, culture, and the world as a whole. These powers constituted a "political world" according to images that Europe projected for itself while positing the non-European as a subordinated other. However, the active consent and participation of a powerful segment of Egyptian society, the Westernized intellectual elite, in the perpetuation of colonial discourse is both conceptually puzzling and politically disturbing. It is puzzling because it calls into question the characterization of the relationship between the colonizer and the colonized as that of constant conflict between two opposed worldviews. This relationship is disturbing because it entailed the active participation of both the colonial authority and colonial subject in the production of a discourse that legitimated and maintained the European-imposed order of exclusion, hierarchy, and submission. This situation is described by Foucault as the "objectification of subject," whereby dominated groups are given a social role and an identity that they themselves actively participate in creating.[8]

Before I explain how the Egyptian liberal reformers were trapped in the language of the Other, and therefore could not provide a compelling notion of national identity and political community, it is necessary to clarify two important points. I am not suggesting that the Egyptian liberal reformers constituted a coherent intellectual group. We may identify three liberal reformist tendencies in Egypt with varying cultural influence, political strength, and attitude about local traditions. The first group of liberal reformers may be called "Muslim reformists," which included figures such as Muhammad 'Abdu (1849–1905), Rashid Rida (1865–1935), and 'Ali 'Abd al-Raziq (1886–1966), who wanted to reform Islamic theological and political traditions from within. 'Abdu and Rida defended Islamic traditions against the prejudiced writings of Cromer, Renan, and Gabriel Hanoteaux on Islam and Muslims, yet they did not shy away from criticizing their own societies and called for profound reforms.[9] A follower of 'Abdu and Rida, al-Raziq argued in a controversial but pertinent book, *Al-Islam wa usul al-hukm* (Islam and the Bases of Political Authority) (1925), that political authority in Islam was not divine.[10] Although the book advocated modern political ideas, it was written within traditional Muslim texts and concepts that radically reinterpreted the foundations of political authority in Islam.

A second group of liberal reformers may be considered "modern nationalists" who were committed to developing the social, economic, and political potential of the Egyptian nation but valorized its Islamic heritage for aesthetic, cultural, or spiritual reasons. This group included social reformers such as Qasim Amin (1865–1908), Muhammad al-Muwailihi (1868–1930), and Huda Sha'rawi (1878–1947), as well as political and business figures such as Mustapha Kamil (1874–1908), Tal'at Harb (1876–1941), Saad Zaghlul (1857–1927), and Ismail Sidqi (1875–1950). Amin, al-Muwailihi, and Sha'rawi all attacked the stagnation of the conservative social order and advocated women's rights but questioned both the colonizer and the colonized. Political and economic leaders, on the other hand, linked national sovereignty to political emancipation and economic independence.[11] Saad Zaghlul, an emblematic figure in the nationalist movement, pleaded for Egypt's independence on the basis of British liberal principles while relentlessly seeking the support of the wider Egyptian community. His advocacy for the nationalist struggle was framed in popular terms but publicly appealed to, and worked with, both Coptic and Jewish leaders.

A third group of liberal reformers, the main focus of this study, may be called "secular modernists" and were more seriously committed to European liberal ideals and principles. This group included literary figures such as Taha Husayn, Muhammad Husayn Haykal, Abbas Mahmud al-Aqqad (1889–1964), and Tawfiq al-Hakim; social critics such as Fathi Zaghlul (1863–1914) and Isma'il Mazhar (1891–1962); Christian Arab émigrés, mainly publishers, such as Salama Musa (1887–1958), Farah Antoun (1874–1922), Jurji Zaydan (1861–1914), and Shibli Shumayal (1860–1917); and political leaders such as Ahmad Lutfi al-Sayyid (1872–1963), publicly known as *utasadh al-jil*, the master thinker of his generation.[12] Although the secular modernists emerged from the same cultural and intellectual colonial tradition as the former groups, their discourse had a distinct feature. In addition to the political and literary works of Rousseau, Comte, Montesquieu, and other European luminaries, the secular liberal reformers were heavily influenced by European writers such as Le Bon, Demolins, Renan, and Taine who advanced "scientific" theories about the superiority of the Aryan race and inferiority of the Semitic mind, morality, and character. In their writings, secular liberal Egyptians uncritically replicated European anti-Arabism and the debasement of the Arabo-Islamic culture. From the beginning, then, the secular liberal reformers were alienated from themselves and from Egypt by their use of the language of the European Other. To use Lacan's metaphor, like an infant caught up in the image of the apparently cohesive and self-similar mother, more than anything else the secular liberal reformers struggled to be everything to the m/other.

Despite my categorization, there are often no clear-cut distinctions between the religious, nationalist, and secular trends of Egyptian liberal reformism. I portray 'Abd al-Raziq, who challenged the divine foundation of political authority in Islam, as a liberal Muslim reformist, but both the Wafd, Zaghlul's nationalist party, and the Liberal Party, the party of the secular liberal trend, defended al-Raziq's book when it was attacked by traditional conservatives and King Fu'ad. I demarcate the differences between these groups not on the basis of institutional affiliation but on how they read and interpreted the European liberal challenge. Institutional politics at that time were fairly erratic and could not provide an adequate or complete understanding of politics in interwar Egypt. For example, *Al-Sufur*, the first weekly periodical to serve as a platform for liberal thinking, which appeared in print in May 1915, was an offshoot of *Al-Jarida*, the official organ of the nationalist Umma Party, which ceased its publication June 1915. The publishers of *Al-Sufur* then founded the Democratic Party in 1919 and soon integrated the (nationalist) Wafd. In 1922 some of the leading members of the Democratic Party joined the Liberal Constitutionalists.[13] What makes the three groups I have sketched "liberals" is their willingness to engage modern Europe and redefine themselves and the world around them and explore possibilities of human emancipation on the basis of new ideas, modern knowledge, and technological progress. What distinguishes the "Muslim reformists" and "nationalist modernists," on the one hand, from the "secular modernists," on the other, is their attitudes about their cultures and traditions. I suggest that while all three groups of reformers showed great interest in their cultural traditions, the secular liberals reinterpreted them, not for cultural renewal but rather to distance Egypt from the Orient and bring it closer to Europe. The secular liberal reformers, who emphasized rationality and individualism, were paradoxically trapped in the cultural order of the Other and therefore could not provide an inclusive notion of national identity and an emancipating notion of political community.

The other point I want to clarify is that I am not suggesting that the secular liberal reformers dominated Egyptian political parties, the parliament, or the government. They were politically influential, but their significance was more importantly literary. Their ideas, memoirs, novels, poems, newspapers, and artwork provide insight into the workings of identity during a period of cultural transformation that formal institutional politics alone cannot grasp. A strict institutional study of parliamentary and party politics during the period may tell us why Egyptian bankers and large landowners collided over taxation or investment policies. They cannot tell us how street demonstrators throwing their *tarboushes* and turbans high in the air in the face of Westernized dignitaries wearing ties and European suits give political conflicts a meta-social or meta-economic dimension that is possibly more determining. For example, the revolt of al-Azhar students and the emergence of religious political movements during the 1930s and 1940s leading to the collapse of constitutional politics cannot be viewed independently from questions of culture, identity, and language that the Egyptian liberal reformers wrote so much and so eloquently about.

Hence, far from being a simple, forceful attempt by the dominant European to govern the Other, the conferring of Western political institutions and values on Egypt involved the formidable participation of the Egyptian political elite. This participation included defining the boundaries of the political community with the purpose of representing Egypt as the European masters wanted it to be represented: imitating Europe, but not quite European.[14] Like the Europeans who defined their "self" against the non-European "other," Egyptian liberals defined their national identity in opposition to the Arabo-Islamic Other. To construct a nation modeled after those in Europe, Egyptian liberals redefined the territorial, historical, racial, and cultural boundaries of the new Egyptian nation.

The Territorial Boundaries

The most fundamental and commonly recognized trait of integrating a national community into a modern, independent state is a clearly defined and delimited territory. States mark the territorial boundaries of their nations by establishing geographic frontiers that delimit the extent of their power and authority over the citizens. The establishment of territorial boundaries, by force or by consent, also serves as a basis for group consciousness and recognition of belonging to one political community. People develop a sense of national identity by differentiating themselves from inhabitants of other and adjacent territories who obey different political and legal orders. According to Ibn Khaldun, the establishment of dynasties depended on the ability of one group to promote and control 'asabiyyah (group solidarity) strongly enough to subdue other existing forms of solidarity among the inhabitants of a given territory.[15] This concept is equally valid for the process of state formation in modern polities. The preponderance of group feeling based on the national territory, for example, is supposed to negate and take precedence over all other forms of affiliation and allegiance.

In modern Egypt, the emergence of territorial nationalism came with the gradual retreat of the cultural and religious bonds with Arabism and Islam.[16] This detachment proved to be problematic. "Let the motherland be the site of our common happiness, which we shall build by freedom, thought and the factory," wrote Rifa'a al-Tahtawi as early as the 1860s.[17] This first expression of Egyptian national identity based on awareness of, and attachment to, the motherland as a distinct territory enclosed within the broader Islamic Umma was revolutionary for its time. Until the collapse of the Ottoman Empire after World War I, in most parts of the Muslim world, religion was the primary source of common identification and subjective understanding among the inhabitants. This meant that Muslims, individually and collectively, were obliged to respond first to the demands of the Ottoman sultan as caliph and to obey the authority of the Islamic state. In contrast, when Tahtawi spoke of *hubb al-watan*, "love of the country," he meant his homeland, Egypt. This identification with the nation was a novelty. Tahtawi exhorted Egyptians to feel the same responsibility and obligations toward their homeland as they did toward the Islamic community. He wrote, for example:

> All that is binding on a believer in regard to his fellow believers is binding also on members of the same watan in their mutual rights. For there is a *national brotherhood* between them over and above the brotherhood of religion. There is a moral obligation on those who share the same watan to work together to improve it and perfect its organization in all that concerns its honour and greatness and wealth.[18]

The political community Tahtawi envisioned was not based on ethnic, linguistic, or religious bonds; he was explicitly referring to the Egyptian nation, *watan*, defined by a geographic territory.[19] When he praised patriotism, he meant the feeling shared by all descendants of ancient Egypt who had been living in the land of Egypt. "The physical constitution of [the present] times," writes Tahtawi, "is exactly that of the peoples of times past, and their disposition is one and the same."[20] Tahtawi was also the first modern Egyptian historian to revive the glories of ancient Egyptian civilization. He presented the Pharaohs as rulers of "great kingdoms" in his patriotic poems, *al-wataniyyat*. This revival of the Pharaonic age and its glories was an important element in the construction of national identity by the Egyptian liberal reformers in the 1920s and 1930s. The process of restoring and glorifying the Pharaonic age in Egyptian history was meant to undermine Egypt's allegiance to Islam or Arabism.

When Egypt fell under British occupation in 1882, despite the upsurge of pro-Ottoman feelings among the 'ulama in response to the Christian intrusion, the sentiments of Egyptian territorial nationalism gained strength among the educated elite. In 1902 Mustapha Kamil, a young nationalist leader, established the newspaper Al-Liwa as the political mouthpiece of Al-Hizb al-Watani, the National Party, in its anticolonial struggle. Mustapha Kamil's territorial nationalism took on an emotional significance. The land of Egypt became the signifier of a lost, coveted, and glorious Egyptian identity. In a 1907 speech, Mustapha Kamil implored his countrymen to commit themselves to the land of Egypt:

Oh you critics, look at it [Egypt], contemplate it, acquaint yourselves with it. Read the pages of its past, and ask visitors to it from the end of the earth: has God created any watan higher of station, finer of nature, more beautiful in character, more splendid in antiquities, richer in soil, clearer in sky, sweeter in water, more deserving of love and ardor than this glorious homeland? If I had not been born an Egyptian, I would have wished to be one.[21]

Like Tahtawi, Mustapha Kamil's conception of territorial nationalism did not necessarily conflict with Islam, or more accurately, religion. Kamil's knowledge of religion was not based on the teachings of Muslim scholars. He was trained as a lawyer in France, and his argument reflected his European education. On the sensitive relationship of nationalism to Islam, Kamil stated:

I do not rely in what I am saying on the teachings of the ancestors, whom the men of the modern age may accuse of ignorance and fanaticism, but I call upon Bismarck, the greatest leader of our time . . . to testify to the truth of this principle. This great man proclaimed indeed with a mighty voice: "if you tore faith from my heart, you will have torn with it my love for the fatherland.[22]

It was clearly not Tahtawi's or Kamil's understanding of what constitutes a nation that influenced most of the Egyptian liberal nationalists of the 1920s and 1930s. For the first reformers, Egyptian identity was still hampered by lingering attachments to the Islamic Umma. Beginning with Ahmad Lutfi al-Sayyid, in the years preceding World War I, this was to change. A more radical and uncompromising ideology of Egyptian nationalism came into being. In 1907, Lutfi al-Sayyid joined a group of "moderate nationalists" to form the Umma (Nation) Party.[23] The newly formed party included many intellectuals who played a significant role in Egyptian politics during the following three decades. Their newspaper, Al-Jarida, became the forum for important and lively debates on the political, cultural, and historical relationships of Egypt to Britain and Europe in general. Unlike the National Party of Mustapha Kamil, which was decidedly anti-British, the leaders of the Umma Party saw some positive aspects to the British presence in Egypt.

For al-Sayyid and his followers, the main problem facing Egypt was its blurred identity, which had been imposed on it during centuries of association with the Arabs and Islam. According to al-Sayyid, the solution was the elaboration of an Egyptian national consciousness and the constitution of a political community based strictly on the boundaries of the Nile Valley. In a series of articles published in March 1907, in the first issues of Al-Jarida, al-Sayyid outlined his ideology of Egyptian nationalism. The basic principle of this ideology was that Egypt was a separate nation from the Islamic Umma. He considered the Ottoman rulers, like the British, foreign intruders in Egypt. "I emphatically reject the suggestion that religion is a suitable basis for political action in the Twentieth Century. Our nationalism must rest on our own interest and not our beliefs," writes al-Sayyid. "[The Egyptians] are all the sons of this land, whether they are brown or white. Most of us realize that we are a nation in our own right."[24]

As a nationalist, al-Sayyid was in fact much more concerned about pan-Islamic, pro-Ottoman activities in Egypt than the colonial policies of the British. He saw in the pro-Turkish groups the forces of despotism and obscurantism who could easily exploit the religious feelings of the people for political ends. Their success could impede the development of an independent Egyptian nation and could perpetuate the allegiance of Egyptians to the Islamic Umma.

By the 1920s and 1930s, al-Sayyid's territorial nationalism was the dominant trend among the liberal Egyptian elite, including Muhammad Husayn Haykal, Taha Husayn, Salama Musa, and Tawfiq al-Hakim. Their rationalization for the need of an Egyptian identity and nation based on territory implied a complete and thorough renunciation of what they perceived as the false, despite its common acceptance, self-image of the Egyptians: belonging to an Arabo-Islamic entity. That image was totally opposed to the ideal European community they dreamed Egypt would become; Islam, it must be remembered, constructs Europe as Other and opponent.

The new collective self-image the liberal intellectuals elaborated for their country was exclusively based on the boundaries of the Nile Valley: "from

Alexandria to the sources of the Nile."[25] They defined the nation by negating the nonterritorial elements of Egyptian identity, the Arabo-Islamic heritage, and by emphasizing the centrality of the land. In this attempt, the Arab was portrayed as alien, other, and inferior to the Egyptian nation and its glorious past. To foster national consciousness, the Egyptian reformers thought it necessary to eliminate the bonds of solidarity and allegiance that could indicate that Egyptians defined themselves otherwise. As Hasan 'Arif writes in the Wafdist newspaper Al-Balagh:

> Whether or not Egyptians intermixed with the Arabs [in the past], the present people of Egypt are radically different from the Arabs in every way. The Egyptian is Arab neither in his [external] form, his mentality, his grasp of moral values and social life, his temperament, nor his customs. The Egyptian nation possesses a self-contained personality which springs from its own environment and long history, which predates Arab history by thousands of years. The Egyptian nation's existence is independent of the Arabs, the Muslims, the Christians, and the entire world.[26]

It was the Islamic and Arab connections, however, that Husayn Haykal and his colleagues were emphatically trying to belittle. By formulating the territorial principle and presenting it as the most important component of Egyptian identity, the Egyptian liberals were rationalizing the rejection of the previously dominant Ottoman-Islamic influence and the creation of a new European image for Egypt.[27]

The Historical Boundaries

Any association with Islam or the Arabs meant a weakening of the link between modern Egypt and Egypt's ancient, glorious Pharaonic past. This past was used as a bridge to link the Egyptian nation to Europe via the Greek heritage. Once the break with the Arabs and Islam was secured, deliberations about Egypt's "true" identity became possible and legitimate. Egyptian history became the privileged space of deliberation and speculation about Egyptian national identity.

To constitute a political community free from the perceived cultural and religious constraints of the Arabo-Islamic heritage, the Egyptian liberals rewrote the history of Egypt by inventing and excluding their own "others."[28] Modern Western historiography developed and progressed in relation to Western culture's perception of its others—"the savage, the past, the people, the mad, the child, the Third World."[29] Michel Foucault argues that from the Renaissance to the Classical Age, the confinement and social exclusion of the leper, the criminal, the poor, and the insane say more about the development of modern Western social institutions and society than about the confined and excluded. As stated earlier, the Europeans also defined themselves vis-à-vis the non-European, Oriental Other. Edward Said posits that the European description of the Orient not only (mis)represented it but constituted Europe itself as the opposite image of the Oriental. This idea of defining self in opposition to the other is also at work in the constitution of national identity and political community. For example, Anne Norton has shown how the Indian, the black, and the woman in their liminal positions were appropriated in the formation of Northern and Southern political identities in antebellum America.[30]

In their attempt to constitute a new political community, the Egyptian liberals wrote a history of Egypt in which the Arabo-Islamic past was either obscured or trivialized. To write the history of a nation or a people implies the transfer of that past into an empty space in which the author can exclude the undesirable, subvert the authoritative, or subordinate the challenging. In a literal sense, to "write" means to construct a sign on a supposedly empty space, the page, which becomes the perverse materialization of something that was or the imposition of something that was not. When Salama Musa, one of the founding fathers of Egyptian liberalism, wrote, "The new Egypt is known by two things: she looks forward to the future and does not care about the past, and turns to the West and does not care about the Orient,"[31] he was renouncing only a select portion of Egypt's past. In fact, Salama Musa and his colleagues were very much concerned with Egyptian history. What he did not care about was Egypt's Arabo-Islamic past.

In the prolific production of articles and books published during the 1920s and 1930s on ancient Egyptian history, the past emerges as the arena of an enormous contest in which Egyptian liberals fought to establish a single, hegemonic view. They sought to become the sole legitimate representatives and interpreters of Egyptian history. Salama Musa proclaimed the past invalid, only to create a new "representative image" of it that brought Egypt closer to its supposedly European origin. The periods where the Arabo-Islamic civilization was too significant to ignore were simply censored, for they made any claim to historical affiliation with the Occident untenable. Conversely, the Pharaonic past, judged more convenient to the Egyptian liberals' new political image of their country, was increasingly evoked and glorified to establish a close civilizational proximity to the West.[32]

What is perhaps most evocative in the development of the Pharaonic revival is the quasi-religious discourse in which it was wrapped. Consider how 'Abbas Mahmud al-'Aqqad, for example, describes his feelings after visiting the Egyptian tombs:

Those (Egyptians) who make the pilgrimage (hajju) to the tomb of Tut-AnkAmon come to it desiring life. . . . . They come to unite one age with another, another world with another, to conquer three thousand years packed with emotions, multitudes of thoughts, and hosts of utopian dreams. They come searching for what is new and alive among the hidden treasures of the tombs and the remains of those who have passed away, not what is ancient and decayed in them.[33]

Salama Musa, who claimed that Egypt did not care about the past, not only enthusiastically supported the dissemination of the ideas of Pharaonic civilization among the people but also refuted the common assertions that the religion of the ancient Egyptians was tyrannical. He argued that it was a sophisticated religion that inspired Judaism, Christianity, and Islam.

The purpose of reviving the Pharaonic past was not only to displace the Arabo-Islamic hold on Egypt. Its other significant aim was to emphasize the influence of ancient Egypt on the cultures of classical Greece and Rome from which dominant European civilization claimed descent. Muhammad Zaki Salih, another proponent of Pharaonism, wrote:

The Greeks, with all their gracefulness of expression and the noble thought processes which they provided; the Romans, with all their forcefulness in administration and the high (example of) determination in government which they have furnished; and even the Anglo-Saxons . . . [pay tribute to] eternal Egypt. They salute Egypt as a soldier salutes his commander or a pupil his teacher. And no wonder, since Egypt is the first teacher of all nations and peoples.[34]

Egypt's glorious past was officially celebrated in May 1928 when the statue Nahdhat Misr (The Revival of Egypt) was unveiled in a festive ceremony attended by King Fu'ad, the British high commissioner Lord Lloyd, representatives of the parliament, the 'ulama of al-Azhar, and the entire cabinet. The sculpture was designed and built by the Paris-trained Egyptian artist Mahmud Mokhtar, who had won a prize in Paris in 1920 for a model similar to the monument erected in Cairo. Made of gigantic granite stones from Aswan, the cradle of ancient Egyptian civilization, and transported on the Nile in the Pharaonic tradition, the sculpture stood in a main Cairo square to become the forceful emblem of a once lost and now reconquered identity.[35] In the opening address of the inauguration, prime minister Mustapha Nahhas described the event in these words:

[The statue represents] the bond uniting different phases of Egyptian history, past, present, and future. It represents the glory of the past, the earnestness of the present, and the hope of the future. It represents a picture of young Egypt preoccupied with the Sphinx so that it may revive through her and she through it, directing its glance towards its old power and copying the glorious precedent of its reawakening. . . . If there is a single nation whose ancient past vindicates its current rebirth, that nation is Egypt.[36]

Nahdhat Misr represents Egypt in the form of an Egyptian woman standing next to a Sphinx, the symbol of the Pharaonic heritage. As a text, the sculpture conveys the message of Pharaonic eternity linking Egypt's past, present, and future, projecting an identity that negates any possibility of temporality, and imposing a material existence of its own. This artistic representation of Egypt primordially addresses the past: a strong Egypt can exist only from the point of view of the glorified and mythologized past. The sculpture reconstitutes and brings to the fore the Pharaonic past symbolized by the Sphinx, while placing to its left Egypt, symbolized by a proud and dignified peasant woman, on whom the artist has inscribed the marks of power mirrored in the Pharaonic headdress. The centrality of the past, conveyed through a careful spatial arrangement of the sculpture, is further intensified by the presence of other details: the throne, the claws, and the colossal size of the Sphinx, together symbolizing majesty, strength, and grandeur. Next to the overwhelming presence of the Sphinx stands Egypt—still, tall, and strong. The striking similarity of the facial expressions of the Sphinx and the woman is unmistakable. The similitude between the two figures is signified by a stern look that conveys a sense of common destiny.

But the calculating association of contemporary Egypt with Pharaonic civilization predates the ceremonial unveiling of Nahdhat Misr. Pharaonic sentiments among Egyptian liberal reformers can be traced back to the late nineteenth century. Tahtawi considered the legitimate heir of the Pharaohs to be Muhammad 'Ali, who is ironically of Albanian origin (1805–49). Tahtawi was also the first modern Egyptian thinker who wrote poems praising the glories of ancient Egypt.[37] However, it was only after World War I, when Egyptology flourished in Europe, that the Egyptian elite began effectively to use the potential power of a Pharaonic affiliation to redefine Egyptian identity. The growing role and prestige of Western Egyptology during the 1920s and 1930s gave momentum to the revival of Pharaonic sentiment and is very important to understanding that revival.

As a discipline, Egyptology developed, like many other Orientalist "disciplines," with the conquest of the East.[38] From the point of view of the Western conqueror, the discovery of ancient Egypt meant the conquest of the exotic Other against which the Occident discovered, defined, and addressed itself. The history of the Other, the non-Western, could be written only from the point of view that appropriated the Orient and reworked it as a body on which the European inscribed his own history.

As captured by a critic of nineteenth-century Orientalist academic painters, Western representation of the Orient addressed, in fact, the West itself:

> After having taken everything they could from Greek and Roman antiquity, painters found in the Orient a new myth . . . a new model in an older civilization. . . . The Orient becomes an exaggerated Italy. [It] is processed and recycled through a Greek and Roman mould in order to become a prehistorical antiquity, closer to the origins of "civilization," that is of the West.[39]

Thus the Orient existed only as a prehistorical entity that evolved, in a long historical process, into the modern West. Ancient Egyptians, like the Mesopotamians, became the prehistoric ancestors of the dominant Western civilization, and their marvelous accomplishments were "honored" only insofar as the modern West could trace its distant origins to that ancient civilization. Accordingly, it was the European who assumed the task of exploring the remains of the ancient Egyptian civilization while excluding indigenous archaeologists and historians from such expeditions.[40] What the Egyptian liberals seem to have missed is that the reason for the European scramble to uncover and decipher ancient Egyptian history and artifacts was to celebrate the triumph of Western civilization, not to pay homage to contemporary Egypt. Egypt remained in the eyes of Europeans a "backward" country reflecting modern Oriental inferiority.[41]

The Racial Boundaries

A particularly striking example of the Egyptian liberals' curious reading of European works on the Orient and its people was their veneration of the books of the notorious French Orientalist Ernest Renan (1823–92). A philologist, Renan attempted to prove scientifically that Islam and its Arabic language were not compatible with philosophic and scientific inquiry.[42] A collection of Renan's pamphlets and a précis of his philosophy were translated into Arabic and published in Cairo in 1929.[43] Most Egyptian intellectuals of the period were familiar with the French positivists and were influenced by Renan's views on race, language, and the making of world civilizations.[44]

Renan's philosophy could have appealed to the Egyptian liberals for two reasons. First, Renan portrayed himself and was perceived as the representative of modern European culture based on scientific knowledge. In *L'avenir de la science*, published in 1890, Renan argued that science, as epitomized in modern European culture, is the key to the future of humanity.[45] At the same time, he argued that owing to the inferiority and the defects of the Semitic "character" and "spirit," the world would inevitably be led, politically and culturally, by the European Aryan race.[46] Second, just as Egyptian liberals accepted Renan's assertion of the inferiority of the Semitic race as an objective scientific truth,[47] they also accepted his appraisal, or rather acknowledgment, that the ancient Egyptians were major contributors to world civilization and therefore could not have been a Semitic people.[48]

Renan's theory of Aryan superiority greatly influenced the Egyptian liberals' view of race. The most prolific, consistent, and enthusiastic proponent of an Aryan affiliation for Egyptians was by far Salama Musa.[49] His exclusively Western education and particular interest in nineteenth-century philosophers could explain his strong position on the question of race.[50] In December 1928, the Egyptian monthly magazine *Al-Hilal* published a controversial article written by Salama Musa under a rather daring title: "The Egyptians Are a Western Nation."[51] The article's purpose was to demonstrate that the Egyptians have the same origins as Europeans. Clearly, Salama Musa had the British in mind as he unequivocally asserts in the opening paragraph:

Perhaps the main cause of our disputes with the Europeans is our illusion that we and the Europeans are complete strangers with no blood ties and a different descent. But the truth, as scientific research has shown, is that the people of the Mediterranean (with its four regions) are descendants of the same origin, and that the ancient Egyptians and ancient British are from the same descent. It is our goal to let the reader know about what has been written on the subject with the hope that this will create an atmosphere of harmony and good-will between the Orient and the Occident. (178)

Quoting from G. Eliot Smith's *The Ancient Egyptians*, Salama Musa confirms again:

Although we can learn a great deal about the appearance and mode of life of the proto-Egyptians from the study of the soft tissues collected from their graves, the study of their skulls assumes a greater importance, because this enables us to compare them with remains of other populations, both in Egypt and elsewhere, which consist of nothing else than the mere skeleton. . . . So striking is the familial likeness between the Early Neolithic peoples of the British isles and the Mediterranean and the bulk of the population: both ancient and modern, of Egypt and East Africa, that a description of the bones of an early Briton of that remote epoch may apply in all essential details to an inhabitant of Somaliland.[52]

To support his argument, Musa includes pictures of four figures representing "proto-Egyptians" and Egyptians' representation of Arabs, and a list of English words that were phonetically similar to the same words in hieroglyphics.[53] Smith, however, uses these figures to show the similarity between the ancient Egyptians and the Arabs. "There is a considerable mass of evidence to show that there was a very close resemblance between the proto-Egyptians and the Arabs, before either became intermingled with Negroid racial elements."[54]

Notwithstanding the "scientific" accuracy of such an assertion, the point is that Salama Musa not only disregards this statement by Smith but changes the comment associated with one of the figures from "a proto-Egyptian as represented in a portrait statuette by a contemporary artist" to "a statue of a proto-Egyptian whose features show its European expressions."[55] As for the table of words, Salama Musa simply states that "it is inconceivable that the commonality between these words could be a coincidence rather than an indication of partnership between the current British people and the ancient Egyptian people" (180).

Having shown the biological similarities between Egyptians and Europeans, Salama Musa goes on to display what he sees as the main difference between them. The real difference between the two people, he argues, is that the Europeans are living in an industrial civilization, while the Egyptians are still in the agrarian age. European cities are filled with factories and machines, and their culture is based on scientific knowledge. Egyptian culture, on the other hand, is restricted to literature in an age where steel, fire, science, and industry are most needed and respected. Musa concludes:

In the end there is no difference between Europe and us; we belong to the same origin. We have the same psychological and mental temperament but our moral values are slightly different from theirs because our economic conditions are different. . . . The European colonization of our country is above all an economic one and the only way to get rid of it is by developing industry and making it the economic basis of the country. The Europeans cannot do without colonization because it is the nature of industry, which leads to the conquest of markets. (181)

Evidence proving the racial connections between Egyptians and Europeans was also presented in various scientific forums and magazine articles. In a lecture to the Egyptian Association of Science in May 1930, Muhammad Sharaf, a prominent Egyptian medical doctor, spoke on the origins of the ancient Egyptians. He began his speech by refuting the findings of a British Egyptologist who claimed that the ancient Egyptians came from Yemen, "which implied that the Egyptians are a Semitic people like the Syrians and the Arabs."[56] The involvement of the medical authorities in these matters and its wide coverage in newspapers illustrates the seriousness with which Egyptian reformers viewed their "origin" and its immediate relevance to their present political situation. Under the provocative title *Al-Misriyyun Umma Ghayr Sharqiyya* (The Egyptians Are Not an Oriental Nation), the magazine published extracts from Sharaf's presentation to underline the scientific ground on which Egyptians claimed a common descent with the Europeans. After explaining the various means used by scientists to designate and classify the various human races—shape of head, hair, skin color—and dismissing them as inaccurate methods of measurement, the author claims that only through blood examinations can one specify the racial descent of a people.[57] Citing the blood tests that were conducted on soldiers during World War I and their contribution to advancing man's knowledge on the racial differences between various people and nations, Dr. Sharaf announced that he had conducted similar tests on 3,064 Egyptians to determine their standing among the human races. According to the article, results confirm that "modern Egyptians descend from the same origin as the ancient Egyptians [despite centuries of intermixing with the Persians, Arabs, and Ottomans] and that Egypt is not an African or an Asian [nation] but rather a European [nation]."[58]

The Cultural Boundaries

Just as Egyptian liberals rewrote their history and "scientifically" reconstituted their racial origins to prove the non-Semitic origin of Egyptians, so they also attempted to scientifically reformulate the distinct national character of Egypt. The works of Gustave Le Bon and Hippolyte Taine provided the conceptual framework for this effort. The general argument advanced by the Egyptian liberals was that Egyptians have a national culture distinct from the rest of the Arabo-Islamic world. According to Husayn Haykal, a prominent literary figure and a proponent of this view, the specific history and environment in which Egyptians lived shaped the general traits of their national character. This interpretation clarified the qualitative difference between the cultural traditions of the Arabs and those of the Egyptians.[59]

The approach to the study of cultural traditions as products of the environment was taken directly from the French philosopher and historian Hippolyte Taine (1828–93), the centennial of whose birth was celebrated by the Egyptian intellectuals in 1928.[60] In the introduction to his monumental five-volume work on English literature, Taine develops the core of his theory of culture:

> Three different sources contribute to produce this elementary moral state—Race, Surroundings, and Epoch. What we call race are the innate and hereditary dispositions which man brings with him into the world. . . . Having thus outlined the interior structure of a race, we must consider the surroundings in which it exists. For man is not alone in the world; nature surrounds him, and his fellow-men surround him. . . . There is yet a third rank of causes . . . beside the permanent impulse and the given surroundings, there is the acquired momentum. When the national character and the surrounding circumstances operate, it is not upon a tabula rasa, but on a ground on which marks are already impressed. Accordingly as one takes the ground at one moment or another, the imprint is different and this is the cause that the total effect is different.[61]

Combining his own analysis with Renan's *Histoire des langues sémitiques* and Montesquieu's *L'esprit des lois*, Taine writes:

> If . . . the general representation in which the conception results is a poetical and figurative creation, a living symbol, as among Aryan races, language becomes a sort of delicately-shaded and coloured epic poem, in which every word is a person, poetry and religion assume a magnificent and inexhaustible grandeur, metaphysics are widely and subtly developed, without regard to positive applications; the whole intellect, in spite of the inevitable deviations and shortcomings of its effort, is smitten with the beautiful and the sublime, and conceives an idea capable by its nobleness and its harmony of rallying round it the tenderness and enthusiasm of the human race. If, again, the general conception in which the representation results is poetical but not graduated; if man arrives at it not by an uninterrupted gradation, but by a quick intuition; if the original operation is not a regular development, but a violent explosion—then, as with Semitic races, metaphysics are absent, religion conceives God only as a king solitary and devouring, science cannot grow, the intellect is too rigid and unbending to reproduce the delicate operations of nature, poetry can give birth only to vehement and grandiose exclamations, language cannot unfold the web of argument and of eloquence, man

is reduced to a lyric enthusiasm, an unchecked passion, a fanatical and limited action. In this interval between the particular representation and the universal conception are found the germs of the greatest human differences.[62]

Haykal's social philosophy clearly echoes Taine's idea of race, milieu, and time:

> The individual does not exist by himself. His existence derives from the environment (al-wasat) in which he lives. Only a complete understanding and knowledge of the natural milieu (al-bi'a al-taabi'iyya), the social milieu (al-bi'a al-ijtima'iyya), the historic condition (al-hala al-tarikhiyyaj), and the beliefs, customs, thoughts, emotions, and trends which flourished under their influence—all these and only these can enable us to understand the writer, the poet, philosopher, or any other person linked to the collective, influenced by it, and affecting it.[63]

Taine's philosophy also influenced Haykal's interpretation that Arabic literature was ill-suited to the Egyptian environment. In a series of articles reviewing two newly published books on the history of Arabic literature, Haykal charges the authors with misrepresenting Arabic literature.[64] Haykal is concerned about two main issues; the first is the question of writing style. Haykal blames Mustapha al-Raafi'i, the author of a book on Arabic literature, for using literary expressions, symbols, and metaphors that were commonly used by the Arab nomads and therefore improper for borrowing by a civilized Egyptian.[65] Haykal's second concern is the very idea of writing a history of Arabic literature. While praising the writing style of Jurgi Zaydan, the author of over twenty-five books on Arab history and literature, Haykal asks why contemporary Egyptians should concern themselves with the literature of the Arabs and "their literary monuments." Haykal rejects the idea that the Egyptians should write the history of Arabic literature just as the French recorded the Greco-Roman literary tradition. Egyptian authors, complains Haykal, think it is a moral obligation to write about the Arabs and their literary history. That is why, he explains, Egyptian literature is filled with redeeming appraisals and mythical glories of the Arabs and Arabic literature. After all, the Arabs have not reached an advanced stage of scientific knowledge, moral values, and political development to deserve such an appraisal.[66]

Haykal wanted a cultural image for Egypt that was distinct from the one associated with the Arab heritage. In all aspects of social life, including language as a mode of social communication, Egypt's distinctiveness was clear and manifest. Egypt's national culture, according to Haykal and his followers such as Ahmad Salim, Ahmad Husayn, Fathi Zaghlul, Niqula Yusuf, Tawfiq al-Hakim, and Taha Husayn, was restricted to the style of life in the Nile Valley. The territorial boundaries became the ultimate signifier of Egyptian cultural identity. These boundaries automatically excluded anyone or anything that did not belong to the regional confines established by these self-appointed representatives of national culture. According to the Egyptian liberals, the Egyptian people had been living for thousands of years under the same climatic conditions and the same natural environment, which together created their character and personality and rendered them a nation distinct from other nations. "The environment gives the people their color, their body structure, their character, and sensations," wrote Ahmad Husayn, a proponent of the Pharaonic character of Egypt.[67] For thousands of years, the natural environment of Egypt had steadily been shaping the beliefs, manners, artistic expressions, and psyches of the Egyptian people. This link between the remote past and the present had not been interrupted.[68]

The Egyptian liberals were concerned that Egyptian culture in general and, more specifically, literature had lost its Egyptian character because it was written and expressed in Arabic. The goal, therefore, was to emphasize the difference between what was written in Egypt and what was produced in Arabia. There was awareness among Egyptians of the role of culture in conveying a national image. Culture in a general sense was understood to reflect people's lifestyle and their social, political, religious, and moral development.[69] Egyptian literature, complained Egyptian literary critics, remained prisoner of the influence of the Arabic and Ottoman heritage, which was considered an alien and harmful growth on the original Egyptian civilization. Moreover, Haykal complains, Egyptian students read more about Arabic poetry and learn nothing about ancient Egyptian writings, which makes it difficult to differentiate between what is Egyptian and what is Arab: "We study Arabic literature which is foreign to us and its imaginations reflect a Bedouin life style with which we have no acquaintance: we do not pray for rain, we do not pitch tents . . . [or] travel with camels and we are not involved in other related practices which characterize the type of civilization reflected in Arabic literature."[70] Egyptians were therefore called on to write, like Victor Hugo or Anatole France, in a specific way for a specific reason—to distinguish themselves from their colleagues in the Arab world. Such literature was called al-adab al-qawrny, "a national literature."

Egyptian national literature was expected to be different from any other Arabic literature. To legitimize the claim of distinctiveness, the Egyptian liberals once again turned to a scientific theory. Muhammad Ghalab, a professor of literature at the University of Lyon, France, and Ahmad Dayf, who completed his doctoral dissertation in Paris, provided that scientific framework. In an article published in 1929, Muhammad Ghalab argues that Egyptian literature was different from Semitic literature.[71] Like the Europeans, Ghalab thought it fair and accurate to portray Oriental and Semitic literature as inferior to the narrative Indo-German tradition and its Greco-Roman precedents. More specifically, Ghalab argues that the Arabs wrote only to satisfy their personal needs and desires but not to study the social, religious, and moral conditions of their nation and people. Despite Renan's extreme and overt anti-Semitism, Ghalab asserts that there is sufficient evidence to support his claim on the striking shortcomings of the Semitic mind. Most of the stories related in the Qur'an, for example, were taken from the Old Testament. These stories also make little mention of the social conditions of the people. As for the so-called Arab philosophy and science, writes Ghalab paraphrasing Renan, they are a historical fallacy, because the Semitic people are incapable of such an intellectual effort. Most of what is called Arab philosophy is a translation of Greek philosophy. In the East, only Persian and Hindu philosophers produced what appeared to be new.[72]

Dayf's dissertation, Le lyricisme et la critique littéraire chez les arabes, also clearly shows the influence of Renan's ideas. Upon his return to Cairo, where he taught Arabic literature at the Egyptian University, Dayf elaborated Renan's concepts and published a book on Arab rhetoric.[73] Like Ghalab, Dayf endorsed Renan's views on the backward and primitive character of Semitic literature and particularly Arabic literature. The next logical step was to disassociate Egyptian literature from the Semitic element and to disclose the misperceptions caused by the unfortunate historical mixing with the Semitic people. This rescue could come only through the elaboration of shakhsiyya Misriyya, an "Egyptian personality."

The desire to resuscitate the Egyptian national character or personality became an obsession that preoccupied Egyptian liberal intellectuals. For thousands of years, complains Tawfiq al-Hakim, a leading literary figure of the period, Egyptians had lost their identity and began to define themselves only through Arab history.[74] Recalling the efforts of Ahmad Lutfi al-Sayyid (1872–1963) to cut off all political links with the Ottoman Empire, al-Hakim calls on Taha Husayn, a distinguished figure in Egypt, and his generation to revive the Egyptian national character through writing. "Your duty," wrote al-Hakim, addressing Taha Husayn, "is to separate [for us, the Arab] element from the [Egyptian element]. We have no choice but to know what an Egyptian is and what an Arab is."[75] Three years after al-Hakim's plea, Husayn published perhaps the most influential essay on Egyptian culture. He entitled his book *Mustaqbal al-Thaqafa fi Misr* (The Future of Culture in Egypt).[76]

The question that Husayn sets out for himself is whether Egyptian culture is Oriental or Occidental. More specifically, Husayn inquires whether "the Egyptian mind [is] Oriental in its imagination, perception, understanding, and judgement of things" or whether it is Western.[77] After proving that Egypt had no regular and organized relations with the East that could have influenced the lifestyle, thought, and political and economic organization of Egypt, Husayn proceeds to demonstrate that ancient Egypt was physically and culturally part of the Mediterranean civilization and developed mutually beneficial contacts with ancient Greece.

The point of Husayn's work was to show that there were more exchanges in arts and politics with ancient Greece than there were with the East. The ancient Greeks, contends Husayn with pride, were in fact honored to have known the Egyptians, whom the Greeks considered their mentors and masters, portraying them with deference in their poetry and prose. Egyptian influence on ancient Greece was not limited to architecture, sculpture, painting, and the various arts but included many other aspects of daily life such as politics. Hence, if one wants to look for the most influential factor in the formation of Egyptian civilization and Egyptian mind, argues Husayn, it would be inadequate to look for sources of influence from the Orient. Rather, one should consider surrounding Mediterranean conditions as determinants of Egyptian cultural traditions. From these historical facts, the reader is led to believe that the ancient Egyptian mind is not an "Eastern mind"; it developed as a result of the prevailing natural and human conditions that brought Egypt in closer proximity to Europe. Husayn acknowledges that Egypt exerted influence on, and was influenced by, neighboring Arab peoples and cultures, but he insists it was with the Greek mind that Egypt interacted most. By making these statements, Husayn wants his countrymen to understand that their culture, mind-set, and character are similar to the Europeans' and therefore the Egyptians "have to learn what the Europeans learn, feel what the Europeans feel, govern like the Europeans govern, work like they work, and live like they live."[78]

When the Egyptian liberals of the 1920s and 1930s wrote about Egyptian history, racial origin, and culture, they presented their "findings" as scientific truths derived from Western knowledge on the Orient. By accepting Western ideas and images of the East as scientific truths, the Egyptian liberals smuggled in their modernist discourse overt racial and cultural discrimination. They came to define themselves mainly from the point of view of the European looking at the non-European Other. The way in which liberal Egyptians defined themselves affected how they defined their political community. In the next chapter, I examine how this intolerant form of liberalism structured the Egyptian liberals' understanding of modern citizenship.

four

The Cultural Preconditions of Citizenship

The Egyptian liberal reformers linked the constitution of Egypt as a modern nation to a redefinition of its geographic, historical, racial, and cultural boundaries. On the basis of "scientific" theories about racial and cultural hierarchies borrowed from modern European thinkers, liberal reformers attempted to validate claims that Egypt was originally a European nation, now disfigured by centuries of Arabo-Islamic domination. Egypt's liberal reformers, the finest and most influential literary and political figures in the Arab world, had set out to "rescue" the country from what they considered an alien and backward cultural heritage. Nothing, then, could have been more troubling to them than the realization that the boundaries of the political community they had envisioned did not quite fit with the everyday reality of the people who were supposed to constitute that community. The manners and conduct of the "masses" in the course of normal, quotidian activities were frantically denounced as incompatible with Egypt's new, "collective" self-image. Any manifestation or sign of native culture, in private or in public, in celebration or in mourning, by an individual or a group, was considered a challenge to the absolute sense of political identity the liberal reformers demanded of their compatriots. These two conflicting images, the country's European vocation and the "primitive" behavior of the masses, stirred passionate arguments that in many ways anticipated the challenge of identity politics in today's liberal democracies. Notwithstanding the culturally prejudiced tone of their discourse, the Egyptian reformers were grappling with a vital question: could the modern notion of citizenship, borrowed from the cultural context of European liberalism, admit cultural difference?

Surprisingly, debates in Egypt on this imminently political question were hardly ever articulated in political terms. In major works by liberal thinkers, there were no serious discussions of, for example, the appropriate form of political authority to incorporate socially and culturally diverse groups as citizens, and there were no deliberations on the priority of individual rights over communal moral or cultural claims.[1] The very concept of citizenship, so central to the political transformation of Egypt at the time, is not treated in any significant work. The rather slim political contribution of Egyptian liberalism may have a practical explanation. Because reformist intellectuals were concerned with immediate, burning political questions, they expressed themselves mainly through newspaper columns to reach a wide audience as quickly as possible. That kind of platform and pressure may have affected the intellectual depth and coherence of their political discourse.[2] But that is not a sufficient explanation. 'Ali 'Abd al-Raziq, a liberal Muslim reformer who was concerned with the same issues, wrote a book that provided the most coherent political justification for the principles of liberal government.[3]

The absence of clear and coherent concepts of public authority, rights, and citizenship in liberal writings has nothing to do with practical concerns or intellectual qualifications. The Egyptian liberals held that in a culturally "backward" society, the masses do not have the capacity to make meaningful choices, and therefore the exclusion of their voices needs no theoretical justification or political explanation. The kind of social and cultural "emancipation" they preached is grounded in a self-evident cultural justification of political subordination. The masses became the object of an arbitrary and authoritative discourse telling them how to dress, how to eat, what to read, what to believe, how to cross the street, how to choose a conjugal partner, how to celebrate a birth, and how to mourn and bury the dead. In short, they were expected to renounce their cultural identities and moral values and assume an alien, "superior" political identity. Except for the simplistic and phony racial theories on the inferiority of Arab culture and the superiority of Western civilization,[4] the Egyptian reformers did not bother to offer the public compelling reasons to give up parts of their cultural identity in order to enjoy citizenship rights.

There was thus no need to assess what aspects of native culture and moral values were illiberal or antidemocratic. Liberal advocates had a specific, ready-made, and expansive notion of the common good. But that is not all. They conflated the good with Western rationalism and unambiguously endorsed state intervention to pursue it. European scientific theories, the liberal reformers believed, provided a way of life different from, and better than, the dominant and irrational popular culture in Egypt.[5] These were not just some naive ideas totally removed from policies; liberal reformers called on the public authorities to play a dominant role. The police, schools, prisons, and hospitals were solicited again and again to enforce strict laws against unwelcome practices such as public celebration of saints, improper mourning, traditional attire, and other unhealthy habits.[6]

This regulation of cultural practices and individual expression appears to contradict modern liberalism's emphasis on the primacy of individual freedom of choice and reluctance to promote a particular conception of the good, and certainly not through the state. In this chapter, however, I argue that the Egyptian liberals' culturally grounded understanding of modern citizenship may not be all that alien to liberalism. The colonial context highlights illiberal and antidemocratic trends within liberalism that are only latent when liberalism does not cross the home frontiers. To develop this argument, I will first consider the Egyptian liberals' curious obsession with social and cultural practices that have no obvious relevance to determining eligibility for citizenship rights. Yet these practices were used to chastise the masses for lacking the prerequisites of citizenship. I call these "the difficult cases" because their link to liberal political principles is subtle. I will then discuss a second set of cultural and social practices that I consider directly relevant to the realization or obstruction of the liberal conception of citizenship. I call these "the telling cases," since they can easily be traced to standard liberal conditions. In both cases, however, the purpose of putting popular beliefs and practices on trial in Egyptian discourse is never to negotiate a balance between collective rights and individual liberty. What informs the reformers' negative portrayal of popular practices is a socially biased and culturally grounded conception of citizenship.

The Difficult Cases

In a recollection of those years of hope and despair, Taha Husayn, whose writings on national literature I examined in the previous chapter, vividly describes his distress upon learning, while returning home on a boat from Marseilles, that cholera was rampant in Egypt.[7] It was a moment pregnant with meanings, since cholera situates Egypt outside the European sphere and links it both to the "sickly" Orient and, metaphorically, to a sick body politic. Aboard the ship, a French newspaper's headlines alarmed the Europeans awaiting their arrival in Egypt and embarrassed the Egyptian passengers. "How could it be?" wondered Taha Husayn. "Cholera is an African disease!" Husayn could not believe his ears. He shrugged his shoulders. "Foolish news from a despicable newspaper! Probably another one of those anti-Egyptian propaganda campaigns, which the French press has been mounting against Egypt and the Egyptian people," he thought. To his astonishment, however, on the third day of the trip, the crew announced that drinking water must be rationed. The ship's water supply had to last until the ship reached Beirut, without replenishment in Alexandria as originally planned. The reason: cholera! How could it be? Cholera—like thick dirty crowds, chaotic streets and markets, backward popular cultural practices, archaic beliefs and values, traditional forms of knowledge—was a distinct mark of African and Oriental primitiveness! Egyptians have a parliament; they have built schools, hospitals, ministries, and a capital to rival Paris, New York, and London! Yet the people, individually and collectively, were not behaving like the civilized citizens they were supposed to be: healthy, productive, rational, and responsive to the demands of the modern state. How had the Egyptians failed? asked Taha Husayn.[8]

If Egypt's proximity to the European model remained removed and uncertain, the masses were to blame. "The masses cannot adjust to the historic changes the country is undergoing," complained the liberal reformers. Because of their inability to adjust, their allegiance to the new Egyptian nation could not be guaranteed. The masses were considered "abnormal," "socially ill," and in urgent need of containment, surveillance, and medical treatment. Egyptian society was viewed as a mixture of pathological groups to be treated, literally, by medical experts to "normalize" their integration as abstract individual citizens into the newly defined political community.[9]

The following discussion illustrates the general tone and scope of the debates among Egyptian reformers on what they thought was wrong with their society and what ought to be done. "The social organism is attacked by germs just like the human body," reads the headline of a major reformist newspaper, summarizing the social problems facing Egypt at the time.[10] The article refers to "criminal behavior" such as popular religious rituals, thick crowds in streets and markets, general "unhealthy" habits, and traditional garb unfit for Egypt's new "collective" self-image. The author reassures the readers that these problems are not unique to Egypt. Governments and people everywhere confront similar concerns and fight them by enforcing rigorous laws against deviant behavior. But governments alone cannot control "social epidemics" and "treat" those who are still "infected" without the cooperation and participation of the general population. Thanks to the increasing number of published articles on the problems of public education, health, morality, and public order and security, says the article, the government began to assume its modern responsibilities.

The intensity of the debates and controversies about the proper behavior in the public sphere suggests, however, that the Egyptian liberals' concern was not related to the intrusive and atomistic social reforms associated with the emergence of modern political power.[11] They were mainly concerned with how the Other, Mother Europe, saw and evaluated Egypt, the child in need of recognition for its "self" definition. Elsewhere in the same issue, an article praised Cairo's police chief for cleaning the city of "drugs, prostitution, gambling, and other humiliating crimes which distort the true image of Egyptians in the eyes of the Europeans and undermine Egypt's efforts towards modernization and progress."[12] This preoccupation with the Other, not the modern will to power, is really what made ordinary social and cultural practices appear suddenly problematic in the eyes of the reformers.

Let us now consider in more detail the social and cultural practices that were considered inappropriate, unhealthy, or even criminal. From a liberal perspective, the Egyptian liberals' most controversial attacks on peoples' collective identities may be those directed at beliefs, rituals, and practices that are in no obvious way incompatible with citizenship. The harsh and prejudiced language used to complain about Sufi celebrations, hysterical mourning, trance dancing, unintelligible singing, and superstitious practices would make most liberals uncomfortable. Yet these issues echo familiar concerns in the European or North American liberal context. Descriptions of Sufi celebrations, for example, call to mind U.S. congressional hearings in the 1950s that were suspicious of a "blacks' song" because its lyrics were unintelligible and the artist was suspected of passing secret codes to the communists. Debates about the modern hat and the fez bring to mind the current "Islamic" head scarf controversy in French public schools. Concern with public health issues is reminiscent of Germany's refusal to include Islamic rituals in slaughterhouses to accommodate the dietary restrictions of Muslim immigrants on the basis of an animal cruelty law passed in the nineteenth century. In both France and Germany, however, the display of the Christian cross in public places is not deemed incompatible with citizenship rights. In sum, views about the social proximity, moral corruption, and cultural degradation of the Other, the immigrant in Europe or the urban poor in Cairo, are often derived not from an objective evaluation of the material reality but predominantly from cultural approximation.

DISCIPLINE AND ORDER

"One of the most alarming problems that the country must face is the question of public security," states an article in *Al-Muqattam*.[13] "There has been an unusual increase of homicides and crimes in some *Muduriyat* [districts]." The author notes that the establishment of public security services throughout the country and the use of "scientific techniques" to deter crimes have been successful. "But this is not enough," he continues; "the government has to mobilize all of its resources to fight crime."

This is one example of a variety of articles that raised the issue of public security, crime, and the reform of the police system. The aim of these articles was to emphasize the importance of modernizing the police force:

> In order to measure progress in controlling crimes, it is necessary to maintain a statistical account of all criminal acts. The publication of cases will discourage other criminals from committing crimes. For this reason, we proposed that the promotion of the public security officers and agents be made conditional upon the reports they keep of various crimes.
>
> In moments of severe economic crisis, crime is comprehensible. But that is not the case today. There are still flaws in the system that encourages crimes. The most serious defect is the outdated system of watchmen. The police have done a very good job fighting drug trafficking and drug use. Their success in this domain encourages us to ask for their help in other domains.
>
> The police should be very proud of their accomplishments in cleaning up the cities from immoral and corrupt behavior. Newspapers have been flooded with letters from the general public praising the police for their fight against social decadence caused by criminals, drug traffickers, communist subversives, and all of those who oppose public order and security. There is no doubt in our mind that this improvement is related to the recent changes in the police administration, especially the gathering and indexing of information about crimes and criminals. This is a proof that we are entering a new age.

The article then contributes to the debate in Egypt on the reform of the police system. The old "watchmen" system was seen by proponents of the reform as archaic and no longer sufficient.

An article in *Al-Muqattam* states: "We are very hopeful about this renaissance [in law enforcement] and we predict a success given more cooperation between the police, the government, and the public."[14] Another article in *Al-Muqattam* describes another danger in the streets of Cairo: street traffic.

The traffic-control system in Cairo is fit for a small municipality, not a capital with large, elegant avenues and public squares. The enormous increase in the number of cars and means of public transportation took place so rapidly that the public did not have the time or the opportunity to adjust to the change. The increasing numbers of accidents is alarming.

Dangers were also found in Egyptian villages far from Cairo's perilous streets:

Those who studied the construction of Egyptian villages know that the reason houses are so tightly packed and the streets are so narrow is to enhance security. By building their homes next to each other, villagers protected themselves from strangers coming into the village. For this reason Egyptian villages are different from all villages throughout the world where villagers put up a space between their houses to grow trees, gardens, and plants. Any reorganization of Egyptian villages to become more orderly must be gradual and contingent upon the stability, order, security, and people's confidence.

But this should not prevent the introduction of small reforms to decrease the major differences between the city and the countryside. The spread of education among the youths and the charm of Cairo and Alexandria with their lights, gardens, and avenues make the cities very attractive to young villagers who are rushing out from the countryside. This could be a dangerous situation for our country because the urban centers in Egypt, unlike in Europe, have a very limited capacity for employment. Egypt will end up with a pool of unemployed youngsters who will resort to theft, crimes, and drugs right here in the cities.[15]

One obvious solution to the problem of urban crowdedness would be to make villages attractive to the rural communities by improving living conditions and building roads, schools, and hospitals and facilitating access to water and electricity. The author of the article seems clearly aware of these issues, but he has something more important in mind. It would also help, he suggests, if the large number of absentee landlords began to spend more time in the village. Why? Because in England "absentee landlords go back to the countryside every season, invite their families and friends, organize festive meals with the villagers, and take care of the village."[16]

The health of the individual became a concern from the perspective of its relevance to the political community as a whole. The physical and psychological well-being of the individual was realized only when he or she was associated with the collective as a citizen. The distinction between health and illness, sanity and insanity, normalcy and deviance was therefore delineated in accordance with the requirements of the political community. Here the connection between political authority, morality, health, and education becomes clear.

In an editorial published in Al-Muqattam in 1925,[17] the director of a prominent hospital recommended that the Ministry of the Interior enlist mental health hospitals and doctors to combat crime and deviant social behavior. A reader wrote to the newspaper in response to this editorial to support the recommendation, citing evidence from an ongoing American experiment:

> How nice it would be if the Ministry of Education [wizarat alma'arif] and the Ministry of Public Health [maslahat al-sihha] could consider following in the footsteps of the Americans so we can together, at the same moment, see the good results.

Most significant is that the author of the article defines deviance as non-adjustment to the fundamental guidelines and maxims of the newly defined political community. Those who could not identify with the norms and characters of the ideal collectivity must be either treated or isolated to protect the rest of society.

> Healthy people are those who can adjust to a style of life, which is in concordance with the morals established by society. Any exception to the accepted moral conduct would be considered delinquency. From this, we can see how the modern method of preventing crimes is based on diagnosing anomalies and treating them in children at an early age. By doing so, we reform the criminal and insulate the social structure.

In the second part of the same article, the author describes how the poor, the ill, and the nonconformists are seen as having weak characters and as such are disposed to commit criminal acts.

> [American doctors] found a correlation between crimes and malnutrition, heart diseases, digestion troubles, and anemia. While these physical disturbances are not directly related to human behavior, they could cause a weakening of the patient's capacity and ability to control himself and therefore to commit a crime in a moment of severe anger.

The popularity of this theory in the United States led to the establishment of what the Americans call "laboratories of behavior" throughout the country. These clinics or laboratories work closely with kindergartens, schools, and parents. Experts follow closely the development of any child whose behavior appears to be deviant, diagnose the illness, and prescribe a treatment according to the severity of the pathological case.

According to the author, the diagnosis and treatment of deviance would prepare men to follow the mores and rules established by society. The author goes on to explain that the scientific research is still at an experimental stage and no immediate results are expected. However, the article predicts that future generations will be able to predict, control, and guide healthy and unhealthy moral behavior and that such work will benefit society as a whole.

Improving public health, like reforming the educational system, was seen as a necessary means to establish control over the individual and constitute the modern citizen. The spread of modern schools and hospitals, with their modern instruments, professional staff, uniformity, and order, also served as symbols of Egypt's transformation into a European nation. The speech by Dr. Muhammad Shahin on the occasion of the inauguration of a new hospital in Dumyat exemplifies this sentiment:

> The opening of this new hospital constitutes another step of renewal and reform in our present renaissance . . . another blessed step which will lead us to take our place among the developed nations of the world. This hospital is living proof that we are worthy of the responsibility we have taken to rule ourselves.[18]

There is no doubt that Egypt had undergone a period of profound social and economic dislocation at the end of the nineteenth century. Cotton cultivation and production, the increased value of agricultural land, rural exodus, cheap labor, the development of enterprise, real estate speculation, growth of the urban populations, slums, poverty, and overcrowding are familiar problems in societies facing industrial transformation, and Egypt was no exception.[19] But the liberal reformers did not treat social decay, health problems, and crimes as issues of social justice. They considered them a grave problem because of what the European Other might say about Egypt. The reformers feared that these problems would remind Europe of Oriental backwardness, even though they were clearly the direct result of a modern colonial process. This concern with the European gaze, rather than with social justice, became more clearly articulated in the liberals' depictions of, and attitudes about, popular cultural beliefs and practices. This is an important point because conventional historiography sees the greatest potential for political and cultural emancipation in Egypt during the period in the secular liberal orientation.

MAWALID, "CELEBRATIONS OF SAINTS"

Some of the most important social events in Egypt are the mawalid, popular celebrations of local saints that provide a moment for individual spiritualism and a social occasion for relatives, neighbors, merchants, and various hangers-on (street children, beggars, and the elderly) to interact. Celebrations of saints commonly take place in old and modest neighborhoods or small villages where Sufis, followers and disciples of mythical religious figures, maintain congregations. Mawalid were particularly targeted in liberal Egyptian discourse because they were considered chaotic, promiscuous, irrational, and filthy, the opposite image of the rational, orderly, productive, and predictable behavior of the modern citizen. But while all sorts of justifications, including unorthodox religious behavior, were advanced to discredit them, there was hardly ever a mention of their incompatibility with the modern notion of citizenship.

The following is a portrayal of mawalid scenes in leading liberal Egyptian newspapers during the 1920s and 1930s:

> The mawalid of al-Hussein begins with the gathering of a filthy group of people who call themselves majadib. They come from all over the country with their long bristling hair, long dirty nails, and torn rags that hide only a small part of their body. They bring tea and coffee pots, the necessary cooking and sleeping materials, and camp around the mosque for days. To demonstrate their jadba [entrancement] and their closeness to God, they deceive the people with clamors that are really nothing but ugly and obscene words.
>
> Yet nobody denounces these people's vulgar character. The usual excuse given is that they are in trance. This gang of criminals who claim divinity has, in fact, no sense of moral or ethical behavior. Among them are found so-called majdubat [women in trance] who have no shame mixing with men, even at night.[20]

The liberal reformers neglected no major institution or argument to put pressure on the government to curtail the activities of Sufi orders. The newspaper Al-Siyasa, which spearheaded the anti-Sufi campaign, repeatedly argued that the manners and rituals of mawalid were alien to the spirit and letter of Islam. The public authorities often made the argument that uncontrolled religious activities constituted a threat to public order and security. The charge of criminality is somewhat understandable. But to call for banning Sufi orders and arresting followers because of their religious unorthodoxy is curious given the Egyptian liberal reformers' known disdain of orthodox religious teachings and institutions. That they felt compelled to call on the 'ulama (official religious scholars) to join in denouncing mawalid celebrations as un-Islamic recalls Napoleon's pamphlet justifying the invasion of Egypt.

> We want to call the attention of His Highness Shaykh Hussein 'Afif, the spiritual head of the mosque and mausoleum of Hussein, to find a solution to this deplorable situation. Because of his responsible position he can forbid these heretical practices. He can rely on the authority of the police and the government, which are also opposed to these embarrassing cults. We remind His Highness that when he was first designated Shaykh of the mosque, he managed to arrest a large number of those who claimed to be in a constant state of trance.[21]

Equally questionable from a liberal perspective is the sudden and obsessive concern with public morality. While positing the alien and un-Islamic origin of mawalid, and calling on the religious establishment to denounce them, the reformers focused on the "perverse" and "pernicious" character of such rituals and practices:

> Today, the mawalid of saints have turned into a bad event. These mawalid have become the nest of perversion, the home of moral corruption, the grave of honorable sentiments, the deathbed of dignity and pride, the place of destructive behavior, and the source of pain, distress, and grief over the fate of this country, which has gone astray to the abyss and is on the verge of reaching the infernal bottom. We are writing these lines on the occasion of Mawalid Sayyid Zin al-'Abidin, which began two days ago amidst foolish dancing and singing on tombs.[22]

Mawalid were considered particularly dangerous because their immorality and vulgarity were so appealing to the masses and threatened to take over society at large:

> Concern with morality forces us to remind the state authorities of what occurs during these mawalid: women dancers violate the sanctity of the dead by performing their dirty acts on top of the tombs, cafes are set up for the occasion among bones and skulls, drunkards gather to enjoy drinks served on tombs turned into bars. These are only a few of the despicable acts which take place during these mawalid. Why are the authorities allowing this type of behavior? Those in charge of public order and security must intervene immediately to save the country from these dangerous people.[23]

Sufi orders were, of course, not new to the country. When the Fatimids ruled an Islamic dynasty in Egypt in the eighth century, they started the custom of public gatherings around popular religious figures whose works were studied and whose miracles, dreams, and poems interpreted. The sudden and swift change was at moments difficult to justify:

> We have to denounce the followers of these once honorable orders. This matter is so important that it is not enough to just call on the police to disperse these groups. It is a question of the expropriation of our religion. These people are dangerous heretical innovators who contradict all aspects of Islamic tradition and therefore undermine the general order and safe inclination [al-nizam al-'amm wa al-zawq al-salim] of our religion.
>
> Late at night in many neighborhoods in Cairo, people see and hear gatherings of people who call themselves "the people of orders" [ahl alturuq]. Sufi orders have nothing to do with these strange people who walk in the streets forming geometric lines banging on their drums and blowing their flutes. This cacophony annoys people. Often they set up circles of zikr [a regular repetition of words praising God] which later turn into sets of ridiculous acting. The main actors are supposedly certified by old Sufi shaykhs [al-sajajid], who grant permission [al-hilakha] to a number of group leaders [al-khalifa], who in turn each gather a group of followers [muridin] depending on his skills. Some of them swallow fire while others eat insects to prove their sanctity [majdub].[24]

The article then uses a scientific analogy to characterize Sufi practices as a bacterial disease that must be contained before it infects the entire community:

> This behavior is not particular to one city, one neighborhood, or one tariqa [Sufi order]. This is the standard behavior in every Sufi order and throughout the country. This is a dangerous social illness, a grave violation of the spirit of our religion. We have to uproot it, avoid it like we avoid bacteria, because it is destructive of our moral values. We ask those in charge [the official religious establishment] to dismantle these groups of heretical innovators.[25]

But the Egyptian liberals' real concern was Egypt's image in the eyes of Europe. These debates and controversies took place shortly before and shortly after Egypt was granted formal independence in 1922. The liberals, who were also nationalists, wanted to prove to Europe that Egyptians could manage their own affairs; the nature of these popular religious celebrations threatened to embarrass the Egyptians' claim of Western sobriety and clarity.

The behavior exhibited at the mawalid, warned a newspaper, is characteristic of a society composed of backward and ignorant people.

> Today is the beginning of a ten-day annual mawalid of Sayyidina al-Hussein. Like the previous mawalid, this one is filled with peculiar events and practices: large crowds, food prepared and sold in the streets, the smell of incense, loud invocations of God from Sufis, and a mixture of other strange voices from the majadib [plural of majdub, a person in trance] All these people will camp around the mosque of Hussein for days.

In the negative portrayals of mawalid in the Egyptian press of the period, there was no word on how these celebrations subverted the political rights and obligations implied in the modern notion of citizenship. Alarmed warnings about the spreading criminality or disfiguration of Islam were just a lure. Liberal reformers were really concerned about the reputation and image of the Egyptian nation abroad, as these discussions clearly suggest:

> The quarter of Sayyidina al-Hussein and other sections of this district, such as Khan al-Khalili and al-Ghuriyya, are very famous among European tourists, who insist on visiting them. It is dishonorable and disreputable that European visitors see these embarrassing and repugnant sights, which confirm their ideas about Egyptians as a backward and ignorant people.[26]

The article was concerned with both the European image of Egypt and the new Egyptian self-image. If Egyptians were to succeed in making Egypt appear less Oriental to Europeans, they had first to convince themselves of their non-Easternness. To do so, the reformers argued, "We should work and do everything we can to change the images the Europeans have formed about us in their minds and books. We have to work together to erase the old images and create new and attractive ones to show to the Europeans that our renaissance is real." Unfortunately, the daily reminders in the street were detrimental to this effort.

Very revealing was the call to take advantage of popular gatherings at mawalid to teach the masses good moral values and the proper social behavior.[27] After emphasizing the economic benefits of mawalid, the author suggests reviving an idea of Edward Browne, "the great Orientalist from Cambridge," who was visiting Cairo at the time of Mawalid Sayida Zaynab, the celebration for a woman saint venerated for her piety and courage. Impressed by the eloquence of a street poet and his simple musical instrument, Browne had suggested that the authorities could use popular storytellers to teach good manners and behavior in the public sphere. "Since street narrators are so venerated by the gullible masses, why not use their popular influence for a good cause? They could be effective in teaching the people good values and principles in a short period of time."[28] And perhaps disguise the state's need to intervene directly in peoples' lives to erase their subversive collective identities and impose a uniform, universal political identity.

MOURNING AND THE PRACTICE OF WAILING

The liberals' attacks on popular cultural practices extended beyond public celebrations of mawalid to target familial expressions of pain during mourning. Liberal reformers portrayed the rituals of the common Egyptian funeral as backward and detrimental to the construction of a modern civilization in Egypt. Once again the reformers looked to Europe for models of appropriate behavior, in this case how to mourn and dispose of the dead. The following two articles discussed funerals and the popular practice of wailing in mourning.

Under the heading "Western Science and Scientific Discovery," *Kawkab al-Sharq* published an editorial advocating cremation and the abolition of funeral processions. The author complains that social conventions disturb his peace of mind and force him to do something he does not value:

> Last night one of my neighbors passed away, and as I was getting ready to go to sleep I became disturbed by what had happened. Not that his death disturbs me, but rather what annoys and frightens me is the bitter idea that I have to walk, again, in his funeral just like I did last week when another neighbor died. A great number of people in this neighborhood walked in my parents' funerals, and I, therefore, have no choice but to walk in the funerals of all of those who will die before me.
>
> There is no way to escape all of these rituals, the worst of which is to feign grief all the way to the cemetery. The whole idea is disturbing. I feel like my freedom has been curtailed because I am somehow forced to conform to the other people's bad habits. These people are liars and hypocrites.[29]

Egyptians should follow the lead of modern European civilization and quietly bury their dead:

> Modern civilization introduced some improvements on how to dispose of dead people; why not use them!? Why not, for example, put the corpse in one car and have the immediate family alone follow in another car so that no-one else is disturbed and reminded of death and its terror.

The truth is that some Muslim families in Cairo began to transport their dead in cars. I witnessed two such cases in one week. I gladly take notice of this practice and hope it will be followed by others until there will be no trace of the old practice.

The author also criticizes the wasteful expenditure of money on elaborate tombs. This expenditure is symbolic of native backwardness and under-development. The author warns that exhortation alone will not convince the people to abandon such bad habits, which prevent the founding of a modern civilization. Rather, these habits must be destroyed, and another solution found to the problem of popular funerals and elaborate tombs—cremation:

> During the war, the European nations and governments realized the benefits of crematoria and decided to use them to solve the problem of dwindling space in the cemeteries. Now every big European city is equipped with electric crematoria that turn corpses into ash in a minute. This way, there will be no more tombs where people go and cry. I don't know what prevents us from copying this practice, which will save us time, effort, and money. I hope the government will support my idea.

The following article, published in *Al-Siyasa*, portrays the popular practice of wailing at funerals as inhibiting the advancement of Egyptian women and the nation.[30] Wailing, first of all, is described as a corruption of conventional Islamic practice. The author is concerned that this corruption will degrade Islam in the eyes of the European observer:

> It is a custom in Muslim funerals that women wail, beat their breasts, and scratch their faces with their nails to express their condolences and mourn with the family of the deceased. This ritual is so important in a funeral that it is considered the most appropriate manner of expressing grief for the lost beloved. The absence of this practice is interpreted as disrespect for the dead person and his or her family.
>
> Those who mourn in this manner often cite the example of the Prophet, who used to cry when one of his kin or close friends passed away. But this despicable habit is really contrary to the rules of Islam, good manners, and human character. Our 'ulama should not remain silent in face of this erroneous interpretation, which degrades our religion in the eyes of Europeans. There is a great difference between the tears of the Prophet, which express a deep, honest, and heartfelt sadness, and the appalling wailing, which expresses a refusal to accept death as a will of God.

Wailing was not only a corruption of Islamic precepts but also an insult to common decency. Moreover, medical experts had proved that wailing was dangerous and harmful. The article is particularly concerned that the persistence of the practice of wailing would inhibit the advancement of Egyptian women. If Egyptian women are to become like European women, they must abandon such "archaic" practices.

> Wailing also provides an opportunity for women to challenge the authority of their husbands. When a woman is wailing nobody can stop her, not even an angry husband threatening divorce. It is the responsibility of the women's liberation movement to investigate this problem. Those who are really concerned about women's liberation and participation in daily activities alongside men should denounce these tactics [wailing] as foolish acting. This wicked theatrical act will not deliver Egyptian women from their weakness, corruption, and lack of awareness. This [act] only makes Egyptian women a target of the mockery and disdain of Western women. If Egyptian women want to adopt Western women's style of dress, education, and active participation, they must first stop such archaic customs as wailing.

As in the articles discussed earlier, the author resorts to the intervention of state authorities to control this dangerous popular practice. Such intervention was deemed necessary for the advancement of the Egyptian nation:

> If the religious, social, and medical considerations are not sufficient to prevent women from wailing, then the only solution is to call on the government to intervene in the name of public health and safety. By outlawing these practices, the government will prove that it is serious about the development and renaissance of the nation.

CONJUGAL LIFE

The battle to conquer the inaccessible world of the individual person went far beyond the reevaluation of social activities such as work to reach the most personal, and seemingly apolitical, aspect of life: conjugal life and the selection of a conjugal partner. Under a revealing title, "How Do We Select a Wife: A Social Scientific Inquiry," the daily Al-Siyasa published an elaborate article on the institution of marriage, the condition of marriage, and the meaning of marriage.[31] In addition to speaking only for the few privileged Egyptian males, and thus excluding women and the impoverished, whose equal representation in the new political community the Egyptian liberals claimed to guarantee, the article is based on a book written by a French author for a French audience.[32] The fact that the author was European provided sufficient grounds to lend its claims universality and scientific credibility. Just as the definition of Egyptian national identity was based on racial scientific theories, so European scientific language and authorship also allowed the Egyptian liberals to justify the devaluation of local social practices. The theme that emerges in the article is again that of the contrast between the animal's instinct and the civilized man's instinct—this time in the sexual or reproductive act. The difference between animal reproduction and human sexuality, it appears, is that human sexuality is a social act that involves a partnership lacking in most animal species. This affiliation implies acceptance of, and commitment to, a set of moral values. "Youth, beauty, and money are ephemeral," says the author. "What counts most in a marital association are the moral standards of the two partners. . . . But how can one find out about the good or bad manners of his mate? We have only the khutba system, and that is not good enough."[33] The khutba is a specific religious sermon about the social benefits and responsibilities of marriage drawn from the Qur'an and customarily addressed by an officiating Muslim judge or any trustworthy practicing Muslim. In sum, the article oddly suggests that the traditional marriage ceremony and institution in Egypt are driven by the individual's sexual desire rather than by conscious, rational thought about an act that affects not only the individual but society at large. I do not wish to suggest that the Egyptian liberals equated the individual in their society to an animal in the state of nature. Rather, the dominant view among the Egyptian liberals was that modern Western society was further removed from the state of nature than was Egyptian society in its current state of development.

THE HAT AND THE FEZ

Clothing was a particularly lively subject during the period, discussed with passion by experts and readers in newspapers that opened their columns to liberal reformers and their opponents. A particularly lively debate surrounded the proper head covering for a modern Egyptian man. In the following article from Al-Hilal, a reader explains why he has chosen to wear a hat rather than the traditional fez.[34] He asserts that the fez, like the veil, is not an "Egyptian" head covering. The veil was introduced by foreign Muslim conquerors; the fez was introduced by the Ottomans. The author clearly expresses his anger against these alien invaders and the imposition of their customs on Egyptian dress.

> I was asked by Al-Hilal to write an essay to explain why I started to wear the hat. This reflection took me back to my childhood when I was in high school, when Qassim Amin's [book] on women and the hijab [veil] appeared. Amin's book made such an impression on me that I began to despise the veil, especially when I

learned that it was not an Egyptian custom but introduced in Egypt by some foreign conquerors (the Muslims). In those days I used to return regularly to the village after school breaks and could not help but notice the uncovered faces of peasant women working in the fields, just like the faces of women statues one could find in the museum. My anger with those foreign Muslim conquerors increased even more.

But if Muslims had invaded Egypt centuries earlier and Egyptian women in rural areas continued to work unveiled in the fields and village markets until the European invasions, as the author testifies, it is not clear whether the problem is linked to Islamic alteration of local customs or to colonial conquest. It seems from the author's own analysis that the colonial encounter was more oppressive and demanding of Egyptians than the Muslims' conquest had been. During World War I, which pitted the British against the Ottoman Empire, says the author, the public's ambivalence about choosing the fez or the hat was somewhat comprehensible. After the war, while some Egyptians began to wear the hat to avoid harassment by Australian soldiers serving in Egypt, the bulk of Egyptians remained attached to the fez as a means to express their opposition to the occupation. Now that Egyptians had "moderated" their views and recognized the benefits of domination by the great British civilization, the choice was clear: wearing the Western hat was a prerequisite to adopting modern political institutions. There was no doubt about the conflation of the political and the cultural in the author's commentary:

> The Egyptians began to harvest the fruits of the renaissance when Egypt adopted the [1923] Constitution and the parliamentary system. . . . I was among those who supported the idea of borrowing from the dominant modern civilization. In the midst of these debates, the summer of 1925, I was in Cairo. With the belief that actions are more effective than words, I decided to make a symbolic gesture by buying a hat.

Besides political considerations, the article argues that wearing the hat is simply healthier than wearing the fez. There was plenty of medical "evidence" concerning the superiority of the European dress:

> In June 1926, al-Rabitat al-Sharqiyya asked the association of medical doctors to give a fatwa on the "hat and fez question." The association of doctors declared that the fez was unhealthy to wear and that only the hat fulfilled the conditions of healthy head covering. That same year in July, I went to a hat merchant and bought a summer hat, took off the fez, and since then I have been wearing the hat.

These were also historical conditions that led me to start wearing the hat. In the final analysis it was for "medical" as well as cultural reasons that I began to wear the hat.

Some of the author's friends commented when they saw him for the first time wearing a hat that "now Orientals [have begun] to think with their heads!" Another one commented, "The conflict is not between the hat and the fez. It is between different modes of thought and tastes."[35]

In April 1930, Al-Hilal printed a pictorial version of the debate between the hat and the fez, showing two pictures: the Egyptian delegation, wearing hats, in London, and the return of the Egyptian delegation, wearing fezzes, to Cairo.[36]

The debate about dress in general was also carried out in the newspapers. In an article in Al-Muqattam, Muhammad Reza expressed his concern about Mustafa Kemal's great efforts to change the Turkish national dress.[37] He suggests other "true aspects of modern civilization" that would be more appropriate for a modern Turkey to adopt. In a subsequent article, another author argues that Muhammad Reza was mistaken, like the rest of the public, in his judgment.[38] Clothing could be used to demarcate a break with the Egyptian past and the beginning of a new cultural age, as was done in Turkey under Atatürk:

I, too, used to think that changing the national costume was silly and a waste of time. But if Reza thinks carefully about this issue, he will understand why Mustafa Kemal is going through such pains to reform Turkish dress. The idea is to sever the Turkish people from their past. Since clothing reflects a specific mind-set and a specific social order, the Kemalist reformers began to change their dressing habits, striving to transform Turkey into a modern civilization and change the course of their nation. By eliminating the symbols of the past (the traditional dress), they prevent the resuscitation of a collective memory. When are Egyptians going to start writing about their renaissance with the same enthusiasm as the Turks?

Addressing those who oppose change, the article continues:

Your sciences, morality, and traditions brought the Orient to the desolate situation in which we find it today. Because of your ideas the Orient today is under the feet of the European civilization. You are responsible for this. Who let the situation deteriorate to the point of allowing the Europeans to dig their claws into the wealth of our nation?

The people, as usual, will side with the winners. In this battle those who favor change will, no doubt, win. There is a big difference between the Waq-Waq theory [in the description of Arab geographers, the name of two different groups of islands—one east of China, the other located in the Indian Ocean] and the Bull's Horn theory, on the one hand, and the scientific theories of the earth's rotation and relativity.[39]

Both of these examples are given to discredit popular and traditional interpretations of the universe in the face of new scientific theories.

What we, those who are in favor of change, want to accomplish is to dispose of those fairy tales and superstitious fables. The problem, then, is not to open more Qur'anic schools, as some argue, but what to teach in schools.

One of the most amazing arguments is that the cause of Oriental backwardness is the Orient's failure to respect the traditions. What a scandalous mistake! Nobody attacked the tradition before we finally realized the dismal nature of our situation. Civilization had not touched the land of Egypt before the rule of Khedive Ismail and Muhammad 'Ali. And despite this there was no serious campaign to stop superstition from poisoning the brains of our people. Only during the last five years did we begin to think seriously about this.

The Telling Cases

ON SACRIFICE

The values of individual members of society, in their work activities or in their reproductive capacities, were determined by their relation to the newly defined political community. It is identification with the political community that gave individuals a purpose and a meaning to their life. The greatness of the Egyptian nation depended on how much sacrifice the Egyptian citizen was willing to make. If Egypt were to look like a European nation, the citizens were expected to show great devotion and make substantial offerings because they had to give up their own personal identity and collective cultural heritage.

"The success of a nation depends on the conviction of its members that they have an obligation toward the collective," states an article in *Al-Muqattam*.[40] "If representative rule is the best system of government, individual sacrifice to the whole is the foundation of a nation's development and stability." Such a demand would seem alien to liberal theory and more appropriate for communitarian doctrines. But the particular kind of political community the Egyptian liberals wanted to build could only be achieved by sacrificing individual autonomy and subordinating the individual's "unworthy" view of the world to a better and more rewarding way of life.

EDUCATION

To open the eyes of the people to the modern European way of life and admit them to the benefits of citizenship, the people must first be educated. An article in *Al-Muqattam* written in 1925 characterized the new age in Egypt by the proliferation of education and schools.[41] The author lauds the great improvements of the educational facilities in Egypt and with more enthusiasm celebrates the positive response of the people to modern education. He says that the newspapers were flooded with letters from parents complaining about the lack of space in primary schools for their children. "This does not surprise us," writes the author, "because we did not expect to place all children in the limited number of schools we have. The point was to create a feeling of need for schools."

The first goal of admitting more children to schools was to make the people value modern education and legitimate the demands of the new political community. The author acknowledges that "the current drive for modern education requires teachers, buildings, money, books, and other equipment, all of which are not readily available." But the positive side of all of this is that "after years of waiting and hesitation, the doors are now open and the people have begun to march along the path cleared by the government."

Though noting the satisfactory progress in the public educational system, the author warns that the goal of education is not merely to graduate students. Rather, education should instill in the students a specific way of thinking and being so that they can fulfill their obligations in society and accomplish the tasks society assigns them. "There is a crucial question which we cannot overlook in the education policy. . . . The first, most important issue is to specify the purpose of education. Is it to prepare the children to pass exams and earn a diploma, or is it to teach them rational thinking and good morality?" asks the author rhetorically. The purpose of education for the author is clear: "mobilize everything to create new rational and good individuals."

Once a conception of morality, happiness, and a specific, superior way of being was established, the purpose of education was for the Egyptian liberal reformer to prepare and produce individuals who could act according to those values.

An editorial published five years later in *Kawkab al-Sharq* elaborates this new role of education in Egypt. Now that Egyptians could control their education system, the goals of education should encompass not merely vocational training but ethics and civic values:

> Ever since education became a specialized field in modern Egypt, the politics of education have been conducted incorrectly because Egyptians did not have a say in the matter. But today Egyptians are responsible for the conduct of their own affairs and must reevaluate the role of education. Egyptian policymakers must think of education in a different light in order to detect the illnesses and remedies of the education problem. Education must be considered in relation to the general requirements of life, ethics, and human development and not simply as a means to obtain a rewarding job.[42]

The editorial offers education as a means to develop the potential of individuals who are willing and motivated to work for the benefit of society as a whole. Education should no longer simply prepare people to work for their daily bread, for God, or for reward in the afterlife. A new rationality should stimulate the pursuit of knowledge. "The purpose of education is related to the meaning of human existence," says the editorial. "What is the purpose of human existence in our culture . . . ? What is the role of the individual in this society . . . ? What is expected from the individual in the world in which we live?" Education, it was believed, should inspire man to construct a new civilization.

> We know . . . that science is making the world more intelligible for us and therefore increasingly under our control. Every new scientific creation becomes integrated in our daily life, at home, in the factory and contributes to the flourishing of our civilization. This is precisely the purpose of human existence in this world: contribute to building a human civilization. The purpose of education, then, is to prepare the individual for this noble cause.

This task, the author argues, requires both intellectual and psychological preparation. By "psychological" the author means "the force that gives birth to all sorts of emotions, morals, manners, and tendencies which we sometimes refer to as things of the heart." Education should therefore focus on both the intellectual and the psychological aspects of the individual.

> Consequently, education should not be viewed as an intellectual exercise only; it is also a "nourishment of the heart." The building of a civilization requires both a material and a moral predisposition. The latter is based on the relationships between individuals and, more importantly, on the relationship between the individual and himself. In education we have to take into consideration these two

forces: the heart and mind. Otherwise we will be a people with no leader, no order, and no goals except the mere satisfaction of our immediate needs.

Implicit in this statement is the recurring theme of Egypt's proximity to nature, where people have no purpose in life, no legal or moral order, and are mostly concerned about their instinctive needs.

To justify his call for these educational goals, the author cites the success of Europe, where he believes exemplary moral behavior has been the key to prosperity. Therefore, in order for Egypt to join the civilized European community, its educational system must promote European morality and teach the good Western ethical values.

> The moral aspect of Western culture is still abundant and protected. That is the key to European prosperity. . . . The foundation of any educational policy should, then, seriously consider both the intellectual and psychological aspects of the individual if we want to join in a world civilization.

Some reformers suggested teaching Latin and Greek to children to cultivate and strengthen the mental capacity of Egyptians.[43] When Taha Husayn, a champion of introducing Latin and Greek studies in Egyptian schools, was nominated minister of education, an angry opponent wrote a letter to warn Husayn that his ideas were not welcome.[44] It was believed that yet another way of improving education in Egypt was to dress children "properly." Again the reformers looked to Europe as a model, as shown in an article that appeared in Al-Muqattam:

> The kind of clothes which pupils wear has a tremendous impact on their performance in school and their general conduct. In some European countries, a teacher noticed the decline of a student who was one of the most brilliant students in the school. Intrigued, the teacher began to look for a possible explanation of his ill performance. He finally found out that the student was wearing an old pair of shoes that his father originally bought for his older brother. This caused discomfort for the student and eventually led to deterioration in his mental capacity.
>
> Given this example, we urge all parents who have several children to refrain from this bad habit, which occurs frequently in some Egyptian families.[45]

In another editorial on the issue of education, the author warns the reader of the dire consequences of the schools' current neglect of the "psychological" aspect in the education of the individual.[46] Without the benefit of formal education outside the home, the masses would be bereft of moral character.

The editorial advocates using schools to reform individuals psychologically and transform them into ideal members of society:

> If the government cannot reform households from inside, it certainly can reach all aspects of daily life through its numerous schools. The government can clean the social environment and protect the children and the youths from those disastrous and perilous characteristics of society.[47]

Significantly, the author avoids granting religious education any role in promoting morality. In fact, the only mention of religion is a vague reference to "religious sentiments." The failure to recognize the potential role of religion was an explicit and characteristic bias of the liberals against any local, Arab, or Islamic conception of morality and ethics. Moreover, as some of the quotations clearly show, individuals were considered "immoral," "corrupt," "ignorant," "egoist," and "aggressive" until they became absorbed in civil society. This position amounted to negating any say or role by members of society whose views of morality and ethics differed from those of Western metaphysical or religious traditions.

The inadequacy of religious schooling to develop a moral individual devoted to the community appeared frequently as a topic in articles dealing with the reform of the education system. In an article entitled "Our Schools and Moral Education: Egyptian Schools Teach but They Do Not Educate," the author criticizes the religious and technical schools on the following grounds:

> In Egypt there are a number of religious and scientific schools [madariss diniyya wa 'ilmiyya] which graduate every year a number of knowledgeable young men. . . . These schools, however, are not good for refining individual character and developing correct human principles and moral virtues of young men. You find very few educated young men who are willing to devote much of their time to social causes such as providing guidance to the uneducated and fighting the social illnesses that destroy this ignorant people. The newly educated people care about one thing only: obtaining a job with the government.[48]

In an article that appeared in *Al-Balagh*, the author advocates the formulation of a national policy on education modeled after those in Europe. The author recommends that the government require students to study the professions of their fathers so that society as a whole will benefit.

> One specific problem needs more attention from both the government and the public. Students decide what they want to study in an anarchic manner. Education

has become a means by which people try to achieve what they could not have otherwise achieved. All parents want their children to become doctors, lawyers, and high government officials.

The result is catastrophic: the sons of merchants, peasants, and manual workers . . . all want to study law. In this way, the country is being deprived of a very good quality, which is prevalent in the West, where sons adopt the profession of their fathers. We find, for example, the sons of doctors study medicine, the sons of architects study architecture, and so on. What will happen to Egypt if the sons of peasants, merchants, and workers want to become doctors, lawyers, and architects? The country will be deprived of factories, fields, and markets because nobody will want to perform those kinds of jobs anymore.

We want to call the attention of the government to this grave problem in the hope that it will take our observations into consideration and it will convince sons to take on the job of their fathers.[49]

What is most provocative in this article is that it reflects the inability of the Egyptian liberal discourse to dissimulate the hierarchical structure of domination it was attempting to impose on Egyptian society. Inadvertently perhaps, the Egyptian liberals casually exposed the myth of the equal opportunity for individuals to fulfill their potential regardless of social background or economic status. This failure comes despite the fact that equality of opportunity is taken for granted in European liberal discourse.

RELIGIOUS BELIEFS

Because Egyptian citizens were to be integrated not as abstract entities but as persons with European cultural and moral qualities, Islamic identity became a particular concern owing to its politically subversive potential. But rather than advocating the conversion of Egyptians to Christianity, which would have been politically counterproductive, the reformers attempted to devalue religious beliefs and knowledge in modern society. "The individual's divine obligations and religious beliefs are no longer pertinent [to leading a good life]," writes a liberal reformer in Al-Muqtataf.[50] In trying to dismiss religious beliefs and portraying them as nonessential to the fulfillment of human needs, the article endorses the political rationale of the imagined collective over the individual's "unworthy" way of life.

The metaphors employed to describe the importance of examining the individual as a subscribing member of the community were taken from the modern sciences: engineering, medicine, and botany. Just as it is difficult for the skilled architect to test the solidity of a building without examining the material structures, explains the author, so it is likewise difficult for the student of society to determine the level of development and weaknesses of a community without examining its foundation: the individual. To contain "social illness" and to control the social mechanisms that breed defiance, modern political authority has to engage individuals in their private lives. For this task, the author proclaims, there is a need for skilled al-ijtima'i (social scientists), not religious scholars. "Even the most skilled doctor could not detect our social maladies without knowing how the various elements of society function." Members of society who did not perform their societal duties as expected were considered sick elements and therefore in need of close supervision. Sick individuals who ran loose without any treatment, it was believed, would harm every member of society. "Just as trees are made of roots, leaves, and branches, each element in the system performs a function to keep the whole tree alive; so is society made of individuals with different skills and degrees of knowledge; each individual must work to keep the whole society alive and healthy." These examples were seen as scientific proof that the individual's active participation in, and submission to, the will of the collective were necessary for the existence and prosperity of the political community.

> There can be no good families without good individuals, there can be no successful societies without successful families, and there can be no advance in a nation without the advance of its people. If a father succeeds in raising his children properly, by educating them, cultivating their tastes, teaching them the good virtues, and eliminating the vices, then he is creating a family unit that deserves its place in society.[51]

To deserve a place in society meant to have new motivations for life, to have a new conception of work, and above all to comply with imported European codes of social conduct and good morality. To qualify for citizenship, Egyptians were expected to repress or "selectively forget," as Ernest Renan suggested, parts of their identities and common memories.

MAN'S NATURAL INSTINCTS AND LABOR

Defining who was a productive member of society in Egyptian liberal discourse depended not on how many commodities or services the individual produced or provided but on the structure within which labor was performed. Industriousness was defined by the shape and substance of its monuments and instruments. Modern tall buildings, factories and schools, bridges and railways, steel and fire all differentiated Western cities from the rest of the world and became the supreme and universal signifiers of civilized man's hard work. In contrast, mosques and *medrasas*, souks and medinas, artisans and bazaars, wood and leather were all properties of the Orient. To the liberal reformers, these institutions and professions were improper symbols of the new nation. They were reminders of native indolence, disorder, and particularism and above all were testimonials to the natives' natural instincts. These native attributes were irreconcilable with the industriousness of the modern individual. "Three things motivate men to work," explains the reformer, "instinct, interest, and duty."[52] Instinct is an animal trait, and man is an animal. What differentiates man from animals is man's ability to speak, learn, and live peacefully among similar associates. It is the transition from the natural stage to civility, the will and competence to transform instincts into obligation, says the author, that give our work meaning and order. Thus instincts must be supplanted by wisdom and reason; otherwise, anarchic work, like any uncontrolled behavior, can lead society to a catastrophic end. Therefore it is necessary to have loyal educators and spiritual guides to teach people how to control their instincts even when it comes to the most basic matter: work. To lose its brute character, the Egyptian population needed to be tamed and policed so that its motivation for work and its social activities as a whole were in accordance with the new requirements of the political community. Noncompliance was seen as an expression of animal rage and deluge.

The intolerance of Egyptian liberal reformers toward popular beliefs and practices cannot be imputed exclusively to colonial racial and cultural prejudices, that is, to views expressed by Europeans once they came into contact with Egypt. As we have seen in chapter 2, most of the colonial views predated the actual colonial encounter. Equally important, the Egyptian liberals' attack on local traditions and practices cannot be viewed independently from classical liberalism with its built-in normative and epistemological assumptions.

In this chapter, I have argued that the social and cultural transformations that Egyptians were expected to endure to become modern citizens were arbitrary and grounded in a cultural definition of citizenship. What informed descriptions of popular social and cultural practices as "dangerous," "immoral," "backward," and in need of containment was a concern with the Other, Europe, not a political manifestation of modern discipline and power.[53] Though these attempted reformations in many ways contradict liberalism's most basic principles, they reveal the difficulty, if not the impossibility, of disentangling citizenship and political community from the cultural, literary, and linguistic traditions that structure them.

The Relevance to Current Debates
on Identity Politics

The activation of identity politics in Western democracies during the last decade has caught liberal theorists off guard. The politicization of cultural, religious, ethnic, and racial claims was thought to be a feature of nondemocratic, nonliberal states. In Western democracies, it was believed, color-blind, culturally neutral citizenship rights had put particularistic affinities to the side. Yet liberal neutrality—the notion that the state can and must derive legitimacy from an undifferentiated citizenry or an abstract will of the people—has become indefensible in the face of mounting evidence. Public institutions in North America and Western Europe are being challenged on a daily basis by "minority" or "identity group" claims that question the cultural neutrality of the state. To cite but a few, the controversy over Affirmative Action for African Americans and the status of Native Indians, Puerto Ricans, and Chicanos in the United States, the problematic incorporation of Aboriginal communities in Australia and Canada, the religious rights of Muslim immigrants throughout Western Europe, and the fight for women's and gay rights everywhere are all forcing liberals to rethink their stand on the role and place of culture in the public arena. Although identity claims come from socially diverse and ideologically incompatible groups, they raise a common question: are the political recognition and incorporation of "minority" cultures good or bad for liberal democracy?

Debates on this issue within the normative and conceptual liberal framework—individual autonomy and choice—overlook an important component of identity: its ambiguous political role. Cultural identity structures nationhood and citizenship, yet it constitutes a challenge to political identity; it is a discourse of resistance when devalued by a state or an invading culture, and a discourse of domination and exclusion when uncontested; it is a discourse of individual empowerment, yet it presupposes a collective; identity gives meaning, yet it is incomplete and subject to negotiation. So coming to terms with identities requires more than assessing the moral worth of culture for each group and figuring out a democratic mechanism to accommodate "difference." The center from which difference is narrated and established is not culturally neutral and therefore must be treated as any other entity making cultural or moral claims. One area from which political theorists could draw insight to appreciate the complexity and relevance of culture to political identity and representation is the colonial context. There "identity politics" reveal that liberalism is not at all immune to cultural claims. This context renders problematic the presumed epistemological neutrality of political liberalism when it comes to making judgments on groups' cultural demands.

In interwar Egypt, I would argue, the appropriation of the modern notions of nationhood and citizenship was grounded in racial and cultural hierarchical assumptions that discriminated against local cultures. That this discrimination took place in a polity where the nationalist elites faithfully espoused liberal principles is particularly intriguing. Egypt, which more than any other Arab country so enthusiastically embraced political liberalism after independence, provides eloquent material to understand how the appropriation of the modern concept of nationhood and citizenship, instead of achieving political emancipation, can result in cultural and social confinement. My consideration of colonial liberalism's conflicting trends—"liberating" the natives from local, traditional tyranny only to subject them to a different form of cultural domination and discrimination—casts doubts on liberalism's general claim to cultural neutrality.

In the colonial context, liberalism promoted arbitrary ideals of "human flourishing" and "conceptions of the good" even as it claimed to liberate the natives from despotic rule and oppressive cultures that offer their people no "context of choice." In Egypt, as in other colonies, there was nothing subtle or ambiguous about liberalism's cultural partiality. Egyptian advocates of liberalism embraced nationhood and citizenship as the only valid identity and thought it was necessary to rewrite Egypt's history, culture, and literature to bring it closer to Europe. They attempted to devalue local social and cultural practices and demonstrate the superiority of the European way of life on the basis of "scientific" theories of race, blood, and language.

The Egyptian reading of European liberalism may have been misguided and excessive. Still, one is tempted to ask: Why was liberalism's cultural neutrality so difficult to grasp in the historical colonial context? Why is it that Egyptian liberals interpreted European liberalism to mean imposing a political identity that is at once absolute and grounded in a particular, alien, and exclusive culture? To address these questions, one must go beyond determining what identity claims are good or bad for liberal democracy or how to accommodate difference while preserving a value-free center.

This book does not claim that politicized identities in today's liberal democracies obey the same logic or are structured by the same power relations as in the colonial context. The social, cultural, political, and economic differences between these two historical situations are too obvious to warrant further explanation. I do suggest, however, that a liberal theory of cultural rights can learn a great deal from the colonial experience because of colonial liberalism's unequivocal cultural claims. This book speaks, then, to both liberal critics and liberal defenders of identity politics. To conventional liberal theorists who hold that cultural affinities are harmful to democracy and therefore can and should be excluded from the political arena, this book presents a challenge. The colonial case I am presenting reveals how the modern notions of nationhood and citizenship are grounded in cultural prejudices that cannot be corrected simply by suspending "culture" and letting "neutral" democratic mechanisms take their course. Nationhood and citizenship are not just political constructions; they are culturally structured and claim absolute sovereignty.

For different reasons, this book also challenges liberal theorists who hold that certain cultural demands and identities are consistent with liberal democratic principles. My critique here centers on their views on the meaning and relevance of cultural membership. Two examples stand out because of their careful specification of what they mean by culture and cultural identity. Will Kymlicka defines what he calls "societal culture" as "a culture which provides its members with meaningful ways of life across a full range of human activities, including social, educational, religious, recreational, and economic life, encompassing both public and private spheres."[54] Avishai Margalit and Joseph Raz think of culture as defining "a variety of forms or styles of life, types of activity, occupation, pursuit, and relationship" and as shaping national cuisines, literature, music, language, architecture, customs, dress, et cetera.[55] According to these appropriately expansive definitions, the relevance of culture to democracy is that it provides a "context of choice" without which individuals may unjustly be barred from making free and informed judgments about vital aspects of their lives.[56] This concept seems like a significant departure from the standard liberal objections to "politicizing" the status and rights of cultural minorities.[57] Yet the proposed political formulation is not innovative. Basically, liberal theorists attentive to minority rights recommend dealing with cultural recognition and representation as well as any other demands articulated by "interest groups." There is a long tradition of associational life and representation in liberal democracies, they argue, which provides sufficient moral, political, and procedural grounds to integrate certain cultural demands—those consistent with liberal democratic principles—as "communities of interest."[58] The problem, however, is that the very notion of representation of interests within the liberal democratic framework is being challenged, regardless of cultural issues. For example, the increasingly nominal character of political representation, declining rates of participation in electoral politics, the domination of business interests in the public political arena, the control of information by big corporations, inadequate social services in poor communities, and similar problems point to a growing gap between democratic practice and ideals. It is therefore difficult to imagine how cultural demands, which are more complicated to figure out than social goods, can be accommodated within the framework of interest group politics.

five

Egypt's Liberal Experiment in Comparative Perspective

I have argued in this book that liberalism's claim to cultural neutrality falls apart in the colonial and imperial contexts. I have shown how the modern notions of nationhood and citizenship the Egyptian liberal reformers borrowed from the West are grounded in biased cultural assumptions, encoded in the very language of liberation and emancipation. Hence this book considers conflicts of identity that emerge in the colonial context vital to understanding the failure of the liberal experiment in postindependence Egypt. Despite various conceptual reformulations and adjustments to empirical findings, current theories of democratization still privilege structural factors and strategic agents acting in their rational interest as the main drive of democratic pact making. Conceptions of democracy and politics that leave out the culture and language that give meaning to citizenship and community overlook an important and complex empirical reality.

When applied to the liberal experiment in Egypt during the 1920s and 1930s, neither the old democratization literature that emphasizes structural prerequisites nor the current theories of democratic transition that emphasize synchronized, agency-based democratic change provide satisfactory explanations. According to the first approach, the problematic establishment and consolidation of liberal democracy in developing countries is attributed to social and economic factors.[1] If democracy has not developed or stabilized in the Third World, the root causes are structural constraints such as the absence of a strong bourgeoisie,[2] low levels of economic development,[3] or the lack of protodemocratic traditions.[4] While these factors were probably crucial to the development of democracy in the West, my reading of the failure of the liberal experiment in Egypt tells a more complex story. In the case of Egypt, the structural prerequisites were certainly not perfect, yet they provided what most specialists would consider a reasonably good environment for the establishment of democratic politics. The economic historians Charles Issawi (1964) and Roger Owen (1969) detail the twin impacts of Egypt's early integration into the world economy: higher urbanization, increasing literacy rates, and better living conditions in parallel with the breakup of traditional economic relations and social structures.[5] Social historians and political economy specialists of interwar Egypt such as Robert Tignor (1977, 1980, 1989), Eric Davis (1983), and Robert Vitalis (1995) concur that there was a dynamic and relatively independent industrial and financial bourgeoisie even if it was linked to international capital.[6] The labor historians Rauf Abbas (1967) and Joel Beinin and Zachary Lockman (1987) document elaborate social differentiations and workers' movements that attest to an advanced process of capital accumulation and class consciousness during the period.[7] Along a similar line of argument, Marius Deeb (1979), Mahmoud Hussein (1977), and Ellis Goldberg (1986) have shown that class politics were well developed by the interwar period.[8] And historical analyses of political institutions in modern Egypt from the 1860s to the late 1930s testify to a long tradition of constitutional and competitive party politics. The works of Egyptian scholars as ideologically diverse as Anouar Abdel Malek, Afaf Lutfi al-Sayyid-Marsot, Tariq al-Bishri, Abd al-Azim Ramadan, and Abd al-Aziz al-Rifaʻi refer to this period in Egyptian history as the era of liberal politics.[9] Yet a democratic regime did not take root.

In a theoretically ambitious book on democratic experiments in various developing countries across the continents, the authors advance a number of factors that they believe are conducive to democratic development.[10] These factors include legitimacy and performance, political culture, social structure and socioeconomic development, associational life, state and society relations, political institutions, and international influences. Of course, no one claims that any one of these factors is sufficient to guarantee the development and stability of democracy. However, a combination of a number of favorable conditions is believed to have a positive impact on the establishment of a democratic process.

The Colonial Legacy Thesis

Since there are very few historical cases where indigenous democracy developed—save in the United States and northwestern Europe—the imposition of representative institutions through colonial rule is considered one of the factors that may have contributed to the development of democracy in postcolonial societies. According to the proponents of this view, two conditions must be met for such a political outcome: the institutions of self-rule created during the colonial period must be preserved, and the colonized people must achieve independence through peaceful means.[11] The classic examples of such a successful transfer of democratic institutions, we are told, are some of the former British and French colonies: India, Nigeria, and Senegal.[12] In the case of India, for example, Atul Kohli makes the point that

> the British inadvertently helped the Indian National Congress, which had grown out of a movement opposed to colonial rule, to become one of the mature forebears of democracy. . . . One has only to contrast the British role in India with that of the Dutch in Indonesia or the French in Indochina to realize how widespread repression forced the nationalist opposition in the latter two cases to be extremist. The extremism of the opposition in turn severely diminished the chances of democratic evolution in Indonesia and Vietnam. The British in India, moreover, left behind a functioning parliament, a cohesive and "apolitical" bureaucracy, and independent judiciary and press.[13]

One can formulate three objections to the colonial legacy thesis. First, on ideological grounds, it implies that the colonial trauma can be justified if the colonial powers did acts of charity, such as introducing institutions that supposedly enhanced the development of democracy in the colonies. Another ideological implication is that colonialism can be beneficial to the colonized people if they do not resort to extremist and violent opposition to colonization. Hence in Zimbabwe, where the political culture in principle accords with democratic institutions, the establishment of democracy is hindered by "the intolerant, violent, and communistic culture of the liberation struggle."[14] Second, the "colonialism continuity" thesis is also based on a conceptual fallacy that permeates the literature on democratic change. This fallacy is the quasi equation of democracy with the political mechanisms that, more often than not, "democratize corruption" by allowing a more open distribution of spoils among the competing elite rather than operating as institutions of democratic representation.[15] Finally, the colonial legacy thesis cannot explain the cases of a Muslim country like Turkey, which was never colonized and is considered democratic. Nor can it account for the development of democracy in countries where the colonial institutions were violently disrupted, as in Chile, where a relatively stable democracy was in place from the 1850s until 1973. Nor can it make sense of the failure of democracy in countries such as Egypt during the 1920s and 1930s, and Morocco during the 1950s and 1960s, where independence was relatively peaceful and the colonial institutions were kept more or less intact.

Egypt's first exposure to Western democratic institutions took place through colonial encounter, first with the French in 1798, then with the British in 1882. Soon after the French military expedition secured its positions in Egypt, Napoleon invited the 'ulama, shaykhs, and notables of Cairo to constitute a nine-member Consultative Administrative Council. Members of the Diwan of Cairo, as it is called in the Egyptian sources, were to be elected freely by the 'ulama, shaykhs, and notables themselves.[16] For the first time in modern Egyptian history, an Egyptian native elite was associated with an elected political body to advise on matters of government. The Diwan was in charge of the civil government in Cairo, but final decisions were to be approved by the French military authorities. The appointment of high civil officials remained the exclusive affair of the French; however, the Diwan had the right to appoint officials in subaltern positions.[17] Furthermore, in 1798, Napoleon established a system of Provincial Administrative Councils and convened a meeting of their representatives in Cairo under the aegis of the newly organized General Council, al-Diwan al-'Am.

In a letter to the General Council, Napoleon stated that the purpose of establishing these political organisms was to accustom Egyptian notables to a system of representative government and advisory councils. He asked the delegates to deliberate and make recommendations on four main issues: the organization, rules, and membership of the provincial councils; the religious and civil courts; the inheritance laws; and the system of taxation and landownership.[18] The General Council had no legislative powers, but it could make propositions to a French committee, headed by Napoleon, which had the final word. Two weeks after the General Council was established, it was suspended because of anti-French disturbances in Cairo in October 1789, but it was reinstated two months later. According to the Egyptian chronicler al-Jabarti, a major problem was constant disputes between the French committee and the Diwan on the question of taxation. French officials, says al-Jabarti, were stubborn and did not want to hear any advice on this matter from natives. The Egyptians complained that they were now paying more taxes to the French authorities than they had to the Mamluk rulers.[19]

After the abrupt departure of the French in 1801, Muhammad 'Ali emerged as the ruler of Egypt following a five-year power struggle with the Mamluks and the Turks supported by the British. He abolished the Cairo Council, the Provincial Councils, and the General Council and ruled autocratically until 1829, when he established an Advisory Council, Majlis al-Mushawara. The council consisted of high government officials, religious scholars, and other notables. Its functions were limited to discussing administrative reforms, modernizing education, and developing public works. In 1834, Muhammad 'Ali created a second body, al-Majlis al-A'la, or the Supreme Council, and in 1837 he established al-Majlis al-'Umumi, the Public Council. The powers of these councils did not extend beyond consultation, and they lacked any influence on the decision-making process.[20] In general, Muhammad 'Ali preferred to rely on an efficient state bureaucracy rather than a representative body to implement his ambitious development schemes.

During the rule of Khedive Ismail (1866–79), the evolution of consultative and representative councils became the precursor to the later development of constitutionalism in Egypt. Certainly, the Consultative Assembly of Deputies had no legislative powers; it could only advise on matters of public works, education, taxation, and landownership. Khedive Ismail had the power to suspend or dissolve the assembly and to ignore or veto the decisions of the deputies. However, deliberations were free and lively, and sometimes proposals from the deputies were approved by the khedive and carried out by the government.[21] In 1877 the assembly began to play a more prominent role in Egyptian politics, as the country faced a severe financial crisis linked to default on European loans. Two years later, as the deputies gained more experience, autonomy, and confidence, they asked for new laws for the assembly. Significantly, they demanded to change the name of the Consultative Assembly of Deputies to Majlis al-Nuwab, the Assembly of Deputies.[22] The new laws contained some clauses important for a nascent democratic process. The deputies were free to express their views; in case of a dispute over any matter between the assembly and the government, decisions were to remain with the assembly. Also, the ministers were to be responsible to the assembly.[23] The assembly further reinforced its self-assertion when a new electoral law, qanun al-intikhab, was introduced to the assembly and approved by the deputies. The new law ordered that every one hundred electors were to appoint an electorate delegate, who would in turn select a deputy to the assembly. The increase in deputy membership to 125, and the concomitant decrease in the number of village headmen owing to less government interference in the electoral process, resulted in more diverse and assertive views in the assembly.[24] Ironically, the British, who claimed to introduce a superior democratic mechanism, interrupted the prominent role of democratic institutions that began with Khedive Ismail.

When the British occupied Egypt in 1882, they abolished the Assembly of Deputies and in 1883 established new institutions modeled after the Viceroy's Legislative Council in India. On the recommendations of Lord Dufferin, the British ambassador in Constantinople, the British created a Legislative Council, Majlish al-Shura, and a General Assembly, al-Jam'iyya al-'Umumiyya. These two bodies remained active until 1912. The Legislative Council consisted of thirty members: the provincial councils elected sixteen deputies for a six-year term; the khedive and the government for an unlimited-period appointed the remaining fourteen members. The president and vice president of the Legislative Council were chosen from the members designated by the khedive and his cabinet. The function of the council members remained limited to consultation on matters pertaining to legislation and the budget.

The General Assembly consisted of members of the Legislative Council, the khedive's cabinet members, and forty-six deputies elected from various Egyptian provinces. Candidates or appointed members to the General Assembly had to be literate, at least thirty years old, and paying at least fifty Egyptian pounds in taxes a year. Although the General Assembly had no legislative powers, the government was compelled to consider its advice on administrative matters, public loans, public works, and taxation. However, the government had the right to reject the recommendations of the assembly simply by providing an explanation.[25]

Although these institutions had an ambiguous mandate, they were flexible enough to accommodate certain demands. After increasing pressure, demands, and petitions from the deputies, the British commissioner in Egypt, Lord Kitchener, introduced two laws in 1913 to redefine the powers of the General Assembly and to improve the system of representation. The new Legislative Assembly, al-Jam'iyya al-Tashri'iyya, included a greater number of elected deputies and representatives from various professional and social groups; it also became more forceful and resolute in holding the government accountable for policy failures. The government had to submit all laws to the assembly for discussion, and the assembly had the right to propose its own projects and to turn down or reformulate projects proposed by the government. In the same spirit, electoral campaigns and competitions for assembly seats changed. For the first time, for example, candidates began to run on defined platforms rather than relying on the support of powerful political friends in the government.

And although the Legislative Assembly did not exert much legislative power, the quality and audacity of speakers such as Saad Zaghlul, Murqus Simeikha Bey, and others were remarkable; they dared to challenge the British using their own language and institutions and encouraged other deputies to follow. The Legislative Assembly debated all issues ranging from court laws, education, freedom of the press, taxation, and landownership to theater and marriage laws.[26] But the last word rested with the colonial authorities. Between World War I and the declaration of Egyptian independence in 1922, the convening of the Legislative Assembly was postponed several times, then officially suspended as Egypt was declared a protectorate and ruled by British martial law.

This brief overview of the colonial representative institutions in Egypt suggests that the country had a long, albeit discontinuous, history of experiments with semidemocratic or semiparliamentary organizations. Most, if not all, of the assemblies and councils had little power and could only advise the government on a limited set of issues and internal matters. Nevertheless, they provided a reasonable institutional framework for debate, competition, and negotiation. These are the traditions that help the emergence of democracy and make it prosper. But democracy did not prosper in Egypt. It did not happen because liberal discourse was more exclusive and nondemocratic than institutions allow us to see.

From a liberal perspective, nondemocratic liberalism may be justified on moral and political grounds if it eventually leads to the establishment of liberal democratic rule in a society where authority relations are based on ethnic, racial, or linguistic clusters. The example of India comes readily to mind, and it can reasonably be compared with Egypt—though Egyptian society is more homogeneous. Both countries were ruled by foreign despotic rulers, the Moguls in India and the Ottomans in Egypt, and both were British colonies with some form of representative institutions—though India was the "jewel in the British crown." In India, it has often been argued, the colonial legacy accounts for the development and consolidation of democracy. The question is whether liberal colonialism did indeed erase "particularistic" affinities. Ongoing ethnic, regional, and religious conflicts point to the contrary. When Muslims, Sikhs, Punjabis, Tamils, or Assamese resort to violence or threaten to secede every time their social and political demands are not satisfied, their actions raise doubts about the legitimacy and efficiency of existing democratic institutions in mediating conflicts. Yet Indian democracy survives, and it seems to do so thanks to, not despite of, the continuing importance of cultural or social clusters. The political process in India functions basically to satisfy, when possible, particularistic demands rather than respond to some abstract notion of universal representation.[27] Ironically, it was the British who contributed to the transformation of these groups, whose demands are perhaps legitimate, into separatist political movements. Jyotirindra Das Gupta, for example, observed: "The colonial rulers in India positively weakened the growth of liberalism by an intensified racialist policy. They hastened the development of reactive communalism, whereby each religious community increasingly came to depend on exclusive mobilization to defend its members' interests."[28]

The Political Institutions Thesis

Next to the colonial legacy thesis, political scientists consider multiparty politics and a sound constitutional structure as essential to the development of democracy in the non-Western, nondemocratic societies. These characteristics are especially important in Third World nations where the socioeconomic conditions and cultural value systems are considered inhospitable to democracy.[29] The multiparty system facilitates the development and consolidation of democracy because it assumes and structures pluralism and competition and provides a vehicle for formal organized opposition that has a stake in preserving the legitimacy of the political system. Furthermore, political parties institutionalize a civic culture through electoral practice and provide political identifications on the basis of platforms with a wide range of social interests, rather than on primordial loyalties.

To prevent the deterioration of a working multiparty system into "polarized pluralism," where the victory of one party means the loss of others, an appropriate constitutional arrangement is considered crucial to regulate political conflicts and give losers the hope that one day they may come to power. Thus a parliamentary system and an independent judiciary are supposed to uphold the legitimacy of the political regime . . . the former by providing the opportunity for party coalition, the latter by holding the government accountable to the people.[30]

While it is an intellectual responsibility to consider the role of political parties and constitutional mechanisms in investigating the failure of democracy in Egypt, I see two major problems at the outset with the thesis. Conceptually, it is reminiscent of the assumptions, methods, and ideology of the orthodox political development literature. Its preoccupation with the diffusion of institutions and structures that led to the development of democracy in the West implies that the discourses that inform and legitimate political authority in different nations are the same or not at all relevant.[31] A related and more obvious problem with the political institutions thesis is that it simply cannot explain the breakdown of democratic institutions even in societies such as Germany, France, and Italy, where the socioeconomic and cultural conditions were favorable.[32]

On this score, Egypt has a rather long tradition of institutionalized political pluralism and elite political activism. One can trace the origins of political parties in Egypt back to the secret societies that sprang up during the 1870s as a reaction to increasing taxation, growing European influence, and the weakening of the autocratic authority of Khedive Ismail.[33] The first political party established in Egypt was the National Party, al-Hizb al-Watani, in 1879. This party evolved from the secret society of Egyptian army officers who resented the favors accorded to Turkish and Circassian officers in the army. The party promised to be more inclusive as it encouraged members of the assembly, representatives of all religious faiths in Egypt (Muslims, Jews, and Copts), notables, merchants, and civil servants to join. The party's program was based on three main points: constitutional reforms, while recognizing the khedive's sovereignty as long as he was "just"; financial reforms, while honoring Egypt's debts to the European creditors; and the rule of law, political freedom, and social justice.[34]

When the 'Urabi revolt broke out between 1879 and 1882, the National Party gained more popular support and a larger membership.[35] However, the British occupation following the military defeat of 'Urabi at Tell al-Kabir and the bombardment of Alexandria marked the end of the National Party. The colonial authorities disbanded it and imprisoned its leaders or forced them into exile.

No significant organized political opposition existed during the first ten years of British rule. Although two new parties were established—the Watani Party of Mustapha Kamil in 1897, and the Umma Party of Lutfi al-Sayyid in 1907—it was between 1919 and 1939 that party politics developed significantly in Egypt.[36] Three main parties were prominent in the Egyptian political scene during this period: the Wafd, the Liberal Constitutionalist Party, and the Watani Party.[37]

On the eve of World War I, Britain officially declared Egypt a protectorate, dismissed Khedive Abbas Hilmi, annulled Ottoman sovereignty, banned all political activities, and declared martial law. At the end of the war, the Egyptian nationalists hoped that the Allied powers would act positively on the issue of Egyptian independence. They formed a *wafd*, the Arabic word for delegation, to plead for complete independence at the Paris Peace Conference in 1919 after failing to convince the British government of the validity of their national demands.

Formed by prominent members of the Umma Party and members of the old Legislative Assembly, the delegation had the endorsements (*tawkilat*) of deputies, provincial councils, religious Muslim and Coptic leaders, notables, professionals, and other social groups who contributed donations. The Wafd organized a central committee with the purpose of collecting subscriptions to support the delegation's trip to Europe and securing the support of the people nationwide. When the declaration of independence was issued in March 1922, the Wafd had already established itself as a political party with a platform, an effective propaganda machine,[38] various internal committees, provincial and local branches, and formally organized associations of students, workers, women, merchants, professionals, and civil servants. In the rural areas, the Wafd had the support of peasants, medium landowners, and large landowners.[39] However, at the national level the party leadership had a significantly larger proportion of large landowners, medium landowners, and professionals than of other groups or classes who lent support to the Wafd.[40]

From its inception, the Wafd based its ideology on the demand of complete and immediate independence from Britain and the establishment of a free and sovereign Egyptian nation. The Wafdist leaders were influenced by a liberal and secular nationalism understood as a "general commitment to . . . remolding society on the basis of a . . . secular conception of the state and rational humanitarian values," rather than on loyalty to a larger pan-Islamic entity.[41] Most of the founders of the Wafd, that is, the Egyptian delegation, were in fact members of the old Umma Party opposed to any allegiance to the Ottoman Empire.[42]

Another basic element of the Wafd's ideology was its adherence to democratic principles of government. Article 3 of the party's statute declares that "the *Wafd* draws its power from the will of the people (*raghba*), expressed directly and through their deputies in elected bodies."[43] I have already mentioned the *tawkilat* that the Wafd sought from various groups, classes, associations, and councils before engaging in negotiations with the British and the European powers at the Peace Conference. And the Wafd remained open to negotiation and compromise with its adversaries. Its leaders called for the election of a national assembly to discuss and act on major national political issues. In one instance, the Wafd called on the assembly to mediate a conflict between Saad Zaghlul, the leader of the Wafd, and Adli Yegen, Sultan Fu'ad's prime minister, over the presidency and mandate of the delegation going to Europe to discuss independence. A second instance concerned the appointment of the Constitution Commission to draft Egypt's first political charter after independence in 1922. The Wafd maintained that only a nationally elected body could draft a free constitution.

It is not clear, however, whether this principled appeal to the nation and claim to represent the Egyptian people as a whole were motivated by democratic ideals or by nationalism. In any case, Saad Zaghlul considered himself the leader of the whole nation rather than of a political party in the parliament and adopted a populist ideology. He began to see political opposition as an attack on the "nation" or on the "will of the people" rather than as a representation of a competing, legitimate political alternative.

THE LIBERAL CONSTITUTIONALIST PARTY

The Hizb al-Ahrar al-Ditsturiyyun was established in 1922 by a group of nationalists who split from the Wafd under the initiative of Adli Yegen, Saad Zaghlul's rival. The purpose of establishing the Liberal Constitutionalist Party was to present a moderate political alternative and a counterweight to the Wafd.[44] At the party's inaugural meeting in October 1922, Adli Yegen, the president-elect of the party, declared in his opening speech that "a constitutional regime was the only appropriate form of government for a civilized nation like Egypt."[45]

The party elected a thirty-member board of directors, eleven of whom were members of the Constitution Commission charged with drafting the text of the 1923 Constitution.[46] The party's organization was limited to the board of directors, who formulated the party's policy with no feedback from provincial committees or local branches. The official organ of the party was *Al-Siyasa*, supplemented by a weekly literary publication, *Al-Siyasa al-Usbu'iyya*. According to Marius Deeb, who investigated the social background of twenty-nine members of the board of directors, seventeen were large landowners (rural notables and absentee landlords), while the remaining members were of urban, middle-class origins.[47] The party had no nationally organized subscription system and relied mainly on the gifts of its wealthy members.

The Liberal Constitutionalist Party's position on independence was based on the concept of *kiyasa* (adroitness, cleverness), which meant accepting the British government's principle of gradual independence. Unlike the Wafd, the liberal constitutionalists did not demand the immediate evacuation of British troops from Egypt. They considered the Wafd's position on this issue too rigid and an obstacle to reaching a political accord with London.[48] The party's program was a platform of eighteen articles, including demands for constitutional change, individual rights, the combating of illiteracy among men and women, improvement in hygiene, financial reforms, and free commerce.[49] In an interesting formulation, the Liberal Constitutionalist Party was committed to a parliamentary system that aimed to liberate "the collective from the tyranny of the individual and . . . the individual from the tyranny of the collective."[50] Unlike the Wafd, which continued to appeal directly to the people, the Liberal Constitutionalist Party was opposed to universal male suffrage because it would give the "populist" and "nationalist" Wafd more political power. The party depended more on the benevolence and maneuvers of the palace and the British for governmental positions than on the constitutional process.[51]

THE NATIONAL PARTY

The Egyptian nationalist leader Mustapha Kamil, known for his advocacy of women's liberation, founded the National (Watani) Party in 1907. Although the party had its own official newspaper, *Al-Liwa'* (the Standard), Mustapha Kamil chose to publish the party's program in the French newspaper *Le Figaro*.[52] The National Party's ideology when it was first established was based on three political principles: the independence of Egypt, the creation of a constitutional government, and social justice. While the party publicly advocated independence from Britain and the establishment of an independent Egyptian nation, the Watani leaders remained attached to the Ottomans and benefited from their support.

The social basis of the Watani Party was primarily the urban middle class and rural notables.[53] The party established its administrative and executive committees in Alexandria, with branches in Cairo and other major urban centers. Despite the small size of its following, the National Party managed to nominate candidates for elections in various cities and in the countryside. However, the party's ideology continued to vacillate between the pan-Islamist, anticolonialist militancy of the younger members and the more restrained stand of the older party founders who interpreted differently the ideas of Mustapha Kamil.

What we learn from party politics in Egypt is that they provided a reasonable human and institutional environment for the flourishing of democratic political pluralism. The nationalist political elite, while torn between the need for national unity in the face of the colonial administration and single-party strategy, never encouraged extremist antiliberal ideologies. The parties and their leaders did not waver in their commitment to play by the rules of the game.

Notwithstanding the ideological, organizational, and social differences among the various political parties in Egypt, they all agreed on an essential point: the need for, and commitment to, a constitutional structure to regulate political life in the country. Soon after the declaration of independence in March 1922, King Fu'ad's Council of Ministers appointed a commission to draft a constitution for Egypt. The thirty members of the Constitution Commission were chosen from landowners, merchants, lawyers, religious leaders, judges, delegates from the old Legislative Assembly, and intellectuals.[54] At the commission's second meeting, a subcommittee of eighteen members was appointed to discuss the general principles of the Constitution. According to Husayn Haykal, this committee included mostly lawyers who believed in "the principles of freedom as understood by the [Europeans] in the nineteenth century," despite their disagreement on the nature of the franchise, the separation of powers, and the representation of minorities. These principles included "the right to private property, inviolability of the domicile, freedom of opinion, and individual liberty."[55]

The Egyptian Constitution was proclaimed in April 1923. It was modeled after the Belgian Constitution of 1830–31 because "Belgium was also a constitutional monarchy with strong French cultural traditions."[56] Although the Constitution gave extensive powers to the king,[57] it was proclaimed after careful preparations, ample debates among learned people (including at least one European lawyer), and a clear dedication to the liberal principles of constitutional government.[58] In fact, the problem with the 1923 Constitution, as Jacques Berque sees it, is that it was "too closely modeled after a Western pattern."[59] Even severe critics of the 1923 Constitution, such as Nadav Safran, who faults the text's ambiguity on religious issues, says that "the Constitution enshrined in every respect the principles of liberal nationalism, which represented in many instances radical departures from the fundamental principles of traditional Islamic doctrine."[60]

The 1923 Constitution provided for the establishment of an Egyptian parliament consisting of a Senate and a Chamber of Deputies, with both the parliament and the king exercising legislative power. The king could veto a bill, but the parliament could override the veto by a two-thirds majority. Three-fifths of the Senate members were to be elected on the basis of a three-stage election; the rest were to be appointed by the king at the recommendation of the prime minister. Members of the Chamber of Deputies were to be elected in a two-stage ballot on the basis of one delegate to each sixty thousand inhabitants.[61]

Although the Wafd and the Watani parties denounced the Constitution Commission and some aspects of the Constitution's provisions, when the 1924 elections approached, both parties participated enthusiastically in the electoral campaigns. The first free Egyptian elections ended with a landslide victory for the Wafdist candidates, giving the Wafd an overwhelming majority in the Chamber of Deputies. Ironically, Saad Zaghlul and his colleagues won the elections by running a campaign that exposed the problems of the newly established constitutional regime. Zaghlul criticized, for example, the electoral laws for being fundamentally incompatible with democracy. He attacked the clause that made eligibility of candidacy to general elections conditional on income. And he argued against Article 78 of the Constitution, which defined social and financial qualifications of candidates to match the social backgrounds of sitting Senate members.[62] The Students Executive Committee of the Wafd played a crucial role in this campaign, explaining to the people the trappings of the established electoral system.[63] But the Constitution was de facto suspended for different reasons.

Nine months after Saad Zaghlul formed a Wafdist government with the backing of an overwhelming majority in the parliament, Sir Lee Stack, the British governor general of the Sudan, was assassinated in Cairo. The British high commissioner issued an ultimatum to the Egyptian government demanding the immediate withdrawal of all Egyptian troops from the Sudan. When Saad Zaghlul refused to comply, British troops occupied the Alexandria customhouse. Saad Zaghlul resigned and the parliament was dismissed.

British involvement in Egyptian politics persisted after that to protect the "vital interests" of the empire. On several occasions—in 1926, 1927, and 1928, for example—Britain intervened directly to circumvent the powers of the elected Wafdist parliament or Wafdist cabinet. The British accused them of violating the agreements of the declaration of independence.[64] King Fu'ad's political power depended greatly on British interference each time democratic elections threatened to undermine his autocratic powers. Free elections meant the weakening of the king's hold on the central administration and the transfer of provincial and municipal councils into the hands of the Wafd. This shift in power could also have crippled the British position in Egypt, since the Wafd was less willing to compromise with the British and did not depend on Britain's support to stay in power.[65]

Indeed, after successive, overwhelming electoral victories, the Wafd and its leaders used their popular support to call for changing "antidemocratic" clauses in the Constitution. The liberals accused the Wafd of attempting to establish a "parliamentary dictatorship."[66] Yet the liberal constitutionalists themselves breached the Constitution and violated a fundamental principle of democratic politics when they accepted, in 1930, the formation of a government by royal decree. Their cabinet became known in Egypt as al-qabda al-hadidiya, the government of the Iron Grip.[67] With the support of the British and the king, they suspended the 1923 Constitution and promulgated a more restrictive one. The new Constitution limited suffrage to those who paid taxes, thereby curtailing the voting rights of the majority of Egyptians who did not own property. Prime minister Ismail Sidqi bluntly justified the new Constitution: "Suffrage is a function, not a right to be exercised by the whole population. Village people, who constitute the bulk of Egypt's population, are absolutely incapable of seeing beyond their horizon."[68]

Although the 1923 Constitution was reestablished in 1936, ongoing conflicts between the Wafd and the opposition parties rallying behind the new monarch, King Faruq, stalled the constitutional process. The Wafd Party suffered from internal political dissent, which culminated in the formation of a more radical splinter group, the al-Wafd al-Saadi.[69] The period from 1935 to 1939 marked, in fact, the end of the Wafd's hegemony in the electoral process and the emergence of new groups who refused to play according to the rules of the liberal constitutional regime. These were the al-Ikhwan al-Muslimun, the Muslim Brotherhood, and Misr al-Fatat, Young Egypt. While members of these groups were behind political assassinations and violent activities, the movement of Islamic revivalism as a whole signaled a rejection of Western constitutionalism on cultural grounds. In 1952, after a series of governmental crises and postponements of parliamentary meetings, the army stepped in and established a military regime, commonly known as Nasser's Free Officers.

The constitutional crises that marred Egyptian politics during the interwar period are not unique and do not tell the full story about the failure of the liberal experiment in Egypt. It is hard to trace democratic development and consolidation to smooth constitutional progress, even in the most solid Western democracies. More to the point, however, constitutional politics could themselves be part of the problem. That is, the purpose of embracing

Western political institutions could stem from a different logic from the smooth regulation of political competition and conflicts. This book suggests that the appropriation of liberal political institutions was in large part informed by a complex interplay of identities in the colonial context. One can find telling glimpses of this problem in the writings of Egyptian specialists who were not concerned with identity politics. Consider how Nadav Safran, for example, intuitively links the liberal experiment in Egypt to a negotiation with the Other, Europe. "The prestige of constitutional democratic government," he observes, "was not so much due to a soundly founded conviction about the merits of the principles of democracy as it was the consequence of the association of democratic forms of government with the success and power of the European nations."[70] Although Safran's aim is to blame the Egyptians for it, his main point is valid. Jacques Berque points to a similar problem when he astutely remarks: "[The 1923] Constitution was too closely modeled on a Western pattern, but that was part of its attraction: its symbolic value was more important than its functional value. . . . It was a form of exorcism."[71] Yet the conventional concern with the institutional and structural prerequisites for democracy seems so irrelevant to the colonial historical context of Egypt. Nowhere is the concern with prerequisites farther off base than when it conflates legitimacy with performance.

The Legitimacy and Performance Thesis

More than in any other type of regime, the stability of democratic regimes depends on the majority of citizens accepting political authority.[72] The question is, how does political authority in democratic polities derive its legitimacy? Larry Diamond, Juan Linz, and Seymour Lipset have an answer:

> Democratic legitimacy derives, when it is most stable and secure, from an intrinsic value commitment rooted in the political culture at all levels of society, but it is also shaped (particularly in the early years of democracy) by the performance of the democratic regime, both economically and politically. . . . Historically, the more successful a regime has been in providing what people want, the greater and more deeply rooted tends to be legitimacy: A long record of successful performance tends to build a large reservoir of legitimacy, enabling the system better to endure crises and challenges.[73]

"What people want" is not always clear. It is readily assumed, however, especially when dealing with underdeveloped Third World countries, that social welfare and economic well-being are what people need most. Hence

Diamond and his coauthors posit an "obvious correlation" between economic performance and democracy.[74] It is therefore not surprising that the discussion on democratic legitimacy is linked to, and dominated by, an emphasis on issues such as "economic policies, inflation, fiscal deficits, and foreign borrowing."[75]

This conceptual conflation of political legitimacy with a regime's capacity to accommodate the socioeconomic needs of various groups makes it difficult to distinguish between the recent literature on the prospects of democracy in the Third World and the old modernization literature. If legitimacy is defined in terms of performance, then it becomes a formula for maintaining the stability of the political order, any political order, not just democracy. This is not to argue that the social and economic performances of a democratic regime are irrelevant to its stability, but rather to suggest that the discussion of these performances is ill placed conceptually. After all, liberal democracy is not about social and economic performance and equality. On the contrary, the main claim of liberal democracy is that all citizens, regardless of their social and economic status, have legally equal political rights. The question, then, is how to make the majority of citizens believe in the legitimacy of the political system, even if some or many of them disagree with the economic and social policies of the rulers. This belief is a necessary condition because, most likely, some group in society will always feel relatively deprived and discriminated against by a government's policies. Any meaningful discussion of democratic legitimacy and the prospect of democracy in the Third World will thus have to make a clear conceptual distinction between legitimacy and performance. Yet even if we accept that legitimacy depends on political and economic performance alone, this does not adequately explain the collapse or survival of democracy.

Although one can credit the Egyptian constitutional regime for at least attempting to institutionalize the ideas of elections, democratic politics, free choice, and a free press,[76] the majority of people could not identify with the constitutional regime and remained largely indifferent to the political intrigues and rivalries that characterized it. What gave the Wafd popular support in the early elections was mainly its anticolonial stand; it attracted the majority of votes in the urban centers and appealed to the sentiments of the peasants in the rural areas. Saad Zaghlul portrayed himself in the electoral campaigns as a *fallah bin fallah*, "peasant son of a peasant," and spoke of "the seizure of power by the fallahin."[77] When the Anglo-Egyptian treaty was concluded in 1936 by the Wafdist government, the party alienated many supporters.[78] I have already mentioned the split of the Saadist group led by

Ahmed Muhammad and Mahmud al-Nuqrashi in 1938. Another splinter party, al-Kutla al-Wafdiyya, was formed by Wafdist dissidents led by Makram Obeyd in 1942, but more significant was the new activism of the Muslim Brotherhood and Misr al-Fatat. They rejected altogether multiparty politics and the traps of the constitutional regime. They undermined the social basis of the Wafd by appealing to the rural populations and the urban masses.[79]

The Class Structure and Socioeconomic Development Thesis

The final major factor I want to consider is the class structure thesis. The development of democracy in Western Europe has historically been linked to the emergence of a bourgeois class.[80] The rise of a powerful and economically autonomous capitalist class prepared the ground for the qualitative transformation of political authority. The bourgeoisie challenged the nobility's claim to state authority on the basis of inherited (later purchased) titles and established representative institutions where nonnobles had equal political rights. What allowed the European bourgeoisie to impose their political demands, the argument goes, was their independence from the monarchical state. Be that as it may, the validity of the thesis that democracy in the West was the product of the political struggle of the bourgeoisie is really of no immediate consequence to students of Third World politics. There seems to be an agreement among students of comparative political development in the Third World that it is unrealistic to hope for a historical reproduction of the European experience in the developing nations. A variety of factors militate against such a scenario: the structure of the world economy, the technological revolution, the predominant position of the state, and the class composition in developing nations are all believed to constitute obstacles to the reproduction of the Western experience.[81]

In many Third World nations, including those in Latin America, the state remains the main sponsor and promoter of economic development. The social class that played a revolutionary political role in the West finds itself in the Third World dependent on the state to provide the financial, social, and basic impetus for its economic projects.[82] This dependence makes it difficult for the privileged segments of civil society to challenge the nature of political authority. The absence of a strong bourgeoisie that can curtail the excessive powers of the state, and the related absence of private, autonomous, and pluralistic initiatives, decrease the chances for the eventual development of democracy. The struggle for democracy is transformed into a power struggle over access to the state, which remains the primary engine for economic advancement. This struggle in turn leads to corruption, authoritarian politics, socioeconomic inequalities, and the fuzzy separation between the private and public sectors of the economy. These features do not constitute a hospitable environment for competitive politics and democracy.

However, there seems to be a way out of this deadlock. One familiar view holds that the process of modernization and economic development generates medium social strata that disrupt traditional structures and impose political changes along the lines of pluralistic politics.[83] According to the proponents of this view,

> an advanced level of economic development, producing greater economic security and more widespread education, is assumed to reduce socioeconomic inequality and mitigate feelings of relative deprivation and injustice in the lower class, thus reducing the likelihood of extremist politics. Increased national wealth also tends to enlarge the middle class, which has long been associated in political theory with moderation, tolerance, and democracy.[84]

The main problems with this proposition, as well as with the modernization literature from which it borrows the argument, are that it is ahistorical and also conceptually questionable. First, there is the valid counterproposition that holds that there are moments where economic development can actually lead to political instability and decay.[85] Second, in many Third World nations, the establishment of constitutional regimes actually predated any significant qualitative change in the economy and the middle-class phenomenon. In the case of Turkey, for example, Orgun Ozbudun concludes after examining the "conventional indicators of socio-economic development" that Turkey was more democratic politically than it should have been.[86] Third, numerous empirical studies show a link between the rise of the middle class and the establishment of military regimes in developing nations.[87] In sum, the political patterns that characterize the contemporary Third World raise serious doubts about the assertion that a positive correlation exists between democracy and economic development or the advent of the middle class.

While the Egyptian economy remained predominantly agrarian until World War II, a nascent bourgeoisie emerged in the interwar era and became a distinct and significant class by the end of the 1930s. Various scholars use different criteria to define the national bourgeoisie in Egypt.[88] If our purpose is to locate the social class that enjoyed relative economic independence from the state and used the existing constitutional structures to defend its interests and to regulate its conflicts with other groups or classes, I would include three groups: the large landowners who invested in financial and industrial enterprises, the financiers, and the local industrialists.[89]

The large landowners were the product of the dramatic transformations in Egyptian agriculture that occurred between 1890 and 1914. This period was characterized by land reforms, the generalization of perennial irrigation, the construction of the Aswan Dam, and the massive expansion of cotton cultivation for export. The immediate result of these transformations was the rise of a small but politically powerful class of absentee landlords. Between 1894 and 1914, wealthy landlords, who represented 0.8 percent of all landowners, controlled 43.9 percent of the cultivable land.[90] The large landowners manifested a strong sense of common interest as early as 1898, when they established the Khedival Agricultural Society, followed by the Union des Agriculteurs in 1911, and the General Agricultural Syndicate in 1921.

When the large landowners established the 1921 syndicate, they had a clearly defined agenda. First, they wanted to establish their own cotton export company and sell directly to the spinners in Manchester and Liverpool. Second, they asked the government to protect the cotton market by limiting the cotton acreage. Third, they sought agricultural credits from the government to allow cotton growers more power to choose the time and the price for marketing their crop. Fourth, they wanted to supplant the role of the government in supervising the agricultural cooperatives. This role would give the landowners a voice in apportioning tax revenues from cotton to various uses and in determining land rents. Except for the elimination of middlemen between growers and spinners, the large landowners obtained most of their demands by inducing the parliament to pass laws in their favor, and by pressuring the government to advance money to cultivators. The state eventually became the major cotton buyer. It was the accumulated wealth of the large landowners that Tal'at Harb, an Egyptian financier, sought to attract to found the Bank Misr group. The enterprise was designed to become the financial tool of the Egyptian bourgeoisie.

The Bank Misr group was established in 1920 by Tal'at Harb, who convinced Egyptian landowners and large merchants to invest in what would be the only all-Egyptian financial institution in Egypt. The group's immediate objective was to bring in noninvested Egyptian capital, or Egyptian capital that would otherwise go to foreign banks with branches in Egypt. The only established national bank, al-Bank al-Ahli, existed primarily for the interests of foreign capital and was managed by non-Egyptians. The long-term objective of Bank Misr was to create the economic basis for political independence by establishing "financial, commercial, agricultural, transport, and insurance companies . . . which would give Egypt a say in its economic affairs."[91] By the late 1920s, Bank Misr emphasized the need to establish a strong industrial sector and proposed the formation of an organization that would include government representatives, industrialists, and financiers. The purpose of this organization was to prepare an industrialization plan that would allow Egypt to manufacture its own products instead of importing them from abroad.

The third segment of the national bourgeoisie was the Egyptian industrialists, organized in the Egyptian Federation of Industries. The federation was founded in 1922 by foreign-born industrialists who had been living in Egypt since the early twentieth century. For example, the founder, I. G. Levi, was born in Istanbul and moved to Cairo in 1903. Although the federation remained a predominantly foreign institution, by the late 1930s Egyptians constituted one-fourth of its total shareholders. In the 1930s, the Federation of Industries had a capital of £E 120 million and employed some 250,000 workers. Like Bank Misr, the federation was established to promote and protect local industry from imported manufactured products. Article 2 of its statutes specified that the federation's objective "was to bring together the important industrial establishments so that industrialists will be able to pursue their common interests and study the means for advancement . . . and if necessary the protection of local industry."[92] By the end of the 1930s, the federation adopted a more flexible attitude toward foreign capital, as Ismail Sidqi, the vice president, argued that foreign investment was necessary for the initial development of industry in Egypt.

Like the General Agricultural Syndicate, the Federation of Industries pressured the parliament to pass laws for protective tariffs and preferential treatments for certain industries, and to only gradually introduce labor reform legislation. Unlike the large landowners, the Egyptian industrialists did not have the total support of the Wafd. Wafdist governments and parliaments were more responsive to trade union demands, as many leaders of the labor movement were affiliated with the Wafd. Moreover, the industrialists were at odds with large landowners on two matters. The first pertained to taxation; the system of capitulation exempted industrial establishments from taxes until 1939. Large landowners complained in the parliament that the agricultural sector was paying the bulk of taxes in Egypt while the industrialists and merchants received a free ride. The industrialists, on the other hand, complained that the overtaxation of small and poor peasants limited the purchasing power of the *fellah* and consequently limited the expansion of domestic markets.

The interests of big Egyptian industrialists also conflicted with those of small industry. The Federation of Industries asked the Ministry of Commerce and Industry, for example, not to encourage small industries to manufacture goods already provided by large industries. In another instance, the federation warned that if taxes were levied systematically on all industries, the small shops would find a way not to pay their share because they were more difficult to inspect. The burden of industrial taxes, the federation complained, would be borne then by large industries only.

Situations arose, however, where the three groups found it necessary to cooperate. For example, there was the attempt by the Egyptian industrialists to gain the support of the large landowners concerning labor laws. By making a parallel between industrial and agricultural workers, the industrialists hoped to prevent the passing of any labor legislation. Bank Misr cooperated with the Federation of Industries on a number of issues, including preferential treatment for locally manufactured goods, the lowering of freight rates for raw materials and local products, the fight against the British Chamber of Commerce in Egypt, and the establishment of joint industrial enterprises.

Furthermore, while the Wafd defended the interests of the large landowners and the petite bourgeoisie, the party was attentive to the nationalist demands of the Egyptian industrial and financial groups. Tal'at Harb and other prominent members of the Egyptian Chamber of Commerce made a convincing argument linking political independence to economic independence. In 1922, for example, the Wafd backed the movement to boycott foreign products. The development of local industrial, commercial, financial, and agricultural enterprises remained a central objective of the Wafd. Wafdist parliaments voted for the allocation of credits, the creation of cooperatives, and the enactment of laws favoring the national bourgeoisie and encouraged private rather than government initiatives in the economy.

In spite of the weak and fragmented structure of the nascent Egyptian bourgeoisie, it was not subordinated to the state and was independent enough to exert political pressure. By raising the banner of economic independence and the protection of purely Egyptian enterprises, the national bourgeoisie secured the support of the political elite. Competition among the various groups took place within the framework of the existing constitutional structure, and most of their demands were of a legislative rather than political nature. In other words, the holding of public office to use the resources of the state for private interests did not pose a particular problem in Egypt at that time. All in all, the national bourgeoisie had a stake in maintaining the constitutional regime, for landowners, financiers, and industrialists could satisfy most of their needs within that framework. The argument that political conditions specific to the Third World prevent the consolidation of pluralistic politics among competing elites is not convincing in the case of Egypt.

To recapitulate, the institutional and structural approaches do not provide a satisfactory explanation for the failure of democracy in Egypt. The Egyptians had a long and diverse practice with semidemocratic colonial institutions that began as early as 1798. After formal independence in 1922, Egypt adopted a constitutional regime and a multiparty system that functioned rather poorly. However, poor functioning is not surprising in a nascent democracy. The political and economic performances of the regime were weak, but again that was not peculiar to Egypt. Finally Egypt had a nascent bourgeoisie that was fragmented but relatively independent, and also significantly involved in the constitutional arrangement to mitigate its conflicts with other groups. Missing in these approaches is the interplay between politics, culture, and identity. The normative appeal of Western liberal democracy is taken for granted. But as we have seen in previous chapters, liberalism is not culture free.

M irroring liberalism's dubious claims to cultural neutrality, Western scholarly works on this period of Egyptian history are no less objective. According to influential interpretations of the Egyptian liberal experiment in the field of Middle East politics, most prominently represented by the works of Nadav Safran and P. J. Vatikiotis, liberal democracy failed in Egypt because Egyptians did not quite understand the ideas of European liberalism.[1] For Safran, the most serious impediment to democratic consolidation in Egypt was the inability of Egyptian political thinkers—both liberal secularists and liberal Islamic reformers—to break from the traditional belief system and embrace a modern political ideology. The Egyptian liberal thinkers failed in this attempt, says Safran, because they "did not grasp the essential meaning and dynamics of democracy and constitutionalism."[2] Vatikiotis, on the other hand, holds that the liberal experiment failed in Egypt because the constitutional process was constantly interrupted to serve partisan political interests. Like Safran, however, Vatikiotis infers from this interference the "unreal hold which liberal European political ideas had over Egyptian leaders."[3] This depiction of the failure of liberalism in Egypt conveniently relieves the colonial order from much accountability and overlooks the cultural tensions and political contradictions that accompanied the imposition of "democratic" institutions under the auspices of colonial authority. It is not surprising that their analyses quite openly support the colonial project in Egypt. Safran, for example, duplicates the British government's own justifications when he portrays the occupation of Egypt as "restoring authority" and "establishing order" in a country "of vital importance for British imperial communications."[4] In a similar manner, Vatikiotis readily accepts the colonial view to justify the British military invasion of Egypt. He writes: "Whoever the Orabi Revolt represented and whatever its aspirations and objectives, it brought about the British occupation of Egypt."[5] The implication is quite clear: the Egyptians provoked the British and brought colonialism upon themselves. Serious scholars of modern colonialism and imperialism must take Vatikiotis's narrative with a grain of salt.

Because Safran and Vatikiotis simply reproduce the British colonial thesis, their assessments lead to the same flawed conclusion: Egyptian leaders failed to appreciate the liberal ideas of European political philosophy and missed a historic opportunity to embrace parliamentary rule. Thus Safran devotes the entire book to demonstrating where the Islamic reformers and Egyptian liberal thinkers went astray. And Vatikiotis, while admitting the British authorities' steady interventions in the democratic process, narrates the political events of the era to argue that the Egyptians were chiefly responsible for the continual political deadlocks and parliamentary crises.[6]

Not all Western scholars considered the failure of the liberal experiment in Egypt the result of native idiosyncrasies. French historians, in particular, appear to be more attentive to the antagonistic impulses that structure political mechanisms inherited from the colonial era. Marcel Colombe points to the ambiguous British commitment to Egypt in general, and to the disproportionate constitutional dispositions in particular.[7] Colombe makes clear at the outset that the British high commissioners in Cairo subordinated their liberal values to the supreme interests of Great Britain. This involved, implies Colombe, the regular and often forceful intervention of the British in the constitutional procedure when the imperial interest required it.[8]

But Colombe's characteristic critical attitude toward the British legacy in Egypt merits attention not just because it exposes maladroit British conduct, or because it delineates a more realistic representation of the political situation in colonial Egypt. Colombe's account is revealing because it somehow betrays the double-edged stance toward colonial liberalism even as he casts a critical picture of the British administration. When French scholars write about the British colonial rule and legacy in Egypt, they implicitly compare it with what could have been a more successful colonial project to "civilize" and transform the Orient in the Western image. This unsaid in French historiography emerges sometimes simply through slippage; sometimes it is more strategically camouflaged under the veneer of universal humanism. But the message is the same: the Europeans had the moral authority and historical responsibility to rescue the natives from their "suffering" and "misery," and this could be accomplished under "good" colonial sponsorship. For example, Colombe begins his book by recalling the great impact of the Napoleonic expedition to Egypt in 1798 and highlights the hopes that the European encounter had brought to the Egyptians. "Bonaparte pulled Egypt out of its lethargy," writes Colombe, but he never mentions Napoleon's notorious burning of entire villages whose populations resisted capitulation to the French flag. Later, Colombe deplores the strong hold of Arab and Islamic "identities" on the Egyptian people, or what he calls "populist xeno-phobia and nationalism," which he views as dangerous obstacles to any political development in the Orient.[9]

Echoing the same fear of the intractable "collective passions" in Egypt, Robert Montagne introduces L'évolution de l'Egypte with these words: "The task of Egyptian statesmen as well as of the cultivated minds of the Orient is to guide the masses whose politicization has been brought up, perhaps too prematurely, by the rapid introduction of democratic principles" (viii–ix). For Montagne and Colombe, the Egyptian masses can comprehend and become eligible for the privileges of democratic rule only after renouncing their "collective passions," in other words, their culture, religion, and iden-tity. To their disappointment, Colombe and Montagne conclude that British rule in Egypt did not lessen the strong hold of native cultural traditions on the Egyptian people. "In their ignorance," comments Montagne, "the [Egyptian] people still obey the simplest sentiments that [the Islamic] faith commands" (ix).

Another interesting account is Afaf Lutfi al-Sayyid's Egypt's Liberal Experi-ment.[10] To be sure, al-Sayyid rejects the colonial claim that liberalism failed in Egypt because the Egyptians are by nature "servile, unaccustomed to self-government, and incapable of appreciating it" (5). She argues that the nega-tive traits that Western scholars attribute to the Egyptian national character and to Islam are one-sided, inadequate, and based on the assumption that an Egyptian cannot become "modern" while remaining a "Muslim." But while al-Sayyid combats the colonial distortion of the "Egyptian character," she ties her argument to the same worldview that she attempts to undermine. For example, she claims that "although the establishment of liberal insti-tutions was thwarted, liberal ideas did flourish and Egyptian society was pushed willy-nilly along the path of progress" (248). She recognizes that colonial liberalism was based on the assumption that the natives would give up their identity and culture to enjoy the rights and privileges of modern citizenship. Yet instead of problematizing these conflicting demands, she attempts to reconcile them by showing exactly the possibility of amending Egyptian identity and character to accommodate the European-imposed requirements of citizenship. This view implicitly subscribes to the colonial claim she seeks to discredit.

The problem with these accounts cannot be redressed through more methodological rigor, conceptual sophistication, or reliable empirical evidence. These works are partial to a particular conception of the political that is contested within the societies they investigate. They therefore miss a central clue of the puzzle they want to reconstitute. It would seem reasonable to consider the founding of the Muslim Brotherhood, Jama'at al-Ikhwan al-Muslimun, by Sheikh Hassan al-Banna in 1928, and the broad popular appeal the movement still commands today, as a principled rejection of politics that discriminate against local cultures. Yet much of the literature on what is called today "political Islam," "Islamic fundamentalism," or "Islamic resurgence" continues to view movements like the Muslim Brotherhood in Egypt simply as a negative reaction against failed politics or social and economic depression. The possibility of modern, legitimate politics within Islamic discursive traditions—or even spiritual flourishing within Islam—is ethically denied and epistemologically censored.

This book contends that culture, language, and identity matter because they provide meaning and inform the political, even in liberal states and societies where the formal political process constantly strives to give an appearance of rational legitimacy. More specifically, I argue that the Egyptian liberal reformers formulated notions of political community and citizenship that excluded the majority of Egyptians. Hand in hand with embracing modern constitutionalism and celebrating the accouterments of parliamentary politics, the Egyptian liberal reformers attempted to redefine the territorial, historical, racial, and cultural boundaries of the new Egyptian political community to which ordinary Egyptians were supposed to owe allegiance. The trouble with this is that most Egyptians had no place in the newly defined political community because it was emphatically defined to link Egypt and Egyptians to a European origin. I suggest that this effacement of "self" was inevitable because the Egyptian liberal reformers borrowed the concepts of nationhood and citizenship from a European liberalism that was complicit in the colonial project. By accepting and normalizing colonial distortions of native culture and history, the Egyptian liberals contradicted the basic political principles of liberalism. To become eligible for the supposed privi-leges of modern citizenship, the Egyptian individual had to be appropriated, transformed, controlled, and alienated from his or her communal identity.

Moreover, I argue that liberalism's contradictory tendencies and cultural biases are inscribed in texts that exist before the colonial situation. One ordi-nary but revealing example was Egypt's 1923 Constitution. The text guaran-tees formal civil and political rights that were compatible with the most liberal constitutions in Europe at the time. Yet the Constitution assumes a political community whose members are not only disconnected from their history and traditions but also believe in the superiority of European culture and social manners and enthusiastically embrace them as their own.

Although these arguments are certainly critical of liberalism's claims to cultural neutrality and universality, it should be clear that they are not incom-patible with the liberal quest for self-emancipation. Yet that quest cannot be the exclusive domain of modern liberalism.

A Moroccan religious reformer by the name of Mohammed Ibn Abdallah al-Muwaqqit al-Murrâkushi (1894–1949), an unfamiliar figure in the exten-sive tradition of Islamic reformism, reveals the low status of the political in Muslim societies through an eloquent silence. In a part chronicle, part liter-ary text, al-Muwaqqit describes the interaction between traditional society and the modern colonial order using the metaphor of a people forced on board a ship, navigated by strangers into the unknown.[11] The European captain of the imaginary ship, an obvious reference to colonial power, makes it clear soon after embarking that he is solely in charge and prohibits indige-nous passengers from positions of command. Al-Muwaqqit, who earned this name from his real-life duty as custodian of ritual time in Marrakech, wrote this text to decry the "apocalyptic" changes taking place under colo-nial rule. Throughout the text, he denounces in the strongest terms those Muslim passengers who mimic European social and cultural habits, and describes the loss of religious traditions as the greatest of all injustices. Curiously, the narrator and his companions are unmoved by the captain's imposed political restrictions, and the text's indifference to the ship's com-mand seems to imply passive submission to colonial political domination. Ultimately what leads the ship/community to wreckage is the loss of self, not the ship being under the command of an alien invader.[12] I suggest that al-Muwaqqit's silence about the captain's formal prerogatives—to the extent that they do not interfere with the community's ritual life and time—reflects something profound and misunderstood about Islamic political traditions: a radical rejection of reason as the sole source of political authority. The captain's command of the ship is depicted in the novel as an arbitrary act despite the author's awareness of its intelligible causes. The ship is navigating the unknown despite the captain's technical knowledge. The captain's leadership is irrelevant to the binding of the community despite his claim to formal political authority. Finally, cultural autonomy is a fundamental demand despite compliance with the captain's interdiction of political activity. In sum, political reason is delegated to an inferior status: it is neither formative nor representative of the collective.

By contrast, confidence in reason as the source of authority, civilization, political community, and cultural conformity is precisely what justified liberalism's complicity with colonial conquest. In many respects, the most serious political challenge to liberalism's claim to cultural neutrality and universal reason remains the various Islamic ethical visions of the political community. The growing political influence of this challenge in contemporary Muslim societies, commonly known as Islamic fundamentalism, suggests a much more complex relationship between the political and religious spheres than current literature on the topic tends to project.

In a provocative theoretical study of the Egyptian Islamic thinker Sayyid Qutb (1906–66), Roxanne Euben observes that beyond the common characterization of Islam as the "Green Peril" in Western public discourse, what is more interesting is Western liberalism's sense of dismay and incomprehension that Islamic political principles have survived the modern era.[13] Euben analyzes Western scholarship on Islamic fundamentalism to argue that this incomprehension permeates a social scientific discourse that explains the appeal to fundamentalist ideas merely as a function of cultural, political, or structural frustration (25–33). Thus the prospect that Islamic fundamentalism might actually articulate an appealing political alternative is conceptually impossible. But through a penetrating analysis of Sayyid Qutb's discussions of reason, divine revelation, interpretation, and community, Euben reveals a coherent "ethico-political vision" that transcends the narrow socioeconomic and political conditions of Egypt to offer a moral critique of modern political assumptions that exclude religious values from political sovereignty.

Euben's theoretical perspective is valuable and relevant to my critique of colonial liberalism in at least two respects. First, she made Sayyid Qutb's rejection of Western rationalism familiar and intelligible to a Western academy all too inclined to dismiss religious, most notably Islamic, critiques as uninformed and irrational. She puts Qutb's apprehension about placing reason at the center of sovereignty on a par with a host of prominent Western critics of the failures of modernity. Euben's study has cleared a significant conceptual hurdle by characterizing apprehensions about Western liberal principles as competing and intelligible—even if problematic—worldviews, not as the final gasps of "exhausted . . . alternatives" (6). Thus to insist on blaming the strong hold of "backward," "irrational" Islamic values and traditions for the failure of the liberal experiment in Egypt, or for the absence of democracy in the Muslim world in general, suggests a narcissistic sense of normative and epistemological self-confidence.

Euben's study of Qutb's fundamentalist views is important in another respect. Her critical examination of social scientific analyses of Islamic fundamentalism reveals the flaw of establishing a causal relation between social and material conditions and the appeal of religious values. She does not deny that Islamic fundamentalist ideas express social and economic pressures, but she problematizes the common denial of Islam's ethical appeal within social scientific studies. In this scholarship, Islamic fundamentalism is depicted as an "irrational" "resurgent" phenomenon that can be understood only in terms of failures. Hence a central element of Islamic fundamentalism, the vision of the ethical community it seeks to establish, is censored. By a similar argument, the view that the liberal experiment in Egypt failed simply because the structural conditions and institutional arrangements were inadequate reproduces the same biased views that take for granted the moral and cultural superiority of liberalism. These views leave no room for doubting the rejection of liberal ideas on intelligible ethical grounds. Hence Euben attempts to explain the fundamentalists' own understanding of the world in their own language. She quotes the Moroccan Islamic reformer Abdessalam Yassin to illustrate the discrepancy between what modernization theory, class analysis, and rational choice theory proclaim and what a theorist activist says:

> For you [the West], this spiritual region remains voluntarily opaque. You do not want to see it. You do not want to look at it. . . . People do not come to Islam as an alternative for their social misfortunes. People come to Islam in response to a call, a call which goes very far and very deep in the human soul. I do not know by which accident of history or by which misfortune "Homo Occidentalus," as you say, has lost this organ, which permits the perception of things that are spiritual. . . . All that he has left are elements of economic, political, and social analysis . . . things that are earthbound in some way. (20)

To be sure, privileging moral values and spirituality over reason and rationality, as Muslim political thinkers and reformers suggest in different

ways, has its own problems. Most notably, morally grounded political principles deny the existence of political conflicts that characterize any political
community. Rather than providing an emancipating alternative to liberalism, the subordination of the political to moral considerations is often used
to legitimate oppressive rule or informal violence. In the Muslim world, the
religious and political battlefields are dominated by conservative clerics in
the service of the state and radical Islamists trying to impose their extremist
vision and interpretation of Islam. Still, our understanding of politics in the
Muslim world would be enriched if we take more seriously Yassin's view that
"social misfortunes" are not the only reason why Muslims might reject
Western political institutions and draw on their own traditions.

Preface

1   Abdelfattah Kilito, "Les mots canins," in *Du bilinguisme*, ed. Abdelkebir Khatibi (Paris: Denoël, 1985). An English version is published as "Dog Words," trans. Ziad Elmarsafy, in *Displacements: Cultural Identities in Question*, ed. Angelika Bammer (Bloomington: Indiana University Press, 1994).

2   President George W. Bush, speaking at the annual dinner of the American Enterprise Institute for Public Policy Research, February 26, 2003, posted April 2, 2003, at www.aei.org.

3   President Bush, discussing freedom in Iraq and the Middle East, remarks by the president at the twentieth anniversary of the National Endowment of Democracy, October 16, posted November 6, 2003, at www.ned.org.

4   Anne Norton, *Ninety-five Theses on Politics, Culture, and Method* (New Haven: Yale University Press, 2004).

5   Louis Althusser and Étienne Balibar, *Reading Capital* (London: Verso Editions, 1979).

Introduction

1   See, for example, Rashid Khalidi, *Resurrecting Empire: Western Footprints and America's Perilous Path in the Middle East* (Boston: Beacon Press, 2004); and Robert Fisk, *The Great War for Civilization: The Conquest of the Middle East* (London: Fourth Estate, 2005).

2   Although Egypt did not have large European colonial settlements, which usually define the term *colony* such as in Algeria, the British occupation of Egypt was more than just formal imperial control of political and economic affairs.

3   Israel Gershoni and James Jankowski, *Egypt, Islam, and the Arabs: The Search for Egyptian Nationhood, 1900–1930* (London: Oxford University Press, 1986).

4   Afaf Lutfi al-Sayyid-Marsot, *Egypt's Liberal Experiment, 1922–1936* (Berkeley: University of California Press, 1977).

5   Jacques Lacan, *Écrits* (Paris: Éditions du Seuil, 1966).

6   See Lewis R. Gordon, "The Black and the Body Politic: Fanon's Existential

Phenomenological Critique of Psychoanalysis," in *Fanon: A Critical Reader*, ed. Lewis R. Gordon et al. (Oxford: Blackwell, 1996).

7 Lacan, *Écrits*.

8 *The Works of Jeremy Bentham*, ed. J. Bowring (London: Simpkin, 1843); James Mill, *The History of British India*, ed. H. H. Wilson (London: J. Madden, 1884); John Stuart Mill, *Three Essays* (Oxford: Oxford University Press, 1975); J. R. Seeley, *The Expansion of England* (Chicago: University of Chicago Press, 1971).

9 Uday Singh Mehta, *Liberalism and Empire: A Study in Nineteenth-Century British Liberal Thought* (Chicago: University of Chicago Press, 1999).

10 Ibid., 17–21.

11 Edward Said, *Orientalism* (New York: Vintage Books, 1979), 42.

12 Said, *Culture and Imperialism* (New York: Knopf, 1993), 263–75.

13 Homi Bhabha, "The Other Question . . . ," *Screen* 24, no. 6 (1983): 18–36; Bhabha, "Of Mimicry and Man: The Ambivalence of Colonial Discourse," *October* 28 (spring 1984): 125–35; Ashis Nandy, *The Intimate Enemy: Loss and Recovery of Self under Colonialism* (Delhi: Oxford University Press, 1983); and Karen T. Hansen, ed., *African Encounters with Domesticity* (New Brunswick, N.J.: Rutgers University Press, 1992).

14 Max Weber, *Economy and Society*, vol. 2, ed. Guenther Roth and Claus Wittich (Berkeley: University of California Press, 1978), 903. For a fuller discussion of this concept, see also 901–26.

15 Max Weber's *The Protestant Ethic and the Spirit of Capitalism* is the classic example of the convergence between modern political institutions and religious models of the covenant.

16 Weber, *Economy and Society*, 921–23.

17 Leonard Binder, "Prolegomena to the Comparative Study of Middle Eastern Governments," *American Political Science Review* 51 (1957); William Zartman, "Political Science," in *The Study of the Middle East: Research and Scholarship in the Humanities and the Social Sciences*, ed. Leonard Binder (New York: Wiley, 1976); James Bill, "Comparative Middle East Politics: Still in Search of a Theory," *Political Science and Politics* 27, no. 3 (September 1994); Mark Tessler, ed., *Area Studies and Social Science: Strategies for Understanding Middle East Politics* (Bloomington: Indiana University Press, 1999); Lisa Anderson, ed., *Transitions to Democracy* (New York: Columbia University Press, 1999).

18 Samuel Huntington, *The Third Wave: Democratization in the Late Twentieth Century* (Norman: University of Oklahoma Press, 1991); Ghassam Salame, ed., *Democracy without Democrats? The Renewal of Politics in the Muslim World* (London: I. B. Tauris); and Tessler, *Area Studies and Social Science*.

19 Max Weber, *The Protestant Ethic and the Spirit of Capitalism*, trans. Talcott Parsons (1905; New York: Scribner, 1958).

20 Patai, *The Arab Mind* (New York: Scribner, 1973); Fatima Mernissi, *Beyond the Veil: Male-Female Dynamics in a Modern Muslim Society* (Cambridge, Mass.: Schenkman, 1975); Fouad Ajami, *The Arab Predicament: Arab Political Thought and Practice since 1967* (New York: Cambridge University Press, 1981); Raphael David Pryce-Jones, *The Closed Circle: An Interpretation of the Arabs* (New York: Harper and Row, 1989);

Elie Keddouri, *Democracy and Arab Political Culture* (Washington: Washington Institute for Near East Policy, 1992); and Bernard Lewis, "Islam and Liberal Democracy: A Historical Overview," *Journal of Democracy* 7, no. 2 (1996): 52–63.

21 William B. Quandt, *Revolution and Political Leadership: Algeria, 1954–1968* (Cambridge: MIT Press, 1969); John Waterbury, *The Commander of the Faithful: The Moroccan Political Elite; A Study in Segmented Politics* (London: Weidenfeld and Nicolson, 1970); Marvin Zonis, *The Political Elite of Iran* (Princeton: Princeton University Press, 1971); Michael Hudson, *Arab Politics: The Search for Legitimacy* (New Haven: Yale University Press, 1977); Robert Bianchi, *Interest Groups and Political Development in Turkey* (Princeton: Princeton University Press, 1984); Philip Khoury and Joseph Kostiner, eds., *Tribes and State Formation in the Middle East* (Berkeley: University of California Press, 1990).

22 John Hall, *Powers and Liberties: The Causes and Consequences of the Rise of the West* (London: Penguin, 1985).

23 Ernest Gellner, "Civil Society in Historical Context," *International Social Science Journal* 129 (August 1991); Bernard Lewis, *Islam and the West* (New York: Oxford University Press, 1993).

24 Ellis Goldberg et al., *Rules and Rights in the Middle East: Democracy, Law, and Society* (Seattle: University of Washington Press, 1993); Augustus Richard Norton, ed., *Civil Society in the Middle East*, 2 vols. (Leiden: E. J. Brill, 1994–95).

25 Diane Singerman, *Avenues of Political Participation: Family, Politics, and Networks in Urban Quarters in Cairo* (Princeton: Princeton University Press, 1995).

26 Anthropologists can do this kind of research, but they are skeptical about causal explanations and generalizations. See, for example, Clifford Geertz, *The Interpretation of Cultures* (New York: Basic Books, 1973).

27 Giacomo Luciani, "Economic Foundations of Democracy and Authoritarianism in the Arab World: The Arab World in Comparative Perspectives," *Arab Studies Quarterly* 10 (1988); Daniel Brumberg, "Authoritarian Legacies and Reform Strategies in the Arab World," in *Political Liberalization and Democratization in the Arab World: Theoretical Perspectives*, vol. 1, ed. Rex Brynen, Bahgat Korany, and Paul Noble (Boulder, Colo.: Lynne Rienner, 1995); Alan Richards and John Waterbury, *A Political Economy of the Middle East* (Boulder, Colo.: Westview Press, 1996).

28 Rex Brynen, Bahgat Korany, and Paul Noble, eds., *Political Liberalization and Democratization in the Arab World: Theoretical Perspectives*, vol. 1 (Boulder, Colo.: Lynne Rienner, 1995).

29 Abdo Baaklini et al., *Legislative Politics in the Arab World: The Resurgence of Democratic Institutions* (Boulder, Colo.: Lynne Rienner, 1999).

one Colonialism as a Historical Phenomenon

1 Uday Singh Mehta, *Liberalism and Empire: A Study in Nineteenth-Century British Liberal Thought* (Chicago: University of Chicago Press, 1999).

2 Edward Said, *Orientalism* (New York: Vintage Books, 1979), 3.

3 One has of course to distinguish "postcolonial theorists" (e.g., Said, Spivak, and Bhabha) from "postcolonial critics" (e.g., Perry, Ahmad, Abdul JanMo-

hamed). See Bart Moore-Gilbert, *Postcolonial Theory: Context, Practices, Politics* (New York: Verso, 1997); and Robert J. C. Young, *Colonial Desire: Hybridity in Theory, Culture and Race* (New York: Routledge, 1995).

4   Spivak's work is much less engaged with Frantz Fanon.

5   Frantz Fanon, *Black Skin, White Masks*, trans. C. L. Markmann (New York: Grove Press, 1967).

6   Aimé Césaire, *Discourse on Colonialism*, trans. Joan Pinkharn (New York: Monthly Review Press, 1972).

7   Ibid., 16.

8   Ibid., 22–23.

9   Cheikh Anta Diop, *Nations négres et culture* (Paris: Editions Africaine, 1955); George G. M. James, *Stolen Legacy: The Greeks Were Not the Authors of Greek Philosophy, but the People of North Africa, Commonly Called the Egyptians* (New York: Philosophical Library, 1954).

10   W. E. B. Du Bois, *The World and Africa* (New York: International Publishers, 1965), and *The Souls of Black Folk* (New York: Dodd, Mead, 1966); Albert Memmi, *The Colonizer and the Colonized* (Boston: Beacon Press, 1991).

11   Du Bois, *The World and Africa*, 78.

12   Memmi, *The Colonizer and the Colonized*, viii.

13   See, for example, Gayatri Chakravorty Spivak, "The Rani of Surmur," in *Europe and Its Others: Essex Conference on the Sociology of Literature*, vol. 1 (Colchester: University of Essex, 1984), 128–45; Lata Mani, "The Production of Discourse on Sati in Early Nineteenth-Century Bengal," in Spivak, *Europe and Its Others*, 107–27; Abdul JanMohamed, "Humanism and Minority Literature: Towards a Definition of a Counter-hegemonic Discourse," *Boundary* 2 (spring–fall 1984): 281–99; Homi Bhabha, "Of Mimicry and Man: The Ambivalence of Colonial Discourse," *October* 28 (spring 1984): 125–33; and Ashis Nandy, *The Intimate Enemy: Loss and Recovery of Self under Colonialism* (Delhi: Oxford University Press, 1983). For a critique of the recent literature on colonialism, see Benita Perry, "Problems in Current Theories of Colonial Discourse," *Oxford Literary Review* 9, nos. 1–2 (1987): 27–58.

14   Nandy, *The Intimate Enemy*, 64–71.

15   Said, *Orientalism*, 2.

16   Edward Said, *Culture and Imperialism* (New York: Knopf, 1993), xii.

17   Ibid., xxv, 239–61.

18   Bhabha, "Of Mimicry and Man," 126.

19   Ibid., 129.

20   Although Bhabha makes no general theoretical claims, his essays in *The Location of Culture* converge on this point. See Homi K. Bhabha, *The Location of Culture* (London: Routledge, 1994).

21   Bhabha, "Interrogating Identity: Frantz Fanon and the Postcolonial Prerogative," in *The Location of Culture*.

22   Octave Mannoni, *Prospero and Caliban: The Psychology of Colonization*, trans. Pamela Powesland (New York: Praeger, 1964).

23   Fanon, *Black Skin, White Masks*, 85.

24 Frantz Fanon, *The Wretched of the Earth*, trans. Constance Farrington (London: MacGibbon and Kee, 1965).

25 On the similarities between early anticolonial critics and postcolonial theorists, see Moore-Gilbert, *Postcolonial Theory*, chapter 5.

26 Fanon, *The Wretched of the Earth*.

27 Fanon, citing Aimé Césaire's *Cahier d'un retour au pays natal*, in *Black Skin, White Masks*, 123–24.

28 On this important difference, see Ronald Judy, "Fanon's Body of Black Experience," and Lewis Gordon, "The Black and the Body Politic: Fanon's Existential Phenomenological Critique of Psychoanalysis," in *Fanon: A Critical Reader*, ed. Lewis R. Gordon et al. (Cambridge: Blackwell Publishers, 1996), 53–73.

29 I maintain that Fanon never abandoned this quest in later writings, only that the means to achieve it changed.

30 To be sure, Fanon declares in the introduction to *Black Skin, White Masks* that "the black must wage his war on both levels," the subjective and objective. But throughout the book, Fanon's main concern is to explain the psychological predisposition of the black in a racist context.

31 Jacques Lacan, *Esquisse d'une vie: Histoire d'un système de pensée* (Paris: Fayard, 1993), 154.

32 The reason why the idea of reestablishing the symbolic order of the colonized does not transpire clearly in Fanon's writings has to do with his initial grounding of colonial hatred in the biological. The ensuing binaries—black-white, colonizer-colonized, settler-native—exclude the possibility of a triangular structure where a self, like an infant, is ambiguously located between the colonial "other," the site of (motherly) desire, and the native "Other," the site of speech where the symbolic (father) reigns supreme. That Fanon does not make this connection remains, however, a puzzle in light of his repeated references to the familial metaphor to describe the colonial situation.

33 Fanon, *The Wretched of the Earth*, 148–205, 206–48.

34 Ibid., 311–16.

35 Frantz Fanon, *Studies in a Dying Colonialism*, trans. Haakon Chevalier (New York: Monthly Review Press, 1965), 36–67.

36 Ibid., 37.

37 Frantz Fanon, "Spontaneity: Its Strength and Weakness," in *The Wretched of the Earth*, 107–47.

38 Ibid., 69–97.

39 For example, Hannah Arendt and others. See Marie Perinbam, *Holy Violence: The Revolutionary Thought of Frantz Fanon* (Washington: Three Continents Press, 1982), 120n1.

40 On the question of violence in Fanon's writings, see Perinbam, *Holy Violence*.

41 Fanon, *The Wretched of the Earth*, 255.

42 See especially "Le séminaire sur 'La Lettre Volée,'" "Au-delà du 'Principe de Réalité,'" "Le stade du miroir comme fondateur de la fonction du Je," and "L'agressivité en psychanalyse," in *Écrits*, by Jacques Lacan (Paris: Éditions du Seuil, 1966).

43 The best available synthesis of the significance and articulation of alienation in Lacan's writings is in Anika Lemaire, *Jacques Lacan*, trans. David Macey (Boston: Routledge and Kegan Paul, 1977); see esp. 78–84 and 176–79.

44 Ibid., 176.

45 Lacan, *Écrits*, 537–41.

46 On the normalizing ramifications of entry into the "Symbolic Order," see Louis Althusser, *Writings on Psychoanalysis: Freud and Lacan*, trans. Jeffrey Mehlman (New York: Columbia University Press, 1996).

47 On Lacan's complex departure from Freud on this point, see Anthony Wilden, "Lacan and the Discourse of the Other," in *The Language of the Self*, by Jacques Lacan, trans. Anthony Wilden (Baltimore: Johns Hopkins University Press, 1968); and Julia Kristeva, *Language: The Unknown*, trans. Anne Menke (New York: Columbia University Press, 1989), 265–77.

48 Lacan, "The Agency of the Letter," and "Discours de Rome," in *Écrits*.

49 On this point, see Elisabeth Roudinesco, *La bataille de cent ans: Histoire de la psychanalyse en France*, vol. 2 (Paris: Éditions du Seuil, 1986), 131–41.

50 Lemaire, *Jacques Lacan*, 83–84.

51 John Stuart Mill, "On Liberty," in *Utilitarianism, Liberty, Representative Government*, ed. H. B. Acton (London: J. M. Dent and Sons, 1972), 38.

52 Ibid., 383.

two **The Colonial Encounter in Egypt**

1 Cited in Anouar Louca, "Contacts culturels avec l'occident," in *L'Egypte aujourd'hui* (Paris: Editions du CNRS, 1977), 109.

2 Ibid.

3 Abd al-Rahman al-Jabarti, *Muddat al-Fransis bi-Misr*, trans. by S. Moreh as *Al-Jabarti's Chronicle of the First Seven Months of the French Occupation of Egypt* (Leiden: E. J. Brill, 1975), 41–52.

4 Ibid., 40.

5 Ibid., 41.

6 Cited in Jean Lacouture and Sirnonne Lacouture, *Egypt in Transition*, trans. Francis Scrape (New York: Criterion Book, 1958), 43.

7 Al-Jabarti, *Muddat al-Fransis bi-Misr*, 47.

8 The complete text of Napoleon's letter is in al-Raafi'i, *Tarikh al-haraka al-qawmiya wa wa-tawwur nizam al-hukm fi misr*, vol. 2 (Cairo: JMA, 1980), 349–50.

9 Ibid., 351.

10 Ibid., 15.

11 Edward Said, *Culture and Imperialism* (New York: Knopf, 1993), 263–75.

12 Afaf Lutfi al-Sayyid Marsot, *Egypt in the Reign of Muhammad 'Ali* (Cambridge: Cambridge University Press, 1984).

13 Timothy Mitchell, *Colonising Egypt* (Cambridge: Cambridge University Press, 1988).

14 Conventional historical accounts of Egyptian political history are obviously aware of Napoleon's short-lived expedition and long-lasting legacy, but they fail

to see the theoretical and analytical relevance of this paradox to understanding the confluence between literary and historical colonialism. See, for example, Ronald Robinson, John Gallagher, and Alice Denny, *Africa and the Victorians* (London: Macmillan, 1981); P. J. Vatikiotis, *The History of Egypt: From Muhammad Ali to Mubarak* (Baltimore: Johns Hopkins University Press, 1985); and Nadav Safran, *Egypt in Search of Political Community* (Cambridge: Harvard University Press, 1961).

15 Juan R. I. Cole, *Colonialism and Revolution in the Middle East: Social and Cultural Origins of Egypt's 'Urabi Movement* (Princeton, N.J.: Princeton University Press, 1993), 31–35.

16 Israel Gershoni and James Jankowski, *Egypt, Islam, and the Arabs: The Search for Egyptian Nationhood, 1900–1930* (London: Oxford University Press, 1986).

17 Abdelfattah Kilito, "Dog Words," in *Displacements: Cultural Identities in Question; Theories of Contemporary Culture*, ed. Angelika Bammer (Bloomington: Indiana University Press, 1994).

18 As quoted in Mitchell, *Colonising Egypt*, 75.

19 Nubar Pasha, as quoted in Mitchell, *Colonising Egypt*, 75.

20 See Albert Hourani, *Arabic Thought in the Liberal Age* (London: Oxford University Press, 1970); and Nikki Keddie, *Sayyid Jamal al-Din al-Afghani: A Political Biography* (Berkeley: University of California Press, 1972).

21 Mitchell, *Colonising Egypt*, 35, 46, 95, 103, 175–76.

22 Ibid., 36–94.

23 Ibid., 104–14.

24 The Earl of Cromer [Evelyn Baring], *Modern Egypt*, vol. 1 (New York: Macmillan, 1908), 298–99.

25 Cited in Jean and Simonne Lacouture, *Egypt in Transition*, trans. Francis Scarfe (New York: Criterion, 1958), 39.

26 Cromer, *Modern Egypt*, vol. 2 (New York: Macmillan, 1908), 228.

27 Jacques Berque, *Egypt: Imperialism and Revolution*, trans. Jean Stewart (New York: Praeger, 1972), 121.

28 Robinson, Gallagher, and Denny, *Africa and the Victorians*; and Vatikiotis, *The History of Egypt*, 141–66.

29 Cole, *Colonialism and Revolution*; and Berque, *Egypt*.

30 Cole, *Colonialism and Revolution*, 235–38.

31 The official justification was the Alexandria riot on June 11, which left 250 Egyptians and 50 Europeans dead.

32 Vatikiotis, *The History of Egypt*, 155–56.

33 Cole, *Colonialism and Revolution*, 205.

34 Cromer, *Modern Egypt*, 2:274–75.

35 Ibid., chap. 39, "The Machinery of Government."

36 Cromer, *Modern Egypt*, 1:152.

37 Berque, *Egypt*, 359.

38 Cromer, *Modern Egypt*, 1:564–65.

39 The 1923 Constitution, which comprises some 170 articles, hardly mentions Islam or religion. The integral text of the French original of the 1923 Constitu-

tion can be found in Hassan Chafik, *Statut Juridique International de l'Egypte* (Paris: Editions Internationales, 1928), 197–222.

40 Vatikiotis, *The History of Egypt*, 271–72.

41 Abdel 'Azim Ramdan, *Tatawur al-Haraka al-Wataniya Fi Misr: 1918–1936* (Cairo, 1968), 339–40.

42 Abdel Rahman al- al-Raafi'i, *Fi A'qab al-Thawra al-Misriyya*, vol. 1 (Cairo, 1947), 46.

43 Muhammad Husayn Haykal, *Mudhakkarat Fi al-Siyassa al-Misriyya: 1912–1937*, vol. 1 (Cairo: Maktabat al-Nahdha al-Misriyya, 1951), 155–65.

44 From the Egyptian side, see al-Raafi'i, *Tarikh al-haraka al-qawmiya wa wa-tawwur nizam al-hukm fi misr*; Abdel 'Azim Ramdan, *Tatawur al-Haraka al-Wataniya Fi Misr*; Luwis 'Awad, *Tarikh al-Fikr al-Misri alHadith* (Cairo: Dar al-Hilal, 1983); Anouar Abdel-Malek, *Egypte: Social Militaire* (Paris: Editions du Seuil, 1962); and Afaf Lutfi al-Sayyid, *Egypt's Liberal Experiment: 1922–1936* (Berkeley: University of California Press, 1977). From the Western side, see Jacob Landau, *Parliaments and Parties in Egypt* (Tel Aviv: Israel Publishing House, 1953); Safran, *Egypt in Search of Political Community*; Vatikiotis, *The History of Egypt*; Berque, *Egypt*; and Leonard Binder, *Islamic Liberalism: A Critique of Development Ideologies* (Chicago: University of Chicago Press, 1988).

45 The Constitution was a faithful reproduction of the liberal principles enforced at that time by many European democracies: equal rights and duties to all Egyptians regardless of race, language, or religion; freedom of property, opinion, and conscience; et cetera.

46 See the discussion by James Boyd White in *When Words Lose Their Meaning* (Chicago: University of Chicago Press, 1980), 192–230.

47 Ibid., 192.

48 This process should be familiar to students of the three scriptural religions: Judaism, Christianity, and Islam. The process is most explicit in Islam, where the constitution of the religious-political Islamic Umma was emphatically based on the act of "reading" and "learning." According to the Islamic tradition, the first sura of the Qur'an, revealed to the prophet Muhammad by the archangel Gabriel, was *Surat al'Alaq*, "The Blood-Clot," also referred to as *Surat Iqraa*, which combines three meanings: Read, Recite, and Proclaim. The sura reads as follows: "In the Name of God, the Merciful, the Compassionate; Recite: In the Name of thy Lord who created, created Man of a blood-clot. Recite: And thy Lord is the Most Generous, who taught by the pen, taught Man that he knew not." Translation of the Qur'an, sura 96, from Arthur J. Arberry, *The Koran Interpreted*, vol. 11 (London: Macmillan, 1965), 345.

49 White, *When Words Lose Their Meaning*. For a similar argument, see also William Harris, "Bonding Words and Polity: The Logic of the American Constitution," *American Political Science Review* 76 (1982): 34–45.

50 Berque, *Egypt*, 363.

51 Roland Barthes, *Mythologies* (Paris: Editions du Seuil, 1957), 197–200.

52 Paul Ricoeur, "The Model of the Text," in *Interpretive Social Sciences*, ed. Paul

Rabinow and William Sullivan (Berkeley: University of California Press, 1987), 73–101.

53 See, for example, Berque, *Egypt*; Safran, *Egypt in Search of Political Community*; and Afaf al-Sayyid, *Egypt's Liberal Experiment.*

54 Amos Peaslee, ed., *Constitutions of Nations*, vol. 1, *Afghanistan to Finland* (Concord: Rumford Press, 1950), 721.

55 Muhammed Husayn Haykal, *Mudhakarat fi al-Siyassa*, 131–33.

56 Jacob Landau, *Parliaments and Parties in Egypt*, 60.

57 Berque, *Egypt*, 459.

58 I cannot resist mentioning again the reaction of al-Jabarti to the Arabic proclamation circulated by Napoleon's soldiers on the day after they invaded Alexandria. While the people of Alexandria were running terrified in the streets wondering what would happen to their lives, al-Jabarti was busy correcting the grammatical mistakes and odd structure of the text circulated by Napoleon. See chapter 4.

59 A similar reading is given by Safran in *Egypt in Search of Political Community*: "Article 1 of the Constitution declared Egypt to be a 'sovereign state, free and independent,' thereby substituting the modern concept of nation-state for the traditional concept of the ummah. Further, it precluded submission of Egypt to any Islamic super state by declaring its sovereignty is 'indivisible and inalienable'" (109–10).

60 Peaslee, *Constitutions of Nations*, 733.

61 Ibid., 728.

three Defining the Boundaries of the Political Community

1   See section 1 ("Etat Moral") of "Les Revendications Nationales Egyptiennes: Memoire Presenté par la Délégation Egyptienne Chargée de Défendre la Cause de l'Indépendance de l'Egypte," in U.S. Department of State, *Records of the Department of State relating to Political Relations between Egypt and Other States: 1910–29,* microfilm 430A. J.

2   The Earl of Cromer [Evelyn Baring], *Modern Egypt* (New York: Macmillan, 1968), 326.

3   Mahmud Abu al-Fath, *Al-Mas'ala al-Misriyya wa al-Wafd* (Cairo, [1921?]).

4   Ibid.

5   "Les Revendications Nationales," sections 2 and 22. In his memoirs, Lashin also describes the feelings of "bitterness and depression" that struck the Egyptian nationalists after learning about Britain's support of Hijazi independence. See Abd al-Khalik Lashin, *Saad Zaghlul ma Dawruhu fi al-Siyassa al-Mesreya* (Cairo: Dar al-Awdah, 1975), 125.

6   Remarking on the Egyptian newspapers' tendency to portray Egypt as a Western nation, a reader from Bethlehem sent a letter to the monthly magazine *Al-Hilal* asking, "Is Egypt a Western or Oriental kingdom?" The editor answered: "Because of her geographic position Egypt is an African Oriental kingdom. But her

scientific and social renaissance supports what Khedive Ismail Pasha has said about Egypt being a piece of Europe." *Al-Hilal*, May 1930, 886. On this issue see, for example, Salama Musa, "Al Shark Shark wal Gharb Gharb," *al-Majalla al-Jadida*, May 1930, 882–88, and "Al-Messreyun Umma Gharbiya," *al-Hilal*, December 1928, 177–81; Muhammad Sharaf, "Layssa al-Messreyun Sameyun," *al-Majalla al-Jadida*, May 1930, 897–900, and "Al-Mesreyun Umma Ghayr Shar-keya," *al-Majalla al-Jadida*, June 1930, 962–64; Mansur Fahmy, "Al-Jensseya al-Mesreya," *al-Sufur*, 1916, 2–3; Abd Razak Sanhuri, "Al-Islam wa Sharq," *Mulhaq al-Siyasa*, October 1932, 16; Abdelhamid Bakri, "Al-Sharq wal Ghrab," *al-Rabita al-Sharqiyy*, February 1929, 15; and Abdelkader Hamza, "Makan Mesr mina al 'Arab wal Qawmeya al 'Arabeya," *al-Balagh*, September 1933, 1.

7   "Les Revendications Nationales," section 17.

8   Michel Foucault developed the concept of "objectification" in three works, mainly *Madness and Civilization*, trans. Richard Howard (New York: Pantheon, 1965); *The Birth of the Clinic*, trans. A. M. Sheridan Smith (New York: Pantheon, 1973); and *Discipline and Punish*, trans. Alan Sheridan (New York: Pantheon, 1977). See Foucault's later remarks on this in "The Subject and Power," in *Michel Foucault: Beyond Structuralism and Hermeneutics*, by Hubert L. Dreyfus and Paul Rabinow (Chicago: University of Chicago Press, 1982), 208–26.

9   Muhammad 'Abdu, *Al-Islam wa al-rad 'ala muntaqidihi* (Cairo, 1928).

10   'Ali 'Abd al-Raziq, *Al-Islam wa Usul al-Hukm* (Beirut: Dar Maktabat al-Hayyat, 1966). With an introduction by Mamduh Haqqi.

11   Eric Davis, *Challenging Colonialism: Bank Misr and Egyptian Industrialization, 1920–1941* (Princeton, N.J.: Princeton University Press, 1983).

12   For an excellent sociological and historical study of this group, see Israel Gershoni and James P. Jankowski, *Egypt, Islam, and the Arabs: The Search for Egyptian Nationhood, 1900–1930* (London: Oxford University Press, 1986).

13   Gershoni and Jankowski, *Egypt, Islam, and the Arabs*, 32–33; P. J. Vatikiotis, *The History of Egypt: From Muhammad Ali to Mubarak* (Baltimore: Johns Hopkins University Press, 1965), 309.

14   On this point see Homi Bhabha, "Of Mimicry and Man: The Ambivalence of Colonial Discourse," *October* 28 (spring 1984): 125–33.

15   Ibn Khaldun, *The Muqaddirnah*, vol. 1, trans. Franz Rosenthal (New York: Pantheon Books, 1958), 327–36.

16   Nabih Abdallah Bayyumi, *Tatawur Fikrat al-Qawmiyya al-'Arbiyya Fi-Misr* (Cairo: Al-Hay'at al-Misriyya al-'Ama lil-Kitab, 1975); Gershoni and Jankowski, *Egypt, Islam, and the Arabs*; and Nadav Safran, *Egypt in Search of a Political Community* (Cambridge: Harvard University Press, 1961).

17   Cited by Anouar Abdel-Malek, *Contemporary Arab Political Thought*, trans. Michael Pallis (London: Zed Books, 1983), 28. We have to keep in mind that Egypt was actually the first country in the Middle East to develop a sense of national identity.

18   Quoted in Albert Hourani, *Arabic Thought in the Liberal Age: 1789–1939* (London: Oxford University Press, 1962), 79.

19   Ibid.

20 Ibid.

21 As quoted in Gershoni and Jankowski, *Egypt, Islam, and the Arabs*, 12.

22 Safran, *Egypt in Search of a Political Community*, 88.

23 Lutfi al-Sayyid used the word 'ummah to denote the nation-state—a territorial and juridical entity. See Vatikiotis, *The History of Egypt*, 500.

24 As quoted in Jamal Mohammad Ahmad, *The Intellectual Origins of Egyptian Nationalism* (London: Oxford University Press, 1983), 106.

25 Literally this definition would include land other than Egypt, but the point was to revive Egyptian identity based on the Pharaonic past, which the reformers felt had been obscured by centuries of Islamic rule.

26 As quoted in Gershoni and Jankowski, *Egypt, Islam, and the Arabs*, 99.

27 At that time the Ottoman Empire had collapsed, and the nation-state was the only viable alternative. This process also occurred in former Ottoman territory in Europe, but the nation-state in Europe did not emphatically exclude Christian or Western characteristics from the political community.

28 In this effort the Egyptian liberals differentiated themselves from the Arabs, the outside "other," and from the local populace, the domestic "other." The latter configuration will be discussed in chapter 4.

29 Michel de Certeau, *L'ecriture de l'histoire* (Paris: Editions Gallimard, 1975), 9.

30 Anne Norton, *Alternative Americas: A Reading of Antebellum Political Culture* (Chicago: University of Chicago Press, 1986), 132–99.

31 Salama Musa, *Al-Majalla al-jadida*, March 1930, 632.

32 See, for example, Marcel Colombe, *L'evolution de l'Egypt: 1924–1950* (Paris: G. P. Maisonneuve, 1951), 121–59, 167–71; and Vernon Egger, *A Fabian in Egypt: Salama Musa and the Rise of the Professional Classes in Egypt, 1901–1939* (New York: University Press of America, 1986), 136–39. See also Gershoni and Jankowski, *Egypt, Islam, and the Arabs*, 164–90; and Bayyumi, *Tatawur Fikrat al-Qawmiyya al-'Arabiyya fi Misr*, 49–75.

33 Gershoni and Jankowski, *Egypt, Islam, and the Arabs*, 170.

34 Ibid., 181.

35 The statue now stands in Giza near Cairo University.

36 Gershoni and Jankowski, *Egypt, Islam, and the Arabs*, 187.

37 See Hourani, *Arabic Thought in the Liberal Age*, 80–81.

38 By the 1820s a race between the French and British consuls in Cairo was already under way to explore Egyptian antiquities for the West. The French won the rivalry when a Frenchman became the director of the Antiquities Service in 1858. This position remained under French control for ninety-four years until Nasser's free officers took over the service after 1952. See Donald Reid, "Indigenous Egyptology: The Decolonization of a Profession," *Journal of the American Oriental Society* (April–June 1985): 234. It is not clear why the French maintained such a long domination over Egyptian antiquities—even during Britain's occupation of Egypt.

39 Olivier Richon, "Representation, the Despot and the Harem: Some Questions around an Academic Orientalist Painting by LeComte-Du-Nouy (1885)," in *Europe and Its Others*, vol. 1 (Colchester: University of Essex, 1984), 2.

40 The German Orientalist Heinrich Bergsch, director of the School of the Ancient Egyptian Language, reports that the French Egyptologist Auguste Mariette, the conservator of Egyptian monuments, "gave the orders to museum officials that no native be allowed to copy Hieroglyphic inscriptions." He feared that native Egyptians, skilled in Hieroglyphics, would threaten his monopoly on Egyptology. Reid, "Indigenous Egyptology," 235.

41 Very revealing was the remark of a French Egyptologist on Khedive Ismail's attitude at the opening of the Museum of Antiquities in 1863. "Being the true Oriental that he [Ismail] was, the loathing and fear which he had of death kept him from entering a building containing mummies." While the ceremonies went on inside, the khedive entertained himself outside in the gardens. Reid, "Indigenous Egyptology," 235. Bayyumi suggested the same idea: "If we examine carefully the Pharaonic orientation [in Egypt], we find that colonialism played a very important role in it." *Tatawur Fikrat al-Qawrniyya al'Arabiyya fi Misr*, 53.

42 Renan's portrayal of Islam and the Arabs can be found throughout his works, and more specifically in *Averroes et l'Averroisme* (Paris: A. Durans, 1856); *L'Islamisme et la science: De la part des peuples semitiques dans l'histoire de la civilization* (Paris: C. Levy, 1882); and most importantly *Histoire generale et systeme compare des langues semitiques* (Paris: Imperiale, 1855).

43 Ali Adham, *Muhawarat Renan al-Falsafiya* (Cairo, 1929).

44 Tawfiq al-Hakim, Mahmud al-Akkad, Salama Musa, Taha Husayn, and Muhammad Ghaleb all shared, with varying degrees of conviction, Renan's negative views of Islamic religion and culture.

45 Ernest Renan, *L'avenir de la science* (Paris: Calmann-Levy, 1890).

46 "In politics as in poetry, in religion as in philosophy, the inclination of the Europeans is to search for nuances, reconciliation, and complexity that are so lacking among the Semitic people." Rough translation of Renan, *L'Islamisme et la science*, 16–18.

47 "The works of greatest importance in nurturing the anti-Arab currents of thought in Egypt in the 1920s were probably Renan's well-known pamphlet *De la part des peuples semitiques dans l'histoire de la civilization* (1862). . . . This anti-Arab note running through Renan's writings on race was eagerly picked up by Egyptian intellectuals searching for a theoretical basis for their own anti-Arab inclinations. In addition, they were flattered by the fact that the same philosopher who so 'scientifically' had condemned the Semites and the Arabs was so fulsome in his praise of ancient Pharaonic Egypt." Gershoni and Jankowski, *Egypt, Islam, and the Arabs*, 101–2.

48 Renan, *De la part des peuples semitiques*, 12.

49 Between 1910 and 1963, Musa published some forty books and wrote for a dozen Egyptian magazines and newspapers.

50 In his *Ha'ula'i 'alamuni*, Musa cites some twenty thinkers who influenced him, none of whom was an Arab or a Muslim. Among them were Renan and Darwin.

51 Salama Musa, "Al-Misriyun Umma Gharbiyya," *Al-Hilal*, 37 (December 1928):

177–81. All citations in this discussion are from this article, unless otherwise specified.

52 This is taken from the original text, G. Elliot Smith, *The Ancient Egyptians* (London: Harper, 1923), 65.

53 Musa took the table from Lilian Eichler, *Book of Etiquette: The Customs of Mankind* (New York: N. Doubleday, 1924), 132–33. The figures were taken from Smith, *The Ancient Egyptians*, 59, 61.

54 Smith, *The Ancient Egyptians*, 61.

55 Ibid., 59, fig. 2.

56 *Al-Majalla al-Jadida*, June 1930, 962–64.

57 Ibid., 962.

58 Ibid., 964.

59 See, for example, Haykal's collection of published articles in various Egyptian newspapers between 1912 and 1925. These articles were subsequently assembled and published in a book by Haykal, *Fi Awqat al-Faragh*, 2nd ed. (Cairo: Maktabat al-Nahdha al-Misriyya, 1968).

60 In 1928 Haykal wrote a tribute to Taine describing him as a great thinker who had done more to propagate the positivist philosophy than Auguste Comte himself: "The world cannot forget [Taine's] contribution to human thought at a critical moment of its development." Husayn Haykal, *Taragim Misriyya wa Gharbiyya* (Cairo, 1929), 233.

61 Hippolyte Taine, *History of English Literature*, vol. 1, trans. H. Van Laun (New York: Worthington, 1889), 17–21.

62 Ibid., 14–15.

63 As quoted in Gershoni and Jankowski, *Egypt, Islam, and the Arabs*, 131.

64 Haykal, *Fi Awqat al-Faragh*, 198–242.

65 A loose translation of Haykal's statements: "It is beyond me why some Egyptians take recourse in unrefined expressions good for the rough nature of Bedouin life but unfit for Egyptians who are more civilized thanks to Egypt's natural environment." Ibid., 205–96.

66 Ibid., 222–24.

67 Ahmad Husayn, "Misr Fir'awniyya," *Al-Muqqattam*, September 6, 1930, 7.

68 Husayn Haykal, "Misr al-Haditha wa Misr al-Qadima," *Al-Siyasa al-Usbu'iyya*, November 7, 1926, 10–11.

69 This idea was voiced in most writings on literature, the history of literature, or literary criticism that were published during this period.

70 Tawfiq Tuwaij, "Tatawur al-Adab al-Misri wa Aghraduhu," *Al-Siyasa al-Usbu'iyya*, May 25, 1929, 17–18.

71 The title clearly reveals the intent of the article: "Egyptian Literature and Its Distinction from Semitic Literature." See Muhammad Ghalab, "Al-Adab al-Misry wa Misatuhu 'an al-Adab al-Samiyya," *Al-Siyasa al-Usbu'iyya*, December 21, 1929, 20.

72 Ibid.

73 Ahmad Dayf, *Muqadima li-Dirasat Adab al-Arab* (Cairo, 1921).

74 Tawfiq al-Hakim, "Ila al-Ductur Taha Husayn," *Al-Rissala*, June 1, 1933, 5.

75 Ibid., 8.

76 Taha Husayn, *Mustaqbal al-Thaqafa fi Misr* (Cairo, 1936). (I am using the 1944 edition.)

77 Ibid., 13.

78 Ibid., 18.

four The Cultural Preconditions of Citizenship

1 Jamal Mohammed Ahmed, *The Intellectual Origins of Egyptian Nationalism* (London: Oxford University Press, 1960); David Semah, *Four Egyptian Literary Critics* (Leiden: E. J. Brill, 1974); Charles D. Smith, *Islam and the Search for Social Order in Modern Egypt* (Albany: SUNY Press, 1983).

2 Nadav Safran, *Egypt in Search of a Political Community: An Analysis of the Intellectual and Political Evolution of Egypt, 1804–1952* (Cambridge: Harvard University Press, 1961), 125–28.

3 'Ali 'Abd al-Raziq, *Al-Islam wa Usul al-Hukm* (Cairo, 1925).

4 Israel Gershoni and James Jankowski, *Egypt, Islam, and the Arabs: The Search for Egyptian Nationhood, 1900–1930* (New York: Oxford University Press, 1986).

5 The most prominent defendant of this view is the Syrian author Salama Musa.

6 Liberal reformist newspapers of the period were filled with editorials, essays, and debates on the backwardness and unhealthy habits of the crowds. See, for example, *Al-Siyasa, Al-Balagh, Kawkab al-Sharq, Al-Muqattam, Al-Hilal,* and *Al-Majalla al-Jadida.*

7 Taha Husayn, *Al-Mu'adhabun fi al-Ard* (Cairo: Dar al-Ma'arif, 1973), 182–92.

8 Ibid., 187–88.

9 These issues were so closely linked in Egyptian liberal discourse that it is hard to find an article treating the question of education, for example, that does not raise the issue of health, order, security, and progress—and vice versa. Of the 150 articles I collected for this chapter, most were actually written by medical doctors. The topics on which M.D.s wrote ranged from the most obvious health issues to education, traffic jams, marriage, leisure time, dress, Islamic law, et cetera.

10 "Afaat al-Ijtirnaa'i: Wa kayfa tuharibuha al-hukumat wa al-shu'ub," *Al-Muqattam,* January 20, 1924, 1.

11 These issues became a preoccupation for the early Egyptian liberal reformers in the late nineteenth century. See Timothy Mitchell, *Colonising Egypt* (Cambridge: Cambridge University Press, 1988).

12 Ibid., 7.

13 "Al-Amn al-Amm," *Al-Muqattam,* September 17, 1925, 1.

14 "Nashat al-Bouliss," *Al-Muqattam,* August 18, 1925, 1.

15 "Isiah al-Qura," *Al-Muqattam,* August 30, 1925, 1.

16 Ibid.

17 "Itiqaa' al-laraaim wa al-linayat bil-Fahssi 'ani al-Atfaal Fahssan Badaniyan wa 'Akliyan," Al-Muqattam, September 25 and 26, 1925, 1.

18 "Al-Mustashfayat wa al-Sihha al-amma," Al-Muqattam, August 7, 1925, 1–2.

19 Jacques Berque, Egypt: Imperialism and Revolution, trans. Jean Stewart (New York: Praeger, 1972), 616–29.

20 "Al-lhtifal bi al-Mawalid al-Husseini," Al-Siyasa, October 17, 1927, 5.

21 Ibid.

22 "Ma'ssat al-Akhlaq," Al-Muqattam, August 7, 1925.

23 Ibid.

24 "Al-Turuq al-Sufiyya: Mukhalafat Rijaluha li al-din, Wajib al-Mashikha wa Wajib al-Hukuma," Kawkab al-Sharq, November 6, 1926, 1.

25 Ibid.

26 Ibid.

27 "Al-Mawalid wa al-Mawassim al-'Amma," Al-Siyasa, January 19, 1927, 1.

28 Ibid.

29 "Ihraqu Juthath Amwatikum," Kawkab al-Sharq, December 7, 1926, 3.

30 "Al-Siyah 'ala al-Mawta," Al-Siyasa, October 12, 1927, 2.

31 Al-Siyasa, October 28, 1927, 3.

32 The book's title, I believe, is Sur le choix des époux. Unfortunately I could not find any information on this book except that it was published in 1923.

33 Al-Siyasa, October 28, 1927, 3.

34 Mahmud Azmi, "Limadha Labistu al-Kuba'a," Al-Hilal 36 (November 1930): 52–56.

35 Ibid.

36 Al-Hilal, April 1930, 898–99.

37 In Al-Muqattam, September 18, 1925, 1.

38 "Al-Aziya' al-Sharqiyya," Al-Muqattam, September 20, 1925, 1.

39 "Al-Aziya' al-Sharqiyya," part 2, Al-Muqattam, September 25, 1925, 1.

40 Al-Muqattam, January 23, 1924, 1.

41 " 'Ala 'Atabat 'asrin Jadid,' " Al-Muqattam, September 18, 1925, 1.

42 "Assas al-Ta'diil al-Manshud fi Nuzum al-Ta'liim," Kawkab al-Sharq, April 14, 1930, 7.

43 Saati' al-Husry, "Al-Thaqafa al-'amma wa Whim al-latiniyya wa al-liyunaniyya," Al-Risala, August 21, 1938, 1625–26.

44 Mubarak Zaki, "Hawla Murakabat al-Thaqafat al-Amma bi-Wizarat al-Ma'arif: Ila al-Ductur Taha Husayn," Al-Risala, January 23, 1939, 2329–31.

45 "Al-Ta'liim wa al-Sihat," Al-Muqattam, October 9, 1925, 1–2.

46 "Assas al-Ta'diil al-Manshud fi Nuzum al-Ta'liim," part 2, Kawkab al-Sharq, April 21, 1930, 6.

47 Ibid.

48 "Madarisuna wa al-Tarbiyya al-Khuluqiyya: Al-Madariss al-Misriyya Tu'allim wa lakinaha la Turabbi," Al-Siyasa, October 27, 1927, 1.

49 "Labudda min Siyassa Thabita li al-Ta'liim," Al-Balagh, October 19, 1927, 1.

50 Abd al-Rahim Mahmud, "Nizamuna al-Ijtimaa'i: Al-Fard," *Al-Muqtataf*, January 1924, 26–29.

51 Ibid.

52 Abd al-Rahim Mahmud, "Nizamuna al-Ijtimaa'i: A'maluna wa al-Bawa'ithu Ilayha," *Al-Muqtataf*, February 1924, 137–39.

53 Fenelon's *Telemaque*, quoted in Mitchell, *Colonising Egypt*, 75.

54 Will Kymlicka, *Multicultural Citizenship: A Liberal Theory of Minority Rights* (New York: Oxford University Press, 1995), 76.

55 Avishai Margalit and Joseph Raz, "National Self-Determination," in *Ethics in the Public Domain: Essays in the Morality of Law and Politics*, ed. Joseph Raz (New York: Oxford University Press, 1994), 114.

56 Will Kymlicka, *Liberalism, Community, and Culture* (New York: Oxford University Press, 1989), 162–81.

57 John Rawls, *A Theory of Justice* (London: Oxford University Press, 1971).

58 See, for example, Kymlicka, *Multicultural Citizenship*, 135–44. An early version of this view can be found in David Truman, *The Governmental Process*, 2nd ed. (New York: Knopf, 1971).

five Egypt's Liberal Experiment in Comparative Perspective

1 See, for example, Seymour Lipset, "Some Requisites of Democracy: Economic Development and Political Legitimacy," *American Political Science Review* 53 (1959): 69–105; Robert Dahl, *Polyarchy, Participation, and Opposition* (New Haven: Yale University Press, 1970); and Larry Diamond, Juan J. Linz, and Seymour Martin Lipset, eds., *Politics in Developing Countries: Comparing Experiences with Democracy* (London: Lynne Rienner, 1990), 9–37.

2 Scholars from various theoretical traditions and ideological persuasions link capitalism with democracy. See, for example, Charles Lindblom, *Politics and Markets: The World's Political-Economic System* (New York: Basic Books, 1977); Barrington Moore, *Social Origins of Dictatorship and Democracy: Lord and Peasant in the Making of the Modern World* (Boston: Beacon Press, 1966); and Samuel Huntington, "Will More Countries Become Democratic?" *Political Science Quarterly* 99, no. 2 (summer 1984): 193–218.

3 Seymour Lipset, *Political Man: The Social Basis of Politics* (Baltimore: Johns Hopkins University Press, 1981); Daniel Lerner, *The Passing of Traditional Society* (New York: Free Press, 1958); S. N. Eisenstadt, "Social Change, Differentiation and Evolution," *American Sociological Review* 29 (June 1964): 375–86; Dahl, *Polyarchy, Participation, and Opposition*; and Huntington, "Will More Countries Become Democratic?"

4 See, for example, Felix Gilbert, ed., *The Historical Essays of Otto Hintze* (London: Oxford University Press, 1975); and Reinhard Bendix, *Kings or People: Power and the Mandate to Rule* (Berkeley: University of California Press, 1977).

5 Charles Issawi, *Egypt in Revolution: An Economic Analysis* (London: Oxford University Press, 1964); Roger Owen, *Cotton and the Egyptian Economy* (London: Oxford University Press, 1969).

6 Robert Tignor, "Bank Misr and Foreign Capitalism," *International Journal of Middle East Studies* 8 (1977): 161–81; Tignor, "Dependency Theory and Egyptian Capitalism, 1920–1950," *African Economic History* 9 (1980): 101–18; Tignor, *Egyptian Textiles and British Capital, 1930–1956* (Cairo: American University in Cairo, 1989); Patrick Clawson, "Egypt's Industrialization: A Critique of Dependency Theory," *MERIP Reports* 72 (November 1978): 17–23; Eric Davis, *Challenging Colonialism: Bank Misr and Egyptian Industrialization, 1920–1941* (Princeton, N.J.: Princeton University Press, 1983); and Robert Vitalis, *When Capitalists Collide: Business Conflict and the End of Empire in Egypt* (Berkeley: University of California Press, 1995).

7 Rauf Abbas, *Al-Haraka al-'ummaliyya fi Misr: 1889–1952* (Cairo: al-Markhaz al-'arabi li-nashr, 1967); Joel Beinin and Zachary Lockman, *Workers on the Nile: Nationalism, Islam, and the Egyptian Working Class, 1882–1954* (Princeton, N.J.: Princeton University Press, 1987).

8 Mahmoud Hussein, *Class Conflict in Egypt, 1945–1970* (New York: Monthly Review Press, 1977); Marius Deeb, "Labor and Politics in Egypt: 1919–1939," *International Journal of Middle Eastern Studies* 10 (1979): 187–203; Ellis Goldberg, *Tinker, Tailor, and Textile Worker: Class and Politics in Egypt, 1930–1954* (Berkeley: University of California Press, 1986).

9 Abd al-Aziz al-Rifa'i, *Al-Dimuqratiyya wa al-Ahzab al-Siyasiyya fi Misr al Haditha wa al-Mu'assirat, 1875–1952* (Cairo: Dar al-Shuruq, 1977).

10 Diamond et al., *Politics in Developing Countries*, 9–37.

11 The authors rely on the following works to make this point: Dahl, *Polyarchy, Participation, and Opposition*; Huntington, "Will More Countries Become Democratic?"; and L. H. Gann and Peter Duignan, *Burden of Empire: An Appraisal of Western Colonialism in Africa South of the Sahara* (Stanford: Hoover Institution Press, 1967).

12 Diamond et al., *Politics in Developing Countries*, 32.

13 Atul Kohli, "Democracy and Development," in *Development Strategies Reconsidered*, ed. John Lewis and Valeriana Kallab (New Brunswick, N.J.: Transaction Books, 1986), 171–72.

14 Diamond et al., *Politics in Developing Countries*, 18.

15 Abdeslam Maghraoui, "A Political Authority in Crisis: Morocco's Mohammed VI," *Middle East Report* 218 (spring 2001): 12–17.

16 Abd al-Rahman al-Raafi'i, *Tarikh al-Harakcah al-Qawmiyah wa Tatawur Nizam al-Hukm fi-Misr*, 5th ed. (Cairo: Maktabat al-Nahdha al-Misriyya, 1955), 93–94.

17 Ibid., 97–98.

18 Ibid., 102.

19 Muhammad Mutawala, *Misr wa al-Hayat al Hizbiya wa al Niyabiya Qablat Sanat 1952* (Cairo: Dar al-Thaqafa li al-Tiba'a wa al-Nashr, 1980), 41–42.

20 Ibid., 51.

21 Ibid., 52; and Jacob Landau, *Parliaments and Parties in Egypt* (Tel Aviv: Israel Publishing House, 1953), 9.

22 Landau, *Parliaments and Parties in Egypt*, 25.

23 Ibid., 26.

24 Ibid., 38.

25 Mutawala, *Misr wa al-Hayat al-Hizbiya wa al-Niyabiya*, 65–72; Landau, *Parliaments and Parties in Egypt*, 41–44; and Abd al-Aziz al-Rifa'i, *al-Dimuqratiyya wa al-Ahzab al-Siyasiyya fi Misr al-Haditha wa al-Mu'assirat, 1875–1952* (Cairo: Dar al-Shuruq, 1977), 34–37.

26 Landau, *Parliaments and Parties in Egypt*, 57.

27 This problem is raised by Jyotirindra Das Gupta on Assam and by Paul Brass on Punjab. See Atul Kohli, ed., *India's Democracy: An Analysis of Changing State-Society Relations* (Princeton, N.J.: Princeton University Press, 1988).

28 Jyotirindra Das Gupta, "India: Democratic Becoming and Combined Development," in *Politics in Developing Countries: Comparing Experiences with Democracy*, ed. Larry Diamond, Juan J. Linz, and Seymour Martin Lipset (London: Lynne Rienner, 1990), 219–20.

29 Diamond et al., *Politics in Developing Countries*, 25–29.

30 Ibid., 28–29.

31 Critical attacks on the political development literature are diverse and substantial. For a concise summary of these critiques, see Ronald Chilcote, *Theories of Comparative Politics: The Search for a Paradigm* (Boulder, Colo.: Westview Press, 1981), 283–87.

32 Juan Linz, *The Breakdown of Democratic Regimes: Crisis, Breakdown, and Re-equilibration* (Baltimore: Johns Hopkins University Press, 1978).

33 Landau, *Parliaments and Parties in Egypt*, 73–83, 101–3.

34 Ibid., 91–92.

35 The revolt was named after Ahmad 'Urabi, an Egyptian army officer who led a popular opposition movement against European interference in the political and financial affairs of Egypt.

36 Marius Deeb argues that the British prevailed in Egypt mainly because of the weakness of the political parties before the nationalist movement of 1919. Deeb, *Party Politics in Egypt: The Wafd and Its Rivals, 1919–1939* (London: Ithaca Press, 1979), 2.

37 I do not include the Union Party (Hizb al-Ittihad), which was formed in 1925 by the Royal Palace. It had very few adherents and played no significant role in competitive politics. I also omit the Socialist Party (later the Communist Party), which was organized as a labor syndicate rather than a political party and was not allowed to participate in the electoral process.

38 The official newspaper of the Wafd was *Kawkab al-Sharq*. Other newspapers that supported its policies were *al-Ahram*, *Al-Balagh*, *Wadi al-Nil*, and *Misr*.

39 Deeb, *Party Politics in Egypt*, 22–24, 26–27, 162.

40 Ibid., 69.

41 Nadav Safran, *Egypt in Search of Political Community* (Cambridge: Harvard University Press, 1961), 275n1, 85–97. See also Albert Hourani, *Arabic Thought in the Liberal Age, 1798–1939* (London: Oxford University Press, 1967), 174–78.

42 The founding members of the Wafd were Saad Zaghlul, Ahmad Lutfi al-Sayyid, Ali Sha'rawi, Abd al-Aziz Fahmi, Muhammad Mahmud (Umma Party), and Abd al-Latif al-Makbati and Muhammad 'Ali (Watani Party).

43 Deeb, *Party Politics in Egypt*, 71.

44 Abd al-Rahman al-Raafi'i, *Fi A'qab al-Thawrat al-Misriyya*, vol. 1 (Cairo: Maktabat al-Nahdha al-Misriyya, 1959), 68.

45 Ibid.

46 Deeb, *Party Politics in Egypt*, 76.

47 Ibid., 77.

48 Abd al-Rahman al-Raafi'i, *Fi A'qab al-Thawrat al-Misriyya* (Cairo: Maktabat al-Nahdha al-Misriyya, 1959), 1:68.

49 Landau, *Parliaments and Parties in Egypt*, 171.

50 *Al-Siyasa*, October 30, 1922, quoted in Deeb, *Party Politics in Egypt*, 80.

51 Al-Raafi'i, *Fi A'qab al-Thawrat al-Misriyya*, 1:68.

52 Landau, *Parliaments and Parties in Egypt*, 111.

53 Deeb, *Political Parties in Egypt*, 80, 188.

54 Both the Wafd and the Watani parties strongly objected to the commission because it was not elected by a representative body.

55 Husayn Haykal, *Mudhakirat fi al-Siyasa al-Misriyya*, vol. 1 (Cairo: Maktabat al-Nahdhat al-Misriya, 1951), 138.

56 Landau, *Parliaments and Parties in Egypt*, 60.

57 The king had the right to select and appoint the prime minister, dismiss the cabinet and dissolve the parliament, postpone parliamentary sessions, and appoint the president and two-fifths of the Senate. P. J. Vatikiotis, *The History of Egypt: From Muhammad Ali to Mubarak* (Baltimore: Johns Hopkins University Press, 1985), 276.

58 Jacques Berque, *Egypt: Imperialism and Revolution*, trans. Jean Stewart (London: Faber and Faber, 1972), 442.

59 Ibid., 363.

60 Safran, *Egypt in Search of Political Community*, 109.

61 Al-Raafi'i, *Fi in A'qab al-Thawrat al-Misriyya*, 1:117–18.

62 Deeb, *Party Politics in Egypt*, 152.

63 Ibid., 154

64 Ibid., 127–29.

65 Ibid.

66 Haykal, *Mudhakirat fi al-Siyasa al-Misriyya*, 214.

67 Afaf Lutfi al-Sayyid-Marsot, *Egypt's Liberal Experiment: 1924–1936* (Berkeley: University of California Press, 1977), 1–11.

68 Berque, *Egypt: Imperialism and Revolution*, 442.

69 Named after Saad Zaghlul, the Wafdist leader who died in 1927. The controversy was over who should get the contract for the electrification of the Aswan Dam. The Saadists opposed giving the contract to the English Electric Company and insisted instead on an open tender for the project. Deeb, *Party Politics in Egypt*, 335.

70 Safran, *Egypt in Search of Political Community*, 187.

71 Berque, *Egypt: Imperialism and Revolution*, 363.

72 Linz, *The Breakdown of Democratic Regimes*, 16–18.

73 Diamond et al., *Politics in Developing Countries*, 9.

74 Ibid., 10, 18–21.

75 Ibid., 1.

76 Afaf Lutfi al-Sayyid-Marsot, *Egypt's Liberal Experiment: 1924–1936*, 241–42.

77 Deeb, *Party Politics in Egypt*, 152.

78 The treaty provided for an Anglo-Egyptian defense arrangement and the mainte-
    nance of British troops in the Suez Canal Zone.

79 The relationship between the two organizations and the young Free Officers
    before they took power in 1952 is well documented. See P. J. Vatikiotis, *Nasser and
    His Generation* (London: Croom Helm, 1978).

80 Moore, *Social Origins of Dictatorship and Democracy*; Lindblom, *Politics and Markets*.

81 See, for example, Immanuel Wallerstein, *The Modern World System*, vol. 2 (New
    York: Academic Press, 1980).

82 Goran Therbom, "The Role of Capital and the Rise of Democracy," *New Left
    Review* 103 (May–June 1977): 3–41.

83 See, for example, Daniel Lerner, *The Passing of Traditional Society: Modernizing the
    Middle East* (New York: Free Press, 1958); and S. N. Eisenstadt, "Social Change,
    Differentiation and Evolution," *American Sociological Review* 29 (June 1964): 357–
    87.

84 Diamond et al., *Politics in Developing Countries*, 18.

85 Samuel Huntington, *Political Order in Changing Societies* (New Haven: Yale Univer-
    sity Press, 1968).

86 Orgun Ozbudun, "Turkey: Crises, Interruptions, and Reequilibrations," in *Poli-
    tics in Developing Countries: Comparing Experiences with Democracy*, ed. Larry Dia-
    mond, Juan J. Linz, and Seymour Martin Lipset (London: Lynne Rienner, 1990),
    214.

87 John J. Johnson, ed., *The Role of the Military in Underdeveloped Countries* (Princeton,
    N.J.: Princeton University Press, 1962); Morris Janowitz, *The Military in the Politi-
    cal Development of New Nations: An Essay in Comparative Analysis* (Chicago: University
    of Chicago Press, 1962). On Egypt, see Eliezer Be'eri, "Social Origins and Family
    Backgrounds of the Egyptian Army Officer Class," *Asian and African Studies* 1, no.
    2 (1966): 1–40; Be'eri, *Army Officers in Arab Politics and Society* (New York: 1970);
    P. J. Vatikiotis, *Nasser and His Generation* and *The Egyptian Army in Politics* (Bloom-
    ington: Indiana University Press, 1961); Monroe Berger, *The Military Elite and
    Social Change: Egypt since Napoleon* (Princeton, N.J.: Princeton University Press,
    1960); and Manfred Halpern, *The Politics of Social Change in the Middle East and North
    Africa* (Princeton, N.J.: Princeton University Press, 1965).

88 Fawzi Jurgi, *Dirassat fi-Tarikh Misr al-Siyassi munthu al-'Asr al-Mamluki* (Cairo,
    1958); Salah Issa, *al-Burjoiziyya al-Misriyya wa Uslub al-Mufawada* (Beirut: Dar Ibn
    Khaldun, 1979); Anouar Abdel-Malek, *Egypte: Société militaire* (Paris: Editions du
    Seuil, 1962); Mahmoud Hussein, *La lutte de classe en Egypte de 1945–1968* (Paris:
    Francois Maspero, 1969); Robert Tignor, "The Egyptian Revolution of 1919:
    New Direction in the Egyptian Economy," *Middle East Studies* 12 (1976): 41–67;
    and Marius Deeb, "Bank Misr and the Emergence of the Local Bourgeoisie in
    Egypt," in *The Middle Eastern Economy: Studies in Economics and Economic History*, ed.
    Eli Kedourie (London: Frank Cass, 1976).

89 This description is based on Tignor, "The Egyptian Revolution of 1919"; and Deeb, *Party Politics in Egypt* and "Bank Misr."

90 Abdel-Malek, *Egypte: Société militaire*, 21.

91 Deeb, "Bank Misr," 70.

92 Ibid., 74.

Conclusion

1 Nadav Safran, *Egypt in Search of Political Community* (Cambridge: Harvard University Press, 1961); P. J. Vatikiotis, *The History of Modern Egypt: From Muhammad Ali to Mubarak* (1969; London: Weidenfeld and Nicolson, 1991).

2 Safran, *Egypt in Search of Political Community*, 246.

3 Vatikiotis, *The History of Modern Egypt*, 320.

4 Safran, *Egypt in Search of Political Community*, 53.

5 Vatikiotis, *The History of Modern Egypt*, 169. In July 1882, British frigates attacked Alexandria and landed troops in Ismailia, where a battle took place between General Wolseley's army and an Egyptian rebel leader, Orabi Pasha. The military confrontation occurred after massive demonstrations were organized in Alexandria in support of Orabi, who had asked the Ottoman governor in Egypt, Khedive Ismail, to abolish the "international surveillance" that had been imposed by Britain and France since 1879, when Egypt stopped paying its debts to the Europeans.

6 Ibid., 273–97.

7 Marcel Colombe, *L'évolution de l'Egypte* (Paris: Editions Maisonneuve, 1951); Jacques Berque, *Egypt: Imperialism and Revolution*, trans. Jean Stewart (London: Faber and Faber, 1972).

8 Colombe, *L'évolution de l'Egypte*, 11–12.

9 Ibid., 275, 277.

10 Afaf Lutfi al-Sayyid-Marsot, *Egypt's Liberal Experiment: 1922–1936* (Berkeley: University of California Press, 1977).

11 *Mohammed Ibn Abdallah al-Mu'aqqit al-Murrâkushi: Les gens du navire*, translated from the Arabic with commentary by Alain Roussillon and Abdallah Saaf (Casablanca: Afrique Orient, 1998). The original Arabic text was published in 1935 in Cairo as *Ashab assafina*.

12 The text's commentators refer in fact to the "Berber Decree" that the French colonial administration enacted in the spring of 1930, which abrogated Islamic civil law in Berber areas in Morocco. The decree was partially canceled following violent protests in 1934, triggering a full-fledged nationalist movement that led to independence in 1956.

13 Roxanne L. Euben, *The Enemy in the Mirror: Islamic Fundamentalism and the Limits of Modern Rationalism* (Princeton, N.J.: Princeton University Press, 1999), 6.

—— selected bibliography

Egyptian Periodicals

Al-Balagh
Al-Fath
Al-Hadith
Al-Hilal
Al-Majalla al-Jadida
Al-Muqattam
Al-Muqtataf
Al-Siyasa
Al-Siyasa al-Usbu'iyya
Al-Sufur
Al-'Usur
Al-Rabita al-'Arabiyya
Al-Rabita al-Sharqiyya
Al-Risala
Al-Siyasa al-Usbu'iyya
Jareeda Misr al-Fatat
Kawkab al-Sharq
Liwa' al-Islam
Majallat al-Hidaya al-Islamiyya
Mulhaq al-Siyasa

Published Works

'Abd al-Raziq, 'Ali. Al-Islam wa Usul al-Hukm. Introduction by Mamduh Haqqi. Beirut:
    Dar Maktabat al-Hayyat, 1966.
Abdel-Malek, Anouar. Egypte: Société militaire. Paris: Editions du Seuil, 1962.
——. Contemporary Arab Political Thought. Trans. Michael Pallis. London: Zed Books,
    1983.
'Abdu, Muhammad. Al-'Amal al-Kamilat. Ed. Muhammad 'Imarah. Beirut: al-Mu'assa-
    sat al-Arabiyya lil-Dirasaat wa al-Nashr, 1972.

Abu al-Fath, Mahmud. *Al-Mas'ala al-Misriyya wa al-Wafd*. Cairo, [1921?].

Adham, Ali. *Muhawarat Renan al-Falsafiya*. Cairo, 1929.

Ahmad, Jamal Mohammad. *The Intellectual Origins of Egyptian Nationalism*. London: Oxford University Press, 1983.

al-Azmeh, Aziz. *Ibn Khaldun in Modern Scholarship*. London: Third World Research Centre for Research and Publishing, 1981.

al-Jabarti, Abd al-Rahman. *Tarikh Muddat al-Fransis bi-Misr*. Translated by Shmuel Moreh as *Al-Jabarti's Chronicle of the First Seven Months of the French Occupation of Egypt*. Leiden: E. J. Brill, 1975.

al-Jabri, Mohammed 'Abid al-Khitab. *Al-'Arabi al-Mu'assir: Dirassat Tahliliya Naqdiya*. Beirut: Dar al-Tali'at, 1985.

———. *Nahnu wa al-Turath: Qira'at fi Turathina al-Falsafi*. Casablanca: al-Markaz al Thiaqafi al-'Arabi, 1985.

al-Raafi'i, Abd al-Rahman. *Fi A'khab al-Thawra al-Misriyya*. Cairo: Maktabat al-Nahdha al-Misriyya, 1959.

———. *'Asr Ismail*. Cairo: Maktabat al-Nahdha al-Misriyya, [1970].

———. *Tarikh al-Harakah al-Qawmiyah wa Tatawur Nizarn al-Hukm fi. Misr*. 5th ed. Cairo: Maktabat al-Nahdha al-Misriyya, 1955.

al-Rifa'i, Abd al-Aziz. *Al-Dimuqratiyya wa al-Ahzab al-Siyasiyya fi Misr al Haditha wa al-Mu'assirat, 1875–1952*. Cairo: Dar al-Shuruq, 1977.

al-Rifa'i, Abd al-Rahman. *Tarikh al-Haraka al-Qawmiya*. Cairo, 1949.

al-Sayyid, Lutfi. *Al-Muntakhabaat*. Cairo: Dar al-Nashr al-Hadith, 1937.

———. *Mabaad'i*. Cairo: Kitab Dar al-Hilal, 1963.

———. *Mushkilat al-Huriyya*. Beirut: Dar al-Rawai'i, 1959.

———. *Safahaat Matwiyya*. Cairo: Matba'at al-Muqtataf wa al-Muqattam, 1946.

———. *Ta'amulaat*. Cairo: Dar al-Ma'arif, 1965.

al-Sayyid-Marsot, Afaf Lutfi. *Egypt's Liberal Experiment: 1922–1936*. Berkeley: University of California Press, 1977.

Althusser, Louis, and Étienne Balibar. *Reading Capital*. London: Verso Editions, 1979.

Arberry, Arthur J. *The Koran Interpreted*. London: Macmillan, 1965.

Arkoun, Mohammed. *Essais sur la pensée Islamique*. Paris: Editions Maisonneuve, 1984.

———. *Pour une critique de la raison Islamique*. Paris: Editions Maisonneuve, 1984.

'Awad, Luwis. *Taariikh al-Fikr al-Misri al-Hadith*. Cairo: Dar al-Hilal, 1983.

'Azzam, 'Abd al-Rahman. *Al-Jami'a al-Arabiyya wa al-Wahda al-'Alamiyya*. Cairo, 1946.

Badr, Gamal Moursi. "Islamic Law and the Challenge of Modern Times." In *Law, Personalities, and Politics of the Middle East*, ed. James Piscatori. Boulder, Colo.: Westview Press, 1987.

Barthes, Roland. *Mythologies*. Paris: Editions du Seuil, 1957.

Bayyumi, Nabih Abdallah. *Tatawur Fikrat al-Qawmiyya al-'Arbiyya Fi Misr*. Cairo: al-Hay'at al-Misriyya al-'Amma lil-Kitab, 1975.

Be'eri, Eliezer. *Army Officers in Arab Politics and Society*. New York: Praeger, 1970.

———. "Social Origins and Family Backgrounds of the Egyptian Army Officer Class." *Asian and African Studies* 1, no. 2 (1966): 1–40.

Bendix, Reinhard. *Kings or People: Power and the Mandate to Rule*. Berkeley: University of California Press, 1977.

Bentham, Jeremy. *The Works of Jeremy Bentham*. Ed. J. Bowring. London: Simpkin, 1843.

Berger, Monroe. *The Military Elite and Social Change: Egypt since Napoleon*. Princeton, N.J.: Princeton University Press, 1960.

Berque, Jacques. *Egypt: Imperialism and Revolution*. Trans. Jean Stewart. New York: Praeger, 1972.

Bhabha, Homi. "Of Mimicry and Man: The Ambivalence of Colonial Discourse." *October* 28 (spring 1984): 125–33.

Binder, Leonard. *Islamic Liberalism: A Critique of Development Ideologies*. Chicago: Chicago University Press, 1988.

Césaire, Aimé. *Discourse on Colonialism*. Trans. Joan Pinkham. New York: Monthly Review Press, 1972.

Chafik, Hassan. *Statut Juridique International de l'Egypte*. Paris: Les Editions Internationales, 1928.

Chilcote, Ronald. *Theories of Comparative Politics: The Search for a Paradigm*. Boulder, Colo.: Westview Press, 1981.

Cole, Juan R. I. *Colonialism and Revolution in the Middle East: Social and Cultural Origins of Egypt's 'Urabi Movement*. Princeton, N.J.: Princeton University Press, 1993.

Collins, J. James. *Fiscal Limits of Absolutism: Direct Taxation in Early Seventeenth-Century France*. Berkeley: University of California Press, 1988.

Colombe, Marcel. *L'évolution de l'Égypte, 1924–1950*. Paris: G. P. Maisonneuve, 1951.

Cromer, the Earl of [Evelyn Baring]. *Modern Egypt*. 2 vols. New York: Macmillan, 1908.

Dahl, Robert. *Polyarchy, Participation, and Opposition*. New Haven: Yale University Press, 1971.

Das Gupta. "India: Democratic Becoming and Combined Development." In *Politics in Developing Countries: Comparing Experiences with Democracy*, ed. Larry Diamond, Juan J. Linz, and Seymour Martin Lipset, 263–322. London: Lynne Rienner, 1990.

Davis, Eric. *Challenging Colonialism: Bank Misr and Egyptian Industrialization, 1920–1941*. Princeton, N.J.: Princeton University Press, 1983.

Dayf, Ahmad. *Muqadima li-Dirasat Adab al-Arab*. Cairo, 1921.

de Certeau, Michel. *L'écriture de l'histoire*. Paris: Editions Gallimard, 1975.

——. *L'invention du quotidien: I. Arts de faire*. Paris: Editions 10/18, 1980.

Deeb, Marius. "Bank Misr and the Emergence of the Local Bourgeoisie in Egypt." *Middle Eastern Studies* 12 (1976): 69–86.

——. *Party Politics in Egypt: The Wafd and Its Rivals, 1919–1936*. London: Ithaca Press, 1979.

Derrida, Jacques. *Of Grammatology*. Trans. Gayatri Chakravorty Spivak. Baltimore: Johns Hopkins University Press, 1976.

Diamond, Larry, Juan J. Linz, and Seymour Martin Lipset, eds. *Politics in Developing Countries: Comparing Experiences with Democracy*. London: Lynne Rienner, 1990.

Duignan, Peter, and L. H. Gann. *Burden of Empire: An Appraisal of Western Colonialism in Africa South of the Sahara*. Stanford: Hoover Institution Press, 1967.

Durand, Jean-Marie. "La destruction symbolique du pouvoir." *Peuples Méditerranéens* 17 (1981): 37–65.

Duverger, Maurice. *Political Parties: Their Organization and Activity in the Modern State*. Trans. Barbara North and Robert North. New York: John Wiley and Sons, 1963.

Egger, Vernon. *A Fabian in Egypt: Salama Musa and the Rise of the Professional Classes in Egypt, 1901–1939.* New York: University Press of America, 1986.

Eichler, Lilian. *Book of Etiquette: The Customs of Mankind.* New York: N. Doubleday, 1924.

Eisenstadt, S. N. "Social Change, Differentiation and Evolution." *American Sociological Review* 29 (June 1964): 375–86.

Euben, L. Roxanne. *The Enemy in the Mirror: Islamic Fundamentalism and the Limits of Modern Rationalism.* Princeton, N.J.: Princeton University Press, 1999.

Fanon, Frantz. *Black Skin, White Masks.* Trans. Charles L. Markmann. New York: Grove Press, 1967.

——. *The Wretched of the Earth.* Trans. Constance Farrington. London: MacGibbon and Kee, 1965.

Foucault, Michel. *Discipline and Punish: The Birth of the Prison.* Trans. Alan Sheridan. New York: Pantheon, 1977.

——. *The Order of Things: An Archaeology of the Human Sciences.* New York: Vintage Books, 1973.

——. "The Subject and Power." In *Michel Foucault: Beyond Structuralism and Hermeneutics,* ed. Hubert L. Dreyfus and Paul Rabinow, 208–26. Chicago: University of Chicago Press, 1982.

Gadamer, Hans-Georg. *Truth and Method.* New York: Seabury Press, 1975.

Geertz, Clifford. *The Interpretation of Cultures.* New York: Basic Books, 1973.

Gershoni, Israel, and James Jankowski. *Egypt, Islam, and the Arabs: The Search for Egyptian Nationhood, 1900–1930.* London: Oxford University Press, 1986.

Gilbert, Felix, ed. *The Historical Essays of Otto Hintze.* London: Oxford University Press, 1975.

Goldberg, Ellis, et al. *Rules and Rights in the Middle East: Democracy, Law, and Society.* Seattle: University of Washington Press, 1993.

Gould, Stephen J. *The Mismeasure of Man.* New York: Norton, 1981.

Guémard, Gabriel. *Les réformes en Egypte.* Paris: Imprimerie P. Barbey, 1936.

Gunnell, John. *Political Theory: Tradition and Interpretation.* New York: University Press of America, 1987.

Halpern, Manfred. *The Politics of Social Change in the Middle East and North Africa.* Princeton, N.J.: Princeton University Press, 1965.

Hansen, T. Karen, ed. *African Encounters with Domesticity.* New Brunswick, N.J.: Rutgers University Press, 1992.

Harris, William, II. "Bonding Words and Polity: The Logic of the American Constitution." *American Political Science Review* 76 (March 1982): 34–45.

Haykal, Muhammad Husayn. *Al-Sharq al-Jadid.* Cairo: Maktabat al Nahdha al-Misriyya, 1963.

——. *Fi Awkhat al-Faragh.* 2nd ed. Cairo: Maktabat al-Nahdha al-Misriyya, 1968.

——. *Hayat Muhammad.* Cairo: Maktabat al-Nahdha al-Misriyya, 1956.

——. *Mudhakirat fi al-Siyasa al-Misriyya.* Vol. 1. Cairo: Maktabat al-Nahdha al-Misriyya, 1951.

——. *Mudhakkarat fi al-Siyaasa al-Misriyya: 1912–1937.* Cairo: Maktabat al-Nahdha al-Misriyya, 1951.

——. *Taraqim Misriyya wa Gharbiyya.* Cairo: Dar al-Ma'arif, 1929.

——. *Thawrat al-Adab.* Cairo: Maktabat al-Nahdha al-Misriyya, 1985.

——. *Zainab.* Cairo: Maktabat al-Nahdha al-Misriyya, 1967.

Hirsch, E. D. *Validity in Interpretation.* New Haven: Yale University Press, 1975.

Hourani, Albert. *Arabic Thought in the Liberal Age: 1798–1939.* London: Oxford University Press, 1967.

Huntington, Samuel. *Political Order in Changing Societies.* New Haven: Yale University Press, 1968.

——. "Will More Countries Become Democratic?" *Political Science Quarterly* 99, no. 2 (summer 1984): 193–218.

Husayn, Taha. *'Ala Hamish al-Sirah.* Cairo: Dar al-Ma'arif, 1966.

——. *Al-Mu'adhabun fi al-Ard.* Cairo: Dar al-Ma'arif, 1973.

——. *Fi al-Adab al-Jahili.* Cairo: Dar al-Ma'arif, 1927.

——. *Hadith al-Masaa'.* Cairo: Dar al-Arab li Bustani, 1983.

——. *Mustaqbal al-Thaqafa fi Misr.* Cairo, 1936.

Hussein, Mamoud. *La lutte de classe en Egypte de 1945 à 1968.* Paris: Francois Maspero, 1969.

Ibn Khaldun, Abd al-Rahman. *The Muqaddimah.* Trans. Franz Rosenthal. New York: Pantheon Books, 1958.

Imarah, Muhammad. *Al-Islam wa Usul al-Hukrn Li 'Abd al-Raziq.* Beirut: al-Mu'assasat al-Arabiyya lil Dirasaat wa al-Nashr, 1972.

Issa, Salah. *Al-Burjoiziyya al-Misriyya wa Uslub al-Mufawada.* Beirut: Dar ibn Khaldun, 1979.

JanMohamed, Abdul. "Humanism and Minority Literature: Towards a Definition of a Counter-hegemonic Discourse." *Boundary* 2 (spring–fall 1984): 281–99.

Janowitz, Morris. *The Military in the Political Development of New Nations: An Essay in Comparative Analysis.* Chicago: University of Chicago Press, 1962.

Johnson, John J., ed. *The Role of the Military in Underdeveloped Countries.* Princeton, N.J.: Princeton University Press, 1962.

Jurgi, Fawzi. *Dirassat fi-Tarikh Misr al-Siyassi Munthu al-'Asr al-Mamluki.* Cairo, 1958.

Kennedy, William. *English Taxation, 1640–1799.* London: Bell and Sons, 1913.

Khalidi, Rashid. *Resurrecting Empire: Western Footprints and America's Perilous Path in the Middle East.* Boston: Beacon Press, 2004.

Kilito, Abdelfattah. "Les mots canins." In *Du bilinguisme,* ed. Abdelkebir Khatibi. Paris: Denoël, 1985.

Kohli, Atul. "Democracy and Development." In *Development Strategies Reconsidered,* ed. John Lewis and Valeriana Kallab, 153–82. New Brunswick, N.J.: Transaction Books, 1986.

——, ed. *India's Democracy: An Analysis of Changing State-Society Relations.* Princeton, N.J.: Princeton University Press, 1988.

Lacouture, Jean, and Simonne Lacouture. *Egypt in Transition.* Trans. Francis Scrape. New York: Criterion Book, 1958.

Landau, Jacob. *Parliaments and Parties in Egypt.* Tel Aviv: Israel Publishing House, 1953.

Laroui, Abdallah. *The Crisis of the Arab Intellectual: Traditionalism or Historicism?* Trans. Diarmid Commell. Berkeley: University of California Press, 1976.

——. *L'ideologie Arabe contemporaine: Essai critique.* Paris: Maspero, 1967.

Lashin, 'Abd al-Khalik. *Saad Zarloul wa Dawruhu fi al-Siyassa al-Misriyya.* Cairo: Dar al-Awdah, 1975.

Lerner, Daniel. *The Passing of Traditional Society: Modernizing the Middle East.* New York: Free Press, 1958.

Lewis, Bernard. "The Impact of the French Revolution in Turkey." *Journal of World History* 1 (July 1953): 105–25.

Lindblom, Charles. *Politics and Markets: The World's Political Economic System.* New York: Basic Books, 1977.

Linz, Juan. *The Breakdown of Democratic Regimes.* Baltimore: Johns Hopkins University Press, 1978.

Lipset, Seymour. *Political Man: The Social Basis of Politics.* Baltimore: Johns Hopkins University Press, 1981.

——. "Some Requisites of Democracy: Economic Development and Political Legitimacy." *American Political Science Review* 53 (1959): 69–105.

Lloyd, Lord. *Egypt since Cromer.* London: Macmillan, 1933.

Louca, Anouar. *Voyageurs et écrivains égyptiens en France au XIXe siècle.* Paris: Didier, 1970.

Mahdi, Muhsin. *Ibn Khaldun's Philosophy of History.* Chicago: University of Chicago Press, 1971.

Mani, Lata. "The Production of an Official Discourse on Sati in Early Nineteenth-Century Bengal." In *Europe and Its Others: Essex Conference on the Sociology of Literature, July 1984,* vol. 1, ed. Francis Barker et al. Colchester: University of Essex, 1985.

Mannoni, Octave. *Prospero and Caliban: The Psychology of Colonization.* Trans. Pamela Powesland. New York: Praeger, 1964.

Mehta, Uday Singh. *Liberalism and Empire: A Study in Nineteenth-Century British Liberal Thought.* Chicago: University of Chicago Press, 1999.

Memmi, Albert. *Portrait du colonisé.* Paris: J. J. Pavert, 1966.

Michels, Robert. *Political Parties.* Trans. Eden Paul and Cedar Paul. New York: Collier, 1962.

Mill, James. *The History of British India.* Ed. H. H. Wilson. London: J. Madden, 1884.

Mill, John Stuart. *Three Essays.* Oxford: Oxford University Press, 1975.

——. "On Liberty." In *Utilitarianism, Liberty, Representative Government,* ed. H. B. Acton. London: J. M. Dent and Sons, 1972.

Mitchell, Timothy. "As If the World Were Divided in Two: The Birth of Politics in Turn-of-the-Century Cairo." Ph.D. diss., Princeton University, 1984.

——. *Colonising Egypt.* Cambridge: Cambridge University Press, 1988.

Montgomery, John D. *Forced to Be Free: The Artificial Revolution in Germany and Japan.* Chicago: University of Chicago Press, 1958.

Moore, Barrington. *Social Origins of Dictatorship and Democracy: Lord and Peasant in the Making of the Modern World.* Boston: Beacon Press, 1966.

Morgan, S. A. *The History of Parliamentary Taxation in England.* New York: Moffat, Dard, 1911.

Musa, Salama. *Ha'ula'i 'alamuni.* Cairo: Salaama Musa lil-Nashr wa al Tawzi', 1965.

——. *Ma Hiyya al-Hadhara?* Beirut: Maktabat al-Ma'arif, 1962.

Mutawala, Muhammad. *Misr wa al-Hayat al-Hizbiya wa al-Niyabiya Qablat Sanat 1952.* Cairo: Dar al-Thaqafa li al-Tiba'a wa al-Nashr, 1980.

Nandy, Ashis. *The Intimate Enemy: Loss and Recovery of Self under Colonialism.* Delhi: Oxford University Press, 1983.

Nasser, Gamal Abdul. *The Charter.* Cairo: Information Department, May 1962.

Norton, Anne. *Alternative Americas: A Reading of Antebellum Political Culture.* Chicago: University of Chicago Press, 1986.

———. *Ninety-five Theses on Politics, Culture, and Method.* New Haven: Yale University Press, 2004.

———. *Reflections on Political Identity.* Baltimore: Johns Hopkins University Press, 1988.

Ozbudun, Orgun. "Turkey: Crises, Interruptions, and Reequilibrations." In *Politics in Developing Countries: Comparing Experiences with Democracy,* ed. Larry Diamond, Juan J. Linz, and Seymour Martin Lipset, 179–99. London: Lynne Rienner, 1990.

Peaslee, Amos. *Constitutions of the World.* Concord: Rumford Press, 1950.

Perry, Benita. "Problems in Current Theories of Colonial Discourse." *Oxford Literary Review* 9, nos. 1–2 (1987): 27–58.

Pocock, J. A. *Politics, Language, and Time.* New York: Atheneum, 1971.

Qutb, Sayyid. *Al-Islam wa Mushkilat al-Hadhara.* Cairo: 'Issa al-Baba al-Halaby, 1962.

Rabinow, Paul, and William Sullivan, eds. *Interpretive Social Science.* Berkeley: University of California Press, 1987.

Ramdan, Abdel 'Azim. *Tatawur al-Haraka al-Wataniyya fi Misr: 1918–1936.* 2nd ed. Cairo: Maktabat Madbuli, 1982.

Razi, Hossein. "Legitimacy, Religion, and Nationalism in the Middle East." *American Political Science Review* 84, no. 1 (March 1990): 69–91.

———. "The Nexus of Legitimacy and Performance: The Lessons of the Iranian Revolution." *Comparative Politics* 19 (1987): 453–69.

Reid, Donald. "Indigenous Egyptology: The Decolonization of a Profession." *Journal of the American Oriental Society* 105 (April–June 1985): 233–46.

Renan, Ernest. *Averroes et l'Averroisme.* Paris: A. Durans, 1856.

———. *Histoire générale et système comparé des langues Sémitiques.* Paris: Imprim. Imperiale, 1855.

———. *L'avenir de la science.* Paris: Calmann-Levy, 1890.

———. *L'Islamisme et la science: De la part des peuples Sémitiques dans l'histoire de la civilization.* Paris: C. Levy, 1882.

Richon, Olivier. "Representation, the Despot and the Harem: Some Questions around an Academic Orientalist Painting by LeComte-Du-Nouy (1885)." In *Europe and Its Others,* vol. 1, ed. Francis Barker et al. Colchester: University of Essex, 1984.

Ricoeur, Paul. "The Model of the Text." In *Interpretive Social Science,* ed. Paul Rabinow and William Sullivan. Berkeley: University of California Press, 1987.

Rodinson, Maxime. *Islam and Capitalism.* Trans. Brian Pearce. Austin: University of Texas Press, 1978.

Rousseau, Jean-Jacques. *The Social Contract, Books I and II.* Trans. Henry Tozer. London: George Allen and Unwin, 1924.

Roussillon, A., and A. Saaf. *Les gens du navire.* Casablanca: Afrique Orient, 1988.

Rustow, Dankwarth. "Transition to Democracy." *Comparative Politics* 2 (1970): 337–63.

Safran, Nadav. *Egypt in Search of Political Community.* Cambridge: Harvard University Press, 1961.

Said, Edward. *Culture and Imperialism.* New York: Knopf, 1993.

——. *Orientalism.* New York: Vintage Books, 1979.

——. *The World, the Text, and the Critic.* Cambridge: Harvard University Press, 1983.

Sartori, Giovanni. *Parties and Party System: A Framework for Analysis.* Cambridge: Cambridge University Press, 1976.

Seeley, J. R. *The Expansion of England.* Chicago: University of Chicago Press, 1971.

Semah, David. *Four Egyptian Literary Critics.* Leiden: E. J. Brill, 1974.

Singerman, Diane. *Avenues of Political Participation: Family, Politics, and Networks in Urban Quarters in Cairo.* Princeton, N.J.: Princeton University Press, 1995.

Smith, Charles D. *Islam and the Search for Social Order: A Biography of Muhammed Husayn Haykal.* Albany: State University of New York Press, 1983.

Smith, G. Elliot. *The Ancient Egyptians.* London: Harper, 1923.

Spivak, Gayatri Chakravorty. "The Rani of Surmur." In *Europe and Its Others,* vol. 1, ed. Francis Barker et al. Colchester: University of Essex, 1985.

Strayer, Joseph. *Studies in Early French Taxation.* Cambridge: Harvard University Press, 1939.

Taine, Hippolyte. *Histoire de la litérature anglaise.* Paris: L. Hachette, 1863.

——. *History of English Literature.* Trans. H. Van Laun. New York: Worthington, 1889.

Taylor, Charles. "Interpretation and the Sciences of Man." In *Interpretive Social Science,* ed. Paul Rabinow and William Sullivan, 25–72. Berkeley: University of California Press, 1987.

Therborn, Goran. "The Role of Capital and the Rise of Democracy." *New Left Review* 103 (May–June 1977): 3–41.

Tignor, Robert. "The Egyptian Revolution of 1919: New Direction in the Egyptian Economy." *Middle East Studies* 12 (1976): 41–67.

U.S. Department of State. *Records of the Department of State relating to Political Relations Between Egypt and Other States: 1910–29.* Microfilm 430A. J.

Valenzuela, Arturo. "Chile: Origins, Consolidation, and Breakdown of a Democratic Regime." In *Politics in Developing Countries: Comparing Experiences with Democracy,* ed. Larry Diamond, Juan J. Linz, and Seymour Martin Lipset. London: Lynne Rienner, 1990.

Vatikiotis, P. J. *The Egyptian Army in Politics.* Bloomington: Indiana University Press, 1961.

——. *The History of Egypt: From Muhammad Ali to Mubarak.* Baltimore: Johns Hopkins University Press, 1985.

——. *Nasser and His Generation.* London: Croom Helm, 1978.

Wallerstein, Immanuel. *The Modern World System.* Vol. 2. New York: Academic Press, 1980.

Waterbury, John. *The Commander of the Faithful: The Moroccan Political Elite; A Study in Segmented Politics.* London: Weidenfeld and Nicolson, 1970.

Weber, Max. *Economy and Society*. Ed. Guenther Roth and Claus Wittich. Berkeley: University of California Press, 1978.

White, James Boyd. *When Words Lose Their Meaning*. Chicago: University of Chicago Press, 1984.

Youssef, Hassan. "The Democratic Experiment in Egypt: 1923–1952." In *Cairo Papers in Social Science: Democracy in Egypt*, ed. Ali Hellal Dessouki. Cairo: American University in Cairo, 1978.

A quoi tient la supériorité des Anglo-Saxons, 47

Arab culture: depreciation in Egyptian Constitution of 1923 of, 53–63; Egyptian liberals' minimization of, 2–3, 9, 67–86; literature of, 82–86; trivialization of, 74–75

Arabic language: Egyptian dialects and, 3; as Egyptian official language, 43

'Arif, Hasan, 73

Aryan superiority, Renan's theory of, 78–80, 160n.46

Assembly of Deputies (Majlis al-Nuwab), 122–23

Aswan Dam, 137, 167n.69

Atatürk, Kemal, 105–6

authenticity, cultural claims of, 22–24; Fanon's critique of, 26–32

authority: Egyptian concepts of, 87–89; Islamic culture and role of, 66–67; language of Egyptian Constitution of 1923 concerning, 59–63; legitimacy and performance thesis and acceptance of, 133–35; in Middle East politics, 12

autocracy, Egyptian Constitution of 1923 as reinforcement of, 55–63

Aventures de Télémaque, 47

Ayubi, Nazih, 12

Baaklini, Abdo, 13

Balkans, myth of Turkish massacres in, 51–52

Bank Misr group, 137–39

Banna, Sheikh Hassan al-, 144

Beblawi, Hazem, 12

behavior, Egyptian cultural attitudes concerning, 94–96, 99–100

Being and Nothingness, 28–32

Belgium constitution, Egyptian constitution modeled on, 58–59, 130

Bentham, Jeremy, 6, 14

"Berber Decree," 169n.12

Bergsch, Heinrich, 160n.40

Berque, Jacques, 51–52, 59, 130, 133

Bey, Murqus Simeikha, 124

Bhabha, Homi, 4, 8, 32; mimicry theory of, 41–42; postcolonial theories of, 14–15, 18, 22–24, 152n.20

Bianchi, Robert, 11

Bilingualism and colonialism, ix–x

Bill, James, 11

Binder, Leonard, 11

biological, Fanon on colonial hatred of, 30–32, 153n.32

Bishri, Tariq al-, 119

black identity, Fanon's discussion of, 26–32, 153n.30

"black psychopathology," Fanon's concept of, 29

Black Skin, White Masks, 15, 24–30, 153n.30

bourgeoisie: absence in Third World of, 119; in Egypt, 119; socioeconomic development thesis and, 135–40

British Chamber of Commerce in Egypt, 139

British Empire: antiquities acquired during Egyptian occupation by, 159n.38; Egyptian independence from, 54, 128–29; Egyptian liberals' biases concerning, 6, 14, 141–48; French analysis of, 142–43; in India, 6, 18–19, 22–24, 124–25; influence in Egyptian Constitution of 1923 of, 53–63; interference in Egyptian politics from, 131–32; occupation of Egypt, 2–3, 5, 47–53, 71, 123–24, 126–27, 142, 149n.2, 166n.36, 169n.5; Ottoman Empire and, 104–6; support for Saudi independence and, 65, 157n.5

Browne, Edward, 99–100

Brumberg, Daniel, 12

brute force, in colonialism, 16

Brynen, Rex, 12–13

Bush administration, "regime change" policy of, x–xi

Byzantine Christians, discrimination against Coptic Christians, 3 capitalism: democracy and, 119; Protestantism and, 11; socioeconomic development thesis and, 136–40

Césaire, Aimé, 4, 15–18, 22, 32; Fanon's critique of, 25–28

Chatterjee, Bakimchandra, 19

Chile, democracy in, 121

cholera, prevalence in Egypt of, 89–90

Christian reformers in Egypt, 67, 71

citizenship: cultural preconditions of, 87–106; education and, 107–11; Egyptian concepts of, xv–xvii, 9–13; identity politics and, 114–17; labor and, 112–13; religious beliefs and, 111–12; sacrifice and, 106–7

civil society, Middle East culture and role of, 11–13

Civil Society Center (Cairo), 13

class structure: Constitution of 1923 and, 131; of Egyptian political parties, 126–29; legitimacy and performance thesis and, 134–35; socioeconomic development thesis and, 135–40

clothing, in Egyptian culture, 103–6, 109

Cole, Juan, 43, 51

Colombe, Marcel, 142–43

colonial continuity thesis, democracy and, 120

colonialism: critical studies of, 5–6, 14–24; denigration of black culture in, 26; Egyptian Constitution of 1923 as symbol of, 56–63; Egyptian liberals' failure and, 141–48; familial metaphor in, 32–36; Fanon's discussion of, 15, 24–32; history in Egypt of, 1–2, 5, 7–8, 37–63; language and, ix–x, 4–5; liberal justification of, 4–6; Orientalist view of, 20–24

colonial legacy thesis, democracy and, 120–25

"Committee of Thirty," Egyptian constitution drafted by, 58–59

common good, Egyptian liberals' concept of, 88–89

community: British suppression of, 51–53; Egyptian Constitution of 1923 as tool for, 56–63; Egyptian liberals' negation of, 9–10; territorial boundaries and integration of, 69–73

Comte, Auguste, 67, 161n.60

constitutional structure: democracy and, 125–26, 130–40; Egyptian liberals' failure and, 141–48; Islamic revivalism and rejection of, 132; legitimacy and performance thesis and, 134–35; socioeconomic development thesis and, 136–40

Constitution Commission (Egypt), 54, 128, 130–31

Constitutive Assembly of Deputies (Egypt), 44–45

Consultative Administrative Council (Egypt). See Diwan (Egyptian administrative council)

Consultative Assembly of Deputies. See Assembly of Deputies

Coptic Christians, marginalization in Egypt of, 3

corruption, colonial legacy thesis and, 120–21

cotton industry in Egypt, 137

Council of Ministers (Egypt), 130

cremation, Egyptian liberals' critique of, 100–102

crime, Egyptian liberals' concern about, 92–100

Cromer, 1st earl (Evelyn Baring), 48–53, 66

cross-cultural fertilization, in Egypt, 8

culture: Césaire on colonialism and, 16–17; citizenship and, 87; Egyptian liberals and role of, 80–86, 87–117, 141–48; Fanon on authenticity in, 26–32; identity politics and, 114–17; Lacan's concept of, 4–5; liberalism and role of, xii–xiii, 1, 4–6; Middle Eastern politics and, 11–13; in postcolonial theory, 15–24; resistance to displacement of, 8

Culture and Imperialism, 22

English Electric Company, 167n.69

Enlightenment: European disillusion with, 26; influence in Egypt of, 44–47

Essai sur la colonization, 16

ethnic conflict, democratic reform and, 124–25

Euben, Roxanne, 146–47

European culture: dominance in Egyptian Constitution of 1923, 53–63; Egyptian liberals' identification with, 3–4, 8–10, 34–36, 44–51, 90–92, 100–102, 109–11, 141–48, 157n.6; Egyptian secular reformers influenced by, 67–86; racial boundaries to, 77–80

familial metaphor, in colonialism, 32–36

Fanon, Frantz, 4–6; critique of colonialism by, 15, 17, 22–24; on language and emancipation, 24–32, 41; phenomenological theory of, 22

Faruq I, 132

fascism, colonialism and, 17, 26

Fatimid dynasty, 98

Fénelon, François de la Mothe-, 47

fez, in Egyptian culture, 103–6

Fhami, Abd al-Aziz, 166n.38

Fikri, 'Abdu'llah, 44

Foucault, Michel: on history, 73–74; "objectification of subject" concept of, 66, 158n.8; political models of, 45–46; postcolonial theory and, 19–22

France, Anatole, 83

France, failure of democracy in, 126

freedom: colonial concept of, in Egyptian Constitution of 1923, 59–63; negritude movement and concept of, 28–32

French colonialism: in Algeria, 2, 5–6, 31–32; antiquities acquired under, 159n.38, 160nn.40–41; British critique of, 49–51; critical theory concerning, 15–16, 142–43; in Egypt, 49–

51, 102–3, 121–22, 142–43; Napoleonic occupation of Egypt, 37–47, 121

Freud, Sigmund, 33–34

Fu'ad I, 54–55, 58, 68, 75, 128, 130–31, 167n.57

fundamentalism, liberals' response to, 146–48

funeral practices in Egypt, 100–102

Gadamer, Hans-Georg, xiii

Gandhi, Mahatma, 6, 19

Gellner, Ernest, 12

General Agricultural Syndicate, 137–38

General Assembly (al-Jam'iyya al-'Umumiyya) (Egypt), 123

General Council of Egypt (al-Diwan al-'Am), 121–22

Germany: failure of democracy in, 126; Orientalism in, 21–22; restrictions on Muslims in, 91–92

Ghaleb, Muhammad, 83–84, 160n.44

Ghose, Aurobindo Ackrod, 19

Gladstone, William, 51–52

Goldberg, Ellis, 12, 119

Gorst, Eldon, 52

Grant, Charles, 23

Granville, 2d earl (Granville George Leveson-Gower), 51

Great Britain, occupation of Egypt by, 2–3

Greek culture, influence in Egypt, 3, 74–77, 85–86, 109–10

"Green Peril," characterization of Islam, 146

Habermas, Jürgen, xiii

Hakim, Tawfiq al-, 65, 67, 72, 83–85, 160n.44

Hall, John, 12

"hallucinatory whitening," Fanon's concept of, 25

Hanoteaux, Gabriel, 66

Harb, Tal'at, 67, 137, 139

hat, in Egyptian culture, 103–6

Haykal, Muhammad Husayn, 60, 65, 67, 72–73, 80–83, 130, 161n.59, 161n.60, 161n.65

health, in Egyptian culture, 89–90, 94–96, 162n.9

Hindu culture, postcolonial view of, 19, 47

Histoire des langues sémitiques, 81

historical boundaries, Egyptian liberals' concept of, 73–77

history, colonialism in, 14–36, 154n.14

Hudson, Michael, 11

Hugo, Victor, 83

Husayn, Ahmad, 83

Husayn, Taha, 60, 65, 67, 72, 83–85, 89–90, 109, 160n.44

Hussein, Mahmoud, 119

"hybridity," native resistance to, 8

Ibn Khaldun, 69–70

Ibrahim (Ottoman bey), 37

identity: citizenship and, 114–17; culture and language linked to, 144–48; denial of, in Egyptian Constitution of 1923, 53–63; Lacan's concept of, 33–36

Imaginary Order, Lacan's concept of, 33–36

imperialism: Egyptian Constitution of 1923 as protection of, 55–63; liberalism and, 4–6; "regime change" policy compared with, x–xi

independence: colonial concept of, in Egyptian Constitution of 1923, 61–63; democratic development in Egypt following, 130–40

India: British rule in, 6, 18–19, 22–24, 123; colonial legacy thesis and democracy in, 120, 124–25; postcolonial view of, 19

industrialists in Egypt, socioeconomic development thesis and, 138–40

Institute of Egypt, 8

"interpreter" class, Bhabha's discussion of, 23

Iran, democratization in, 13

Iraq: British rule in, 2; failure of regime change in, x–xii

"Iron Grip," government of (al-qabda al-hadidiya), 132

Islamic culture: colonial denigration of, 143–48; Egyptian Constitution of 1923 minimization of, 53–63; Egyptian liberals' critique of, xv–xvii, 2–3, 9–10, 67–86, 98–102; "modern nationalist" reformers and valorization of, 67; "Muslim reformists" proposals concerning, 66; Ottoman Empire and, 104–6; public gatherings in, 98–100; Renan's negative views of, 77–80, 160n.44; revivalism movement for, 132; status of politics in, 145–48; territorial boundaries and, 69–73; textual community in, 156n.48; traditional invocation of, 60; trivialization of history of, 74–75

"Islamic" head scarf controversy, 91–92

Islamic Umma: Egyptian nationalism and, 71–72, 159n.23; political purpose of, 61, 156n.48

Ismail, Tawfiq, 50–51

Ismail (Khedive), 43–45, 47, 50–51, 66, 122, 126, 157n.6, 160n.41, 169n.5

Iswai, Charles, 119

Italy, failure of democracy in, 126

Jabarti, Abd al-Rahman al-, 7–8, 37–41, 121–22, 157n.58

James, G. G. M., 17

JanMohamed, Abdul, 15

Jordan, democratization in, 13

Judaism, context in colonial Muslim society of, 17–18

judiciary independence, democracy and system of, 125–26

Kader, Abdel (emir), 8, 41

Kamil, Mustapha, 67, 71–72, 129

Kawkab al-Sharq, 100–102, 107–8, 166n.38

Keddouri, Elie, 11

Kemal, Mustafa, 105

Khedival Agricultural Society, 137

Khoury, Philip, 11

khutba, Egyptian practice of, 103

Kilito, Abdelfattah, ix, 44

kingly powers, in Egyptian Constitution of 1923, 130–31, 167n.57

Kipling, Rudyard, 18–19

Kitchener, 1st earl (Horatio Herbert), 52, 123

kiyasa (adroitness, cleverness), Egyptian concept of, 129

Kohli, Atul, 120

Korany, Bahgat, 13

Kostiner, Joseph, 11

Kristeva, Julia, postcolonial theory and, 19

Kurayyim, Muhammad, 38

labor, in Egyptian culture, 112–13

Lacan, Jacques, 8; familial paradigm of, 32–36; Fanon inflenced by, 15, 23–24, 29–30; influence on Egyptian liberals, 68; Oedipal metaphor of, 5–6, 33–36; "symbolic order of language theory," 4–5, 30–31, 153n.32

Lane, Edward, 47

language: Fanon's discussion of, 24–32; identity politics and, x, 144–48; Lacan's "symbolic order of," 4–5, 30–31, 33–36, 153n.32; political role of, in Egyptian Constitution of 1923, 55–63; in postcolonial theory, 14–15, 18–24; resistance and emancipation using, 4–5, 38–47

L'anthologie de la poésie nègre et malgache, 28

La reforme intellectuelle et morale de la France, 16

Lashin, Abd al-Khalik, 157n.5

Latin America, democratization in, 135–36

L'avenire de la science, 78

Le Bon, Gustave, 67, 80–81

Le Figaro (French newspaper), 129

legislation, liberal rationalization of colonialism and, 6

Legislative Assembly (al-Jam'iyya al-Tashri'iyya), 123–24, 127, 130

Legislative Council (Majlish al-Shura) (Egypt), 123

legitimacy and performance thesis, democratic development and, 133–35

Le lyricism et la critique littéraire chez les arabes, 84

L'esprit des lois, 81

Levi, I. G., 138

Lévi-Strauss, Claude, 34

L'évolution de l'Egypte, 143

Lewis, Bernard, 11, 12

Liberal Constitutionalist Party (Hizb al-Ahrar al-Ditsturiyyun) (Egypt), 126, 128–29

liberalism in Egypt: citizenship and, 87–89; colonialism and, xi–xii, 1–2, 4–6, 51–53, 65–86; cultural boundaries of, 80–86; Egyptian Constitution of 1923 and failure of, 53–63, 132–33, 156n.45; failure of, 1, 7–8, 132–33, 141–48; historical boundaries in, 74–77; identity politics and, 114–17; non-democratic forms of, 124; racial boundaries of, 77–80; territorial boundaries of, 69–73

Liberal Party (Egypt), 68

Linz, Juan, 133

Lipset, Seymour, 133

literature: colonialism in, 14–36, 154n.14; cultural boundaries in, 81–86, 161n.69–71; of Egypt liberal reformers, 67–86; historical references in, 76–77; national identity defined through, 8–10, 81–86

lived-experience, Fanon's concept of, 28–29

Lloyd, 1st baron (George Ambrose), 75

local texts, colonialist appropriation of, 41–47

Luciani, Giacomo, 12

Lyotard, Jean-François, 19

Mahmud, Muhammad, 166n.42
Makbati, Abd al-Latif al-, 166n.42
Malek, Anouar Abdel, 119
Mamluks, in Egypt, 2–3, 37–38, 42, 122
Manners and Customs of the Modern Egyptians, 47
Mannoni, Octave, 18, 24
Mariette, Auguste, 160n.40
Markmann, Charles, 28–29
marriage, in Egyptian culture, 102–3
Martinique, colonization in, 25–26
masculinity, in British imperialism, 19
mass culture: Egyptian concepts of, 87–89, 162n.6; Western view of, 142–43
mawalid (celebration of saints), 96–100
Mawalid Sayida Zaynab (celebration of a woman saint), 99–100
Mazhar, Isma'il, 67
Mediterranean identity, Egypt's adoption of, xv–xvii
Mehta, Uday, 6, 14, 22
Memmi, Albert, 4, 17–18, 26
mental health, Egyptian cultural view of, 94–96
Mernissi, Fatima, 11
metaphor of self-emancipation, 4
Michelet, Jules, 37
Middle East: language and identity politics in, x; political theory concerning, 10–13
military control, in Egypt, 46–47
Mill, James, 6
Mill, John Stuart, xii, 6, 36
mimicry: as colonial strategy, 22–24, 41–42; native resistance to, 8
Ministry of Commerce and Industry (Egypt), 139
Misr (newspaper), 166n.38
Mitchell, Timothy, 45–47
modernization: legitimacy and performance thesis and, 134–35; socioeconomic development thesis and, 136–40
"modern nationalists," Egyptian liberal reformers as, 67–68
Mogul Empire, 124

Mokhtar, Mahmud, 75
Montagne, Robert, 143
Montesquieu (Charles-Louis de Secondat), 67, 81
Morocco, democratization in, 13, 121
mourning, wailing as symbol of, 100–102
Mubarak, 'Ali, 44
Muhammad, Ahmed, 135
Muhammad 'Ali, 3, 8, 42–46, 76, 122, 166n.42
Murad (Ottoman bey), 37
Musa, Salama, 60, 67, 72, 74–75, 78–79, 160nn.44; 49–50
Muslim Brotherhood (al-Ikhwan al-Muslimun), 132, 135, 144
"Muslim reformists" in Egypt, 66–68
Muslim society: autonomous associations in, 12; colonial denigration of, 142–43; modernism and, x; status of politics in, 145–48
Mustaqbal al-Thaqafa fi Misr (The Future of Culture in Egypt), 85
Muwailihi, Muhammad al-, 67
Muwaqqit al-Murrâkushi, Mohammed Ibn Abdallah al-, 145

Nahdhat Misr (Revival of Egypt) statue, 75–76
Nahhas, Mustapha, 75–76
Nandy, Ashis, 18–19, 47
Napoleon, invasion of Egypt by, 7–8, 37–47, 97, 121–22, 143, 154n.14, 157n.58
Nasser's Free Officers, 132, 167n.79
national identity: in Arab literature, 81–86; citizenship and, 114–17; colonial concept of, in Egyptian Constitution of 1923, 61–63; cultural boundaries of, 80–86; Egyptian concepts of, xv–xvii, 2, 9–13, 158n.17; Egyptian liberals' idea of, 66–86; historical boundaries of, 73–77; minimization of Arab and Islamic elements in, 9–10; religion as threat to, 98–100
nationalism: Bhabha's suspicion of, 24;

Egyptian Constitution of 1923 as barrier to, 54–63; "modern nationalists" in Egypt and, 67–68; role of culture in, 15; Said's discussion of, 22; territorial boundaries of, 69–73

National Party (al-Hizb al-Watani) (Egypt), 71–72, 126, 129, 131

native culture, Egyptian liberals' disparagement of, 87–88

Nazism, disillusion with Enlightenment and, 26

negritude movement, 26–32

newspapers, as Egyptian liberals' platform, 88–89, 162n.6

Nigeria, colonial legacy thesis and democracy in, 120

Noble, Paul, 13

Norton, Anne, xiii

Norton, Richard, 12

Nuqrashi, Mahmud al-, 135

Obeyd, Makram, 135

"Observations on the State of Society among the Asiatic Subjects of Great Britain," 23

Oedipus complex, Lacan's discussion of, 5–6, 33–36

Operation "Iraqi Freedom," 1–2

Orabi Pasha, 169n.5

order, Egyptian cultural attitudes toward, 92–93

Orientalism: cultural boundaries in, 84–86; Egyptian liberals' denial of, 9–10, 64–65; Egyptology and, 76–77, 160n.40; Egypt's inclusion in, xv–xvii, 5, 7–8, 34–36, 47; Middle East politics and perspective of, 12–13; postcolonial theory and, 20–24; racial boundaries and, 77–80

Orientalism, 14, 20–24

Other: Egyptian liberals and language of, 66–69, 73–74, 132, 159n.28; Lacan's concept of, 34–36, 42

Ottoman Empire: British annulment in Egypt of, 127; cultural boundaries in,

83–86; Egyptian integration into, 2–3, 37–39, 42–47, 51–53, 124; Egyptian nationalism and rejection of, 72–73, 84, 127, 159n.27; fez as symbol of, 103–6; Napoleonic doctrine and, 7; Saudi independence from, 65

Owen, Roger, 119

Ozbudun, Orgun, 136

Paris Peace Conference, 64, 127–28

parliamentary institutions: democracy and, 125–26; in Egyptian Constitution of 1923, 130–32; Liberal Constitutionalist Party support of, 129

Parry, Benita, 15

party politics in Egypt, democracy and, 125–40

Pasha, Nubar, 44

Patai, Raphael, 11

Patriot Act, xii

patronage politics, in Middle East, 11

Pharaonic culture and literature, Egyptian revival of, xvi–xvii, 59–60, 70–77, 83, 159n.25

pluralist politics, socioeconomic development thesis and, 136–40

police system, Egyptian reforms of, 92–93

political community: analysis of Egyptian Constitution of 1923 and, 53–63; citizenship and, 88–89; cultural biases in, xiii–xvii; failure of Egyptian liberals concerning, 65–86; historical boundaries to, 74–77; territorial boundaries and, 69–73

political development literature, shortcomings of, 126

political institutions thesis, democracy and, 125–26

political theory: asymmetry of power in Napoleonic occupation of Egypt and, 37–47, 154n.14; boundaries of, in post-independence Egypt, 64–86; in Islamic culture, 66–67. See also democracy

postcolonial theory, overview of, 14–24

power: colonialism and exercise of, 17; Egyptian Constitution of 1923 and redistribution of, 55–63, 130–31; Napoleon's invasion of Egypt and asymmetry of, 38–47; social reforms and, 91–92, 162n.11

Prospero and Caliban: The Psychology of Colonization, 24–25

Protestantism, capitalism and, 11

Pryce-Jones, David, 11

psychoanalytic theories of colonialism: Fanon's discussion of, 30–32; Lacan's Symbolic Order paradigm and, 33–36; limitations of, 4–5; postcolonial theory and, 18–24

psychological aspects of education, Egyptian liberals' concern for, 109–11

Public Council (al-Majlis al-'Umumi) (Egypt), 122

public health, Egyptian liberals' concern with, 91–96

Quandt, William, 11

Qur'an: colonial context for study of, 7; as literary source, 84; marriage discussed in, 103; Napoleonic invocation based on, 40–41; textual community depicted in, 156n.48

Qutb, Sayyid, 146–47

Raafi'i, Mustapha al-, 82

racial boundaries: Egyptian political community and, 77–80; in United States, 91

racism, Fanon's discussion of, 25–32

Ramadan, Abd al-Azim, 119

Raziq, 'Ali 'Abd al-, 66, 68, 88

reason, liberalism's confidence in, 146–48

"regime change" policy, imperialism and, x–xi

religion: democratic reform and, 124–25; education and, 110; in Egyptian culture, 111–12; purposes of, in

Egyptian Constitution of 1923, 61–63

Renan, Ernest, 8, 16, 41, 66–67, 112; racial boundaries in work of, 77–78, 81–82, 84, 160n.42, 160n.46

resistance: against European cultural hegemony, 8; language as tool for, 4

Reza, Muhammad, 105

Richards, Alan, 12

Ricoeur, Paul, xiii

Rida, Rashid, 66

Rifa'i, Abd al-Aziz al-, 119

Roman culture, influence in Egypt of, 74–77, 109

Rousseau, Jean-Jacques, 67

Roy, Rammohun, 19

rural communities, Egyptian liberal's view of, 93

Rushdie, Salman, 22

sacrifice, Egytpian cultural notion of, 106–7

Saddam Hussein, liberal views of, xi–xii

Safran, Nadav, 130, 132, 141–42

Said, Edward, 4–5, 7–8, 32; Orientalist theory of, 14–15, 18, 20–24; on textual and historical colonialism, 41, 47

saints, Egyptian mawalid celebration of, 96–100

Salame, Ghassam, 11

Salih, Muhammad Zaki, 75

Salim, Ahmad, 83

Sartre, Jean-Paul, 28–29

Saudi Arabia, independence of, 65, 157n.5

Saussure, Ferdinand de, 34

Sayyid-Marsot, Ahmad Lutfi al-, 67, 71–72, 84, 119, 126, 143–44, 166n.42

science: cultural boundaries for, 80–81, 87, 98–100, 110–11; Egyptian religious beliefs and, 111–12; influence on Egyptian liberal reformers of, 67–68; racial boundaries imposed in, 77–80

"secular modernists," in Egypt, 67–86

ABDESLAM M. MAGHRAOUI is a political scientist based in Washington. He holds a Ph.D. in comparative politics from Princeton University.

Library of Congress Cataloging-in-Publication Data

Maghraoui, Abdeslam.
Liberalism without democracy : nationhood and citizenship in Egypt, 1922–1936
    Abdeslam M. Maghraoui.
p. cm.—(Politics, history, and culture)
Includes bibliographical references and index.
    ISBN-13: 978-0-8223-3800-0 (cloth : alk. paper)
    ISBN-10: 0-8223-3800-9 (cloth : alk. paper)
    ISBN-13: 978-0-8223-3838-3 (pbk. : alk. paper)
    ISBN-10: 0-8223-3838-6 (pbk. : alk. paper)
1. Liberalism—Egypt—History. 2. Democracy—Egypt—History.
3. Egypt—Politics and government—1882–1952. I. Title. II. Series.
    JC574.2.E3M34 2006
    320.96209′042—dc22
                    2006014258